Ascend to Mount Zion

"Worship at His Footstool"

Book III of the Barnabas Series
Cho Larson

Albertville, AL

Published by Warner House Press of Albertville, Alabama USA

Copyright © 2023 Cho Larson
Cover Design and Illustration © 2023 Ian Loudon, OKAY Media
Interior Design © 2023 Warner House Press

All rights reserved. No part of this book may be used or reproduced in any manner whatsoever without written permission, except in the case of brief quotations in critical articles and reviews. For more information, contact

Warner House Press
1325 Lane Switch Road
Albertville, Alabama 35951
USA

Published 2023
Printed in the United States of America

Cover image used under license from Shutterstock.com.

Unless otherwise noted, all scripture quotations are taken from HOLY BIBLE, NEW INTERNATIONAL VERSION®. Copyright © 1973, 1978, 1984 by International Bible Society. Used by permission of Zondervan Publishing House.

Scripture quotations marked NKJV are from the New King James Version®. Copyright © 1982 by Thomas Nelson. Used by permission. All rights reserved.

Scripture quotations marked NLT are from the Holy Bible, New Living Translation, Copyright © 1996, 2004, 2007, 2013, 2015 by Tyndale House Foundation. Used by permission of Tyndale House Publishers Inc., Carol Stream, Illinois 60188. All rights reserved.

26 25 24 23 1 2 3 4 5

ISBN: 978-1-951890-50-6

Dedicated to:
All "Prisoners of Hope."
(Zechariah 9:12)

"He makes my feet like the feet of a deer; he causes me to stand on the heights."
(2 Samuel 22:34)

"Who may ascend the mountain of the LORD? Who may stand in his holy place?"
(Psalm 24:3)

"You have come to Mount Zion, to the city of the living God, the heavenly Jerusalem."
(Hebrews 12:22)

Contents

The Ascent Begins Here	i
Part I: Children of the Resurrection	**1**
Chapter 1: A History of Worship	3
Chapter 2: A Heart for Gathering	13
Chapter 3: True to Our Purpose	23
Part II: A Repentant Cry	**31**
Chapter 4: Cain's Offering	33
Chapter 5: Out of Focus	41
Chapter 6: It's in the Bulletin	49
Chapter 7: The Reality of Experience	57
Chapter 8: Testimony Time	65
Chapter 9: Cleanse the Temple	73
Part III: Children of Zion	**81**
Chapter 10: Abel's Sacrifice	83
Chapter 11: Dressed and Ready For Battle	91
Chapter 12: Crossing the Threshold	99
Part IV: Awaken the Dawn	**107**
Chapter 13: Where We Gather	109
Chapter 14: Come Together With Purpose	117
Chapter 15: Exalting God in a Storm	127
Chapter 16: The Object of Our Worship	135
Part V: Strengthen the Foundations	**143**
Chapter 17: A Call to Order	145
Chapter 18: A House of Prayer	153
Chapter 19: Water Baptism	161

Chapter 20: The LORD's Table	171
Chapter 21: Teaching the True Word	181
Chapter 22: Proclaiming the True Gospel	189
Chapter 23: Ministries of Spiritual Gifts	197
Chapter 24: Awesome Offerings	209
Part VI: Children of Promise	**219**
Chapter 25: Songs of Victory	221
Chapter 26: Worthy Exaltations	229
Chapter 27 : Our High Priest's Ministry	235
Chapter 28: Our High Priest's Prayer	241
Chapter 29: Forgiveness	247
Part VII: Praise of Children and Infants	**255**
Chapter 30 : Lift up Holy Hands	257
Chapter 31: Sing a New Song	265
Chapter 32: A Sweet-Smelling Fragrance	271
Chapter 33: A Redeemed People	279
Chapter 34: Songs of Rest	287
Chapter 35: The Watchman Calls Out	295
Part VIII: Faithful to the Temple's Design	**303**
Chapter 36: From the Beginning to Forever	305
Chapter 37: Put Your Feet in the Water	313
Standing on the Summit	**321**

The Ascent Begins Here

First, rest on your backpack for a minute and listen up to a basecamp briefing. If you follow your guide's instructions the ascent will be an awesome and inspiring journey of a lifetime to God's holy mountain where we gather to worship. Ignore them, and there will be pitfalls along the way.

Our purpose as sons and daughters of resurrection is to find a greater knowledge of Jesus Christ, our High Priest. By the powerful work of the cross He raises us up as worshipers of our heavenly Father in spirit and truth. In Christ we are joining the worshipful ascent to Mount Zion, the city of the Living God. To help you with your ascent, each teaching is presented in bite-size portions with applicable Scriptures. We will be considering many Old Testament Scriptures because they provide us "on whom the culminations of the ages has come" with examples and warnings.[1]

The Old Testament regulations for worship were written out in intricate detail. Every article for worship had specific dimensions, and the handling requirements were rigorous. Today's churches often think that we just gather and let our spirit lead where it will. But while the gospel has no burdensome laws, it calls us to a higher standard.

Prepare yourself for a good spiritual workout. Our learning steps are not like taking a leisurely afternoon stroll on the beach. It's more like hiking the Mist Trail to Half Dome at Yosemite National Park. Our goal isn't to establish an excessively high human standard of conduct, but to lift up worship as a part of everyday life and to enrich our gatherings for worship, service, and ministry and to glorify God's holy name. Our purpose is not to make a mystical ascent into the divine, but to keep our feet on the ground while lifting holy hands to worship in the presence of Jesus our High Priest.

Every denomination has its own emphasis and worship style. Calvary Chapel focuses on expository teaching and praise songs. Presbyterians express their faith by hearing the Word proclaimed and singing out with hymns and praise songs. Lutherans focus on the Word and sacraments and sing out with

---

1. 1 Corinthians 10:11.

beautiful hymns of the church. Baptists concentrate on preaching the gospel, soul winning, and singing both contemporary and traditional worship. Charismatic churches emphasize ministry gifts of the Holy Spirit and inspirational worship with hands lifted in praise.

With so many different styles of worship, Bible students may ask, "What does true and real worship look like?" The clear and simple answer is that it looks like Christ Jesus, our LORD and Savior. Indeed, when the fullness of Christ Jesus is revealed to us in all His glory and majesty, true worshipers ascend to His holy presence, entering into worship that is spiritual and real. We are set free and our exaltations flow out as beautifully as living water from the Rock.

Do you want to know the design for God's holy temple?
Rejoice!
Have you resolved to fit into the temple's plan?
Knock!
Is your desire to offer praise and worship that please the LORD?
Give thanks!

Come, enter into the joy of worshipping the LORD God Almighty in all his splendor.

Let my people go, so that they may worship me. (Exodus 8:1)

Part I

Children of the Resurrection

"Blessed are those who dwell in your house;
they are ever praising you."
(Psalm 84:4)

Like steps up the mountain the Scriptures in this part of our ascent offer a brief history of worship and defines the elements of worship.

Chapter 1: A History of Worship

Key Scriptures:

- "Seth also had a son, and he named him Enosh. At that time people began to call on the name of the LORD" (Genesis 4:26).
- "Abraham planted a tamarisk tree in Beersheba, and there he called on the name of the LORD, the Eternal God" (Genesis 21:33).
- "On coming to the house, they saw the child with his mother Mary, and they bowed down and worshiped him. Then they opened their treasures and presented him with gifts of gold, frankincense and myrrh" (Matthew 2:11).
- "When the day of Pentecost came, they were all together in one place. Suddenly a sound like the blowing of a violent wind came from heaven and filled the whole house where they were sitting. They saw what seemed to be tongues of fire that separated and came to rest on each of them. All of them were filled with the Holy Spirit and began to speak in other tongues as the Spirit enabled them" (Acts 2:2–4).

We press on to reach the first milestone on our ascent with a historic roadmap unfolded before us. The Bible maps the path of heavenward worship from the days of Adam, Eve, Seth, and Enosh to the present-day church. The shadow of the cross is evident in the beginning. The path of history begins with the fall of mankind and reaches a summit as the Holy Spirit founds the church with a baptism by fire. Now, let's follow the map to see the countless places where the modern-day church gathers in Jesus' name.

A prayer according to Isaiah 60:1:

Arise and shine out with the light of your coming
so that your glory may rise upon us.

The First Sacrificial Offerings

Worship of God, the Creator of all the heavens and earth, began with Adam and Eve as they communed with God, walking with Him in the garden of Eden. Then, by faith, Abel was compelled to bring a sacrificial offering that sent up sweet-smelling fragrances to the LORD. Later, in Levitical worship under the Law, burnt offerings were offered with the fatty portions of the sacrifices belonging to the LORD alone. This was to acknowledge God who provides abundantly from the fat of the land. Their sacrificial offerings looked back to God's grace shown to fallen man, and forward to Christ who paid the final and all-sufficient sacrifice for sins of the world.

A sacrifice of the firstborn from the flock was always an unblemished sacrifice—the best and strongest of the flock. This offering acknowledges God's abundant grace when He slayed an animal to provide a covering for Adam and Eve's sin. Israel's firstborn animal sacrifices looked forward with faith to a promised Redeemer who was to come to save His people.

We, like Abel, stand in awe as we consider our heavenly Father's abundant grace and mercy toward His people. But we have a better sacrifice, a Savior who purchased our salvation with His innocent blood, pardons our sins, and gifts us with an eternal promise. This amazing truth compels us to truly worship and exalt the God of glory.[1] He sent His only Son to die in our place so that we might "live through Him."[2] True worshipers lift up voices in praise because our Redeemer is preparing a place for us. Rejoice because He is coming back as our Bridegroom returning for His bride. Abel looked forward to Christ as he worshipped God. Today, we exalt our heavenly Father in the light of Christ.

> *In the course of time Cain brought some of the fruits of the soil as an offering to the LORD. And Abel also brought an offering–fat portions from some of the firstborn of his flock. The LORD looked with favor on Abel and his offering.* (Genesis 4:3–4)

Sacrificial Worship Restored

The waters receded from a world-wide flood. All the animals could finally come out of the ark onto dry land. The flood waters had cleansed the earth of wretched and rampant depravity that defiled God's perfect creation. God set this remnant free on the earth and offered them a new beginning. Then Noah built a stone altar and sacrificed acceptable animals as a fragrant sacrifice to the LORD. God accepted his sacrifice and then Noah and his family received

---
1. Psalm 92:4.
2. 1 John 1:9.

covenantal instructions regarding the life blood of men and animals. He renewed His command to "be fruitful and increase in number; multiply on the earth and increase upon it.[3]" Then a rainbow appeared in the sky as a sign of God's promise to never again destroy the earth by flood.

> *Then Noah built an altar to the LORD and, taking some of all the clean animals and clean birds, he sacrificed burnt offerings on it. The LORD smelled the pleasing aroma and said in his heart: "Never again will I curse the ground because of humans, even though every inclination of the human heart is evil from childhood. And never again will I destroy all living creatures, as I have done.*
> (Genesis 8:20–21)

A Covenantal Sacrifice

When the LORD manifests Himself to a person and their fearsome awe finally subsides, their strength returns so they may worship and exalt the Almighty One, whose radiance and glory is far beyond anything imaginable. Yahweh appeared to Abram to cut a covenant with him and he built an altar of uncut stones where he worshipped. He received God's promise of a land flowing with milk and honey and acknowledged this promise in sacrificial worship. This altar of uncut stones testified of his trust and reliance upon God Almighty who appeared to him. In building an altar he received the LORD's promise by faith and looked forward to what he was yet to receive in deed.

Then Abram went on from there as a sojourner in a land not yet his own where he built another stone altar for sacrifice and God was well pleased. He offered a sweet-smelling, fragrant sacrifice at a place called the "House of God."

> *The LORD appeared to Abram and said, "To your offspring I will give this land." So he built an altar there to the LORD, who had appeared to him. From there he went on toward the hills east of Bethel and pitched his tent, with Bethel on the west and Ai on the east. There he built an altar to the LORD and called on the name of the LORD.*
> (Genesis 12:7–8)

Worship at a Historic Crossroad

Many years later, Abram, now called by God, Abraham, commissioned his trusted servant to go back to his family in their homeland to find a bride for his son Isaac. Studying this account gives us the impression that the servant prayed every step of the way. He was sent on a mission, and he prayed for direction and success.

---
3. Genesis 9:7.

He went on his journey with Abraham's authority. His continuous prayer gave him godly wisdom. Yahweh gave light for every step of his path. He found the wellspring where Abraham's relatives collected water. Once again, he prayed to the LORD for success. Even before he finished praying, Rebekah approached the well with her water jar. When he asked for a drink for himself, she offered him a cup of cool water and then watered all ten of his camels until they were fully satisfied. This obedient and prayerful servant played a significant role as God prepared the way to establish a holy nation to worship Him.

Abraham's servant immediately gave her a nose ring and two gold bracelets. Then he bowed down to worship the LORD. At this historic crossroad for the nation of Israel, Abraham's servant bowed down to worship God who provided a bride for Isaac.

> *I bowed down and worshiped the Lord. I praised the Lord, the God of my master Abraham, who had led me on the right road to get the granddaughter of my master's brother for his son.*
> (Genesis 24:48)

Worship In Synagogues

The word "synagogue" doesn't appear in the Old Testament, but they existed as early as fifth century BC. They began as simple local gatherings and only later became formal structures. Local synagogues served as a location to come together for prayer, study, teaching, and discussion. In their meetings, the men were taught so they could serve as teachers for their families.

Synagogues functioned as community centers for spiritual growth where rabbis, priests, and teachers of the Law gathered. In their meetings they read the Law of Moses and the Prophets, and received instruction for living. Local synagogues often offered temporary lodging for strangers, serving as a hostel. Those who were sick could come to synagogue where apothecary services would be administered for healing.

A synagogue was the place Jesus chose to declare God's purpose for sending Him; "To proclaim good news to the poor, freedom for the prisoner, recovery of sight for the blind, to set the oppressed free, and to proclaim the year of the Lord's favor."[4]

> *He [Jesus] went to Nazareth, where he had been brought up, and on the Sabbath day he went into the synagogue, as was his custom.*
> (Luke 4:16)

---

4. Luke 4:18–19.

Worship at the River

John the Baptizer prepared the way for the promised Messiah, prophesying at the shoreline of the Jordan River where he baptized repentant souls. Jesus taught the people and His disciples baptized those who believed and received Jesus as Redeemer. Later, when Paul arrived at Philippi, he went outside the city to the river, where he expected to find a place where people would come to pray.[5] Still today, gathering down by the riverside makes a beautiful sanctuary for worship where we can sing in harmony with God's river of delights.[6] Indeed, every ascent to Mount Zion begins at the "river whose streams make glad the city of God, the holy place where the LORD Most High dwells."[7]

The great old hymn of the church rings out with a welcoming refrain, "Shall we gather at the river?"[8] The words echo an age-old practice of gathering to worship on the shoreline. Many of those who heard the gospel believed in Jesus the Son of God as their LORD and Savior could be baptized immediately. Centuries later, many slaves in America's southern states followed this practice: preaching, singing, and baptizing in the river's flowing water.

On the Sabbath we went outside the city gate to the river, where we expected to find a place of prayer. We sat down and began to speak to the women who had gathered there.
(Acts 16:13)

Worship in Homes

Early Christians gathered to pray, worship, and sing psalms in Jerusalem's temple courtyards or in local synagogues every day of the week, and especially on the first day of the week.[9] But the religious leaders opposed them, became abusive, and expelled those who worshipped Christ as Savior. Then Jesus' followers found that homes offered the safest and most readily available gathering places.[10] Imagine the incredible blessing of being welcomed into a neighbor's house where you would hear words of eternal life, drink from springs of living water, and be invited to partake of the bread of life.

---

5. Acts 16:11–15.
6. Psalm 36:8.
7. Psalm 46:4.
8. Written by the American poet and gospel music composer, Robert Lowry (1826–1899).
9. Acts 2:46, 20:7, 1 Corinthians 16:2.
10. Acts 18:5–7.

Should churches today return to gathering in homes? Would going back to this practice restore the church to its first love?[11] Would the intimate atmosphere of worshipping in homes wake up the church? A few American churches have abandoned large gatherings in huge auditoriums and only meet in homes. There are advantages and disadvantages to this practice.[12] Moving into houses cannot offer a perfect solution for a crumbling church. Paul's apostolic leadership presents a variety of perfect examples for our gathering places. As a church builder, he served churches that met at the river's side, in homes, and in synagogues. He discipled and strengthened the church no matter where they gathered.

> *You know that I have not hesitated to preach anything that would be helpful to you but have taught you publicly and from house to house.*
> (Acts 20:20)

Worship under Persecution

In our day, persecution of the Christian church has hit that proverbial exponential curve. While the American church remains relatively safe compared to third world countries, we have experienced dramatic assaults. One of the most heinous was the Birmingham Church bombing on September 15, 1963 that killed four young girls and injured many more. Recently, in the first three months of the year there were sixty-nine hostile acts against Christian churches in the United States.[13]

Hebrews chapter eleven tells the stories of many overcomers who are champions of our faith. The persecution of God's people began with Abel who was murdered by his own brother. Noah, the preacher of righteousness, built an enormous ark surrounded by a world filled with ungodly people hostile to Creator God. Abraham's family lived in tents as strangers in a foreign land of promise. The accounts of God's faithful servants include Isaac, Jacob, Joseph, Moses, Rahab, Gideon, Barak, Samson, Jephthah, David, Samuel, and the prophets. Many of them died without ever receiving what was promised. Some were tortured, stoned, burned, or even sawn in two. And yet, they were all faithful to their calling.

When we are persecuted because we bear the name of Christ, we must always remember that our Savior is the champion of the oppressed. He is an ever-present help. He leads us beside still waters and restores our soul. We can take heart knowing the LORD of the armies of heaven declares: "Do not touch my anointed ones; do my prophets no harm."[14]

---

11. Revelation 2:4.
12. The author asserts that a fully functioning church needs fifty maturing Christians to minister and serve in their spiritual gifts.
13. Family Research Council report released April 10, 2023.
14. Psalm 105:15.

And the God of all grace, who called you to his eternal glory in Christ, after you have suffered a little while, will himself restore you and make you strong, firm and steadfast. To him be the power for ever and ever. Amen.
(1 Peter 5:10–11)

State Sanctioned Worship

Constantine became the first Roman emperor to convert to the Christian faith. Under his rule, Christianity became the endorsed religion for the empire. His influence had a part in the Edict of Milan in AD 313 that provided acceptance of Christianity in the Roman Empire. By his decree, in the year AD 325, he convened the first Council of Nicaea that established the Nicene Creed's statement of Christian faith.

A true confession of the Christian faith serves as a bond to bring people together in Christ and eliminate the confusion created by winds of false doctrine. But the government's sway over religion loomed ever larger, continuing into the Holy Roman Empire. Even today, the government's shadow covers the church in many European countries.

Let us hold fast the confession of our hope without wavering, for he who promised is faithful.
(Hebrews 10:23)

Worship in Historic Grandeur

Between the twelfth and sixteenth centuries, God's people in Europe gathered to worship in great cathedrals with towering spires. Beginning in the fifteenth centuries, these saints lifted their voices to the great music of renaissance composers. Medieval master builders built great Gothic cathedrals inspired by man's deep-felt need for religious expression. They carved stone, set massive pillars in place, and erected steeples that pointed to the heavens, as if to pierce the barrier between heaven and earth. Their towering steeples, porticoes, and archways projected upward as if to catch the eyes of heaven to reach down to help humankind in their woeful estate.

Statues of the apostles and stained glass windows offered illiterate worshippers an opportunity to picture Christ's birth, miracles, crucifixion, and resurrection. Lancet style stained glass windows filled such churches with vibrant colors to portray the light of the Spirit. But still, while the glass and statues served as colorful illustrations of Bible history, they fell short when the gospel message was not declared or heard.

But the righteousness that is by faith says: "Do not say in your heart, 'Who will ascend into heaven?'" (that is, to bring Christ down).
(Romans 10:6)

Come as You Will Worship

Is modern-day worship more conformed to the world than to Christ? Do we raise our hands on Saturday night and dance to Alice in Chains, and then lift our hands and sway to the worship leaders music on Sunday morning? Think about how we worship today. Children of the Most High God must not lift their hands to glorify a rock star and then extend a hand to exalt the resurrected Christ.[15] Saturday night's chains have no place in gatherings for worship and praise.

James warns us that a spring cannot flow with both fresh water and salt water.[16] He is not only talking about cursing. His epistle emphasizes this truth, pointing out that a fig tree cannot bear olives, nor can a grapevine grow figs. In the same way, our worship must separate what is holy from all that is common. Divided loyalties puts us in danger of the Spirit of Christ saying, "Away with the noise of your songs!"[17] Discordant worship is unacceptable because it is irreverent and sated with disdain.

Therefore, since we are receiving a kingdom that cannot be shaken, let us be thankful, and so worship God acceptably with reverence and awe.
(Hebrews 12:28)

The path of world history is the story of Creator God who gathers a people who call on the name of the LORD. The historic record begins with creation, man's fall, and the first revelation of God's abundant grace and mercy. Then, our heavenly Father's loving kindness and longsuffering nature continue to be evident through a history of war, expanding empires, failed nations, and political chaos. As states are raised up and thrown down, it becomes evident that God is LORD, and sovereign over all. Bible history makes it clear that our heavenly Father always maintains a remnant of people who come as true worshippers to exalt the great I AM.

Christ is still head of the today's church. We are called to follow Him rather than worship trends that do not separate what is holy from what is common. We are called to take an account of our gatherings and ask, "Are we walking in Abel's footsteps, or defaulting to Cain's vegetable style of worship?"

---

15. Leviticus 10:10, Ezekiel 44:23.
16. James 3:11.
17. Amos 5:23.

> "I am the Alpha and the Omega," says the LORD God, "who is, and who was, and who is to come, the Almighty." (Revelation 1:8)

Chapter 1 Q&A

A History of Worship

1. Whose story is told in the record of the world's history? Why is it so important to recognize this thread woven into all historic records?

   _____
   _____
   _____

2. What is the one element that defines every generation's ascent to worship?

   _____
   _____
   _____

3. What part do sacrificial offerings have in the history of calling on the name of the LORD?

   _____
   _____
   _____

4. As the modern-day church takes an account of itself, what are the most important questions we must ask?

   _____
   _____
   _____

My Journey's Journal:

Chapter 2: A Heart for Gathering

Key Scriptures:

- "One thing I ask from the LORD, this only do I seek: that I may dwell in the house of the LORD all the days of my life, to gaze on the beauty of the LORD and to seek him in his temple" (Psalm 27:4).

- "If anyone speaks, they should do so as one who speaks the very words of God. If anyone serves, they should do so with the strength God provides, so that in all things God may be praised through Jesus Christ. To him be the glory and the power for ever and ever. Amen" (1 Peter 4:11).

Think about the woman who dragged her feet along the dusty path while lugging her water jug all alone to the town's only watering hole in the heat of the day. The sun blazed down on her and dust from the path stuck to her feet. Just the thought of lifting a heavy jar full of water from the deep well must have weighed her down. Then, when she got there, Jesus directed her to a spring of living water that she couldn't see. In this segment of our ascent, we'll walk in her footsteps and put aside that heavy water jug. We'll see the powerful effect of gathering to worship, minister, and serve in the church may flow out from our spirit like an everlasting fountain.

Verse by verse we'll see that true worshippers exalt the LORD God in all His glory, just as He has revealed Himself to us in the holy Scriptures. We'll step into a shower of blessings as we ascend to worship in Christ Jesus' living and active presence. Step by step through the Bible our understanding is opened so we may enter through the gates of worship with great confidence to offer our sacrifices of praise.

A Prayer According to Isaiah 63:7:

Oh LORD, give us songs of praise to tell of your lovingkindness. Give us words to praise you for your mighty deeds. Give us hearts to exalt you, for your abundant compassions.

We are led into eternally joyful worship by our High Priest, Jesus Christ, and the Holy Spirit. In His presence our gatherings are beautifully orchestrated. He helps us block out the world's noise so our hearts may overflow with justice like a river with an unstoppable flow of righteousness[1]. To enter His true and real worship we give up all personal agendas. Our own interpretation of what it means to worship no longer measures up. Like prophecy, worship doesn't have its origin in the desire of man. We must come as living sacrifices,[2] placing on the altar all the baggage we brought in through the front doors.

It's important to understand that true worship is impossible for mortal souls apart from the ministries of the Spirit of Christ. True worshipers worship from their spirit by means of the Holy Spirit. The Spirit of Jesus overflows from our spirit so we may bow to worship, exalt, and glorify our heavenly Father. By the power of Jesus' name, we are lifted from the corruption of the world into the realm of the Spirit so we may enter into genuine worship.

You make known to me the path of life; you will fill me with joy in your presence, with eternal pleasures at your right hand.
(Psalm 16:11)

All our earthly cares are set aside as we gather to worship. When we prescribe acts of reverence according to our own way of thinking, the flame of worship gets snuffed out and the lingering curl of smoke blows away.[3] Christ Jesus, our High Priest, provides a better way. He lifts us up to worship in His presence. From this vantage point a worshiper's eyes are opened to see His true glory. Our eyes are shielded from darkness and our hearts are prepared to enter heaven's sanctuary where our Redeemer ministers before us. When we come to offer thanksgiving and praise, we don't come like horses with blinders to keep us focused on the path ahead. We don't need a bit in our mouths to turn us in the right direction. Our greatest need is to humble ourselves in the sight of the LORD so that He will lift us up to worship with the angels in the presence of a holy God. This is the high and holy place we enter for worship.[4]

Blessed are those whose strength is in you, whose hearts are set on pilgrimage. As they pass through the Valley of Baka, they make it a place of springs; the autumn rains also cover it with pools. They go from strength to strength, till each appears before God in Zion.
(Psalm 84:5–7)

---

1. Amos 5:24.
2. Romans 12:1.
3. Matthew 15:9.
4. Psalm 144:2.

Rejoice for our ever-present help has come. By the power of the Word and the Holy Spirit, He has shown us our sin, our sinfulness, our need of Christ, and brought our hearts to repentance. Our God is faithful and just to forgive us our sins and to cleanse us of all unrighteousness.[5] In Christ our hands are washed clean so that we may lift up holy hands to praise and exalt our heavenly Father. Our hearts overflow with praise to God who is mighty in battle. He is worthy of all praise because He shields and protects His very own sons and daughters who are called by His name.

Our LORD Jesus brings us before the Father, and He rejoices over us as a Bridegroom rejoices over his bride.[6] Our Savior gathers us as a flock and sings His new song to us because He delights in us. How could we not worship and sing in harmony with the voice of our Good Shepherd?

"Do not fear, Zion; do not let your hands hang limp. *The LORD your God is with you, the Mighty Warrior who saves. he will take great delight in you; in his love he will no longer rebuke you, but will rejoice over you with singing."* (Zephaniah 3:16–17)

True worship is powerfully effective. It strengthens the connections between every part of the body of Christ.

Consider our solar system with its sun as the bright star at its center. Because of its gravitational force, everything revolves around this glowing star. The Milky Way's stars spin in their orbits, appearing as a river of light in the night sky. Every planet in our solar system receives its light from the sun and is perfectly placed to move in their paths, orchestrated by a mighty Conductor. The gravitational pull of these planetary orbs affects the orbits of other spheres that circle around the sun.

Now reflect on worship in the light of the Son who leads the universal church to exalt the LORD God Almighty.

a. Our praises are in tune with the truths of the Scriptures and in accord with the true nature of God as He has revealed Himself. The Spirit of Christ is the "gravity" that draws us to worship God in His presence so we may draw others to our Savior.

b. We exalt our LORD God, led by our High Priest and the Spirit of Christ to sing hymns, psalms, and spiritual songs. He inspires us so we may shower blessings upon all those with whom we interact in our daily lives.

c. The Spirit of Christ is actively present to speak to His people and His servants who proclaim what He has said to the congregation according to their need.

---

5. 1 John 1:9.
6. Zephaniah 3:17, 2 Corinthians 4:14.

d. Those who are gathered to worship sing out and lift up holy hands. They hear God's word ministered to them and partake of Christ at the LORD's Table. Christ Jesus ministers to us and we are strengthened to minister and serve others.

e. In our assemblies, the Holy Spirit lavishes gifts and empowers His people with various spiritual abilities as He desires: to preach, teach, prophesy, minister Jesus' healing touch, and encourage one another. When we express our reverence and awe in song and proclamations of God's Word, the Holy Spirit's power puts wings on our gospel shoes.

f. In our worship gatherings, the saints lift up their prayers in accord with Jesus' name. Our prayers are treasured like fragrant incense in heaven's golden bowls, and then everything we need for life and godliness is showered down upon all those who gather. Our petitions and intercessions directly affect the lives of friends, family, the weak and helpless, and to meet urgent needs in every nation.

g. Every element of worship adds to our faith, goodness, and knowledge. Self-control is added to our knowledge. Perseverance is added to self-control, and to perseverance, godliness and brotherly kindness. Then the greatest of all gifts is added to brotherly kindness—the gift of love.[7]

> *As the secrets of their hearts are laid bare, they will fall down and worship God, exclaiming, "God is really among you!" What then shall we say, brothers and sisters? When you come together, each of you has a hymn, or a word of instruction, a revelation, a tongue or an interpretation. Everything must be done so that the church may be built up.*
> (1 Corinthians 14:25–26)

True worship is contagious. During the pandemic of 2020 we were warned that singing served as a major spreader of the virus. The greater truth is that in our worship gatherings, even one person singing out from their spirit with psalms, choruses, and hymns is spiritually contagious. One voice in harmony with Jesus' new song exalts our Father and reveals Christ's holy presence, and soon there will be many voices joined together.

> *Let the message of Christ dwell among you richly as you teach and admonish one another with all wisdom through psalms, hymns, and songs from the Spirit, singing to God with gratitude in your hearts.*
> (Colossians 3:16)

---

7. 2 Peter 1:5–7.

When we gather to lift up the High and Exalted One, our High Priest ministers mercy and grace to the lowly, reviving the heart of the oppressed.[8] He has forgiven us, cleansed us, and now advocates for us. He adorns us as a bride so He may present us before the throne of grace. We approach the Father with confidence in our time of need because Jesus is present with us and intercedes on our behalf. Our LORD Jesus is ever present and yet He is manifested in greater measure in our time of need. His holy presence is active among us, overflowing with heaven's treasures in our gatherings so we may worship, serve, and minister before Him.

In His presence we minister with great confidence. With the Master Builder at our side, we are like young apprentices practicing a trade under our father's guiding hand. We sing out with conviction because our Redeemer is at our side and we simply raise our voices in harmony.

Let us then approach God's throne of grace with confidence, so that we may receive mercy and find grace to help us in our time of need.
(Hebrews 4:16)

Gates of thanksgiving welcome us into worship. The congregation considers His mighty deeds, the wonders of His creation, His power and might to save, and this inspires us to exalt the LORD Almighty. As we worship together, we enter into the realm of God's kingdom, remembering His great promise of salvation. Then, in reverent awe we see His mighty arm at work on behalf of all those who will dwell in Him and abide in Christ.

God's people enter into true worship with reverence and awe because our God is a consuming fire. Six days a week we face hardships and trials that refine us. We are being purified into the finest vessels of silver and gold. The hardships of this world serve to polish us into precious, brilliant building stones of God's kingdom. Then we come into God's rest as tried, tested, and proven servants. God's enemies are consumed by His fiery presence, but refined saints pass through the fire into peace, comfort, and rest.

Therefore, since we are receiving a kingdom that cannot be shaken, let us be thankful, and so worship God acceptably with reverence and awe, for our "God is a consuming fire."
(Hebrews 12:28–29)

Worship isn't reserved for one hour on Sunday morning. It flows out to become a part of our everyday lives. When we wake during the night, praise breaks the grip of dark dreams. The bright morning sun pierces the horizon to warm our hearts and fill us with anticipation for heaven's blessings that

---
8. Isaiah 57:15.

overtake us as we apply our hands to do our job.[9] A quick breakfast during the chaos of packing the kid's lunches and getting them to the school bus is a precious moment of thanksgiving for the blessings of family and God's provision.

A thermos of hot coffee, a bologna and cheese sandwich, and a juicy apple at lunch time offer a moment to lift our eyes above the fray and offer up thanksgiving from our hearts. The time we spend snarled in traffic on the way home isn't wasted because this offers us extra time to pray and honor God who makes straight the way before us.[10] When the kids are tuckered out and tucked in their beds, the moment offers a special opportunity for passing on to them a legacy of worship, prayer, and praise before they close their eyes in slumber. In the quiet, waning moments of the evening we may find this is the best time to talk to our heavenly Father and lift our hands to Him—for He is holy, holy, holy.

Heaven's angels never tire of worshiping God Almighty. They are surrounded by His glory and eternal holiness. May we never become weary of lifting our hands to worship the LORD Most High in His presence as we prepare to worship forever with angelic choirs.

> *Each of the four living creatures had six wings and was covered with eyes all around, even under its wings. Day and night they never stop saying: "'Holy, holy, holy is the LORD God Almighty,' who was, and is, and is to come."* (Revelation 4:8)

In every sense of the word, when we gather to worship and praise our Father in heaven, we prepare ourselves for that great day when our LORD Jesus returns for His bride. We become hearers of the Word as we sing the words of holy Scripture. What we hear inspires us to do what the Word teaches.[11] By the power of the Word and the Holy Spirit we come to know our LORD Jesus so that we may walk in His footsteps and follow the path of the LORD's favor.[12]

Prayers of the people serve as a vital part of our worship gatherings. In a very real sense, we carry our everyday pleas into congregational worship where all who are gathered agree together. Our petitions are presented before the throne of grace in accord with Jesus' name.

Consider the reality and power of our intercessions. The twenty-four elders bow down to worship the Lamb of God. They have harps to sing our Redeemer's new songs, and yet they treasure the prayers of the saints in golden bowls like fragrant incense.

---

9. Deuteronomy 28:23.
10. Proverbs 3:6.
11. James 1:22.
12. Psalm 90:17.

Heaven collects our petitions in priceless bowls as if to weigh them on the scales of justice.[13] The incense of our effectual and fervent appeals tips the balance on heaven's scale of justice and the oppressive burdens of the kingdom of darkness give way to God's favor.[14] Even unjust judges must give way to heaven's justice.[15]

And when he had taken it, the four living creatures and the twenty-four elders fell down before the Lamb. Each one had a harp and they were holding golden bowls full of incense, which are the prayers of God's people.
(Revelation 5:8)

The door to real worship in a gathering of God's people is open to those who put aside personal agendas and ambitions. This doorway isn't opened by common means. Instead, repentant hearts see their need of Christ and enter to worship, washed clean and wrapped in Christ's robe of righteousness.

The power of God's Word keeps our voices true, like a tuning fork that brings us into harmony with Christ Jesus' new song. Then, in His holy presence, the darkness is driven back so we may enjoy our Savior's showers of blessing.

As we come together to worship in Jesus' name, our love for each other grows and strengthens our union in Christ. In the presence of our high priest, we receive His ministering touch and we're covered in the shadow of His wings so we may go out with singing. Every voice of praise, every truth we are taught, and every gospel message proclaimed stays with us through the week and serves to prepare us as a bride for His coming.

> Praise our God, all you his servants, you who fear him, both great and small! (Revelation 19:5)

---

13. Job 3:16.
14. Proverbs 16:11.
15. Luke 18:7–8.

Chapter 2 Q&A

A Heart for Gathering

1. Describe the door that opens the way to worship. How is it opened to us?

   _____
   _____
   _____

2. Why are contrite hearts so vital as we gather to worship?

   _____
   _____
   _____

3. How does assembling for worship affect the work of the Great Commission?

   _____
   _____
   _____

4. What joys and blessings are yours as you join with people of faith to bow down in worship and lift up holy hands in praise?

   _____
   _____
   _____

My Journey's Journal:

Chapter 3: True to Our Purpose

Key Scriptures:

- "Yet a time is coming and has now come when the true worshipers will worship the Father in the Spirit and in truth, for they are the kind of worshipers the Father seeks. God is spirit, and his worshipers must worship in the Spirit and in truth" (John 4:23–24).

- "For we who worship by the Spirit of God are the ones who are truly circumcised. We rely on what Christ Jesus has done for us. We put no confidence in human effort" (Philippians 3:3 NLT).

This part of our ascent opens the way for us to walk according to the perfect law of freedom that compels the kingdom's royal priests to fulfill our purpose in Christ's royal priesthood, declaring God's praises.[1] In sermon, song, and service we proclaim the Good News of Jesus Christ and His saving grace. We are children of Zion who broadcast the truths of God's eternal Word to a world torn by sin's chaos. We are edified as true worshipers so we may be delivered from assaults by a dark world. As children of resurrection, we speak out and sing out the truths that have changed our lives forever. As children of hope, we overflow with resounding notes of eternal assurance that drive back the enemies of God's kingdom.

Verse by verse through 1st John chapter 1, we'll see the powerful effect of the breath of the Spirit who gives wind to our spirit as we ascend God's holy mountain. With each step we shout out with praise and exaltations before our God as we gather to worship.

> A prayer according to Matthew 21:16:
>
> Oh LORD our God, may our lips be like those of children and infants from whom you have called forth your praise.

---

1. 1 Peter 2:9.

Hearers and doers of the Word look intently into the perfect law of freedom.[2] What we have heard and believed compels us to fulfill our purpose; to praise, honor, and glorify the Great I AM. True worshippers fulfill Christ's command to proclaim the good news that has changed our lives and our eternal destiny. Our praise is rooted in the beginning and our voices ring out into eternity with a victorious song. We treasure the truths we have heard; truths established in the beginning by the Word who spoke, and it came to be.[3] All who overcome in Christ and stand firm on the Rock, hold onto His promises that carry us through to the end of time.

The testimony declared by Jesus' disciples remains true to the Word of creation who spoke and all things stood firm. Immanuel's called, chosen, and faithful followers stand with Him in victory.[4] They rejoice in Christ who is victorious and will reign with Him forever and ever.[5]

As Jesus' royal priesthood, the Church lifts her hands and voices to declare His praises. We are the true worshipers whom the Father seeks. By the power of the Word and the Holy Spirit, and through the waters of baptism, we are raised up as children of resurrection. God's sons and daughters live according to saving faith and rise up victorious in Jesus Christ. We grow in grace and knowledge to strengthen us in soul and spirit. We wait upon the Holy Spirit's anointing, gifting, and empowering work to cloth us with power so we may go out with authority to proclaim the Word and make disciples.

That which was from the beginning, which we have heard, which we have seen with our eyes, which we have looked at and our hands have touched–this we proclaim concerning the Word of life.
(1 John 1:1)

Children of Zion boldly and joyfully broadcast a heartfelt witness of what the LORD has done for them. We spread the word that brings order into a chaotic and sin-torn world. Our witness fulfills Christ's Great Commission command to fill and subdue the earth.[6]

As new creations in Christ we enter by faith into God's eternal rest.[7] God uses our testimony of Christ, our Savior, to open other people's eyes to see into eternity and grab hold of the blessings of this present life and see the world around us from an eternal viewpoint. We give witness of Christ who is ever present with us to deliver us from the clutches of this world's darkness and bring us into the eternal light of life.

2. James 1:25.
3. Psalm 33:9.
4. Revelation 17:14.
5. Revelation 5:10.
6. Habakkuk 2:14.
7. Hebrews 4:10–11.

The life appeared; we have seen it and testify to it, and we proclaim to you the eternal life, which was with the Father and has appeared to us.
(1 John 1:2)

Children of resurrection speak out about what they have seen and heard—the true gospel of our LORD and Savior, Jesus Christ. We are candid about our weaknesses and failings, and delight to speak of the work that God's grace and mercy have accomplished in our lives. By His grace and mercy, the chains of our sins, our weaknesses, and failings break away and we are made overcomers in Christ. We know the power of the blood of the Lamb of God who takes away even the stain of our sin, and the sins of the whole world.

What we have believed is not limited to a get-me-out-of-trouble religion. Even when it feels like the consequences of our sin linger too long, we hold on to God's promise that our LORD is ever-present with us in our times of trouble to deliver us from our accusers. But that's just a good beginning. We are adopted as sons and daughters of the Most High God and brought together as brothers and sisters of our LORD Jesus. We are brought into a family of fellowship where we fed on the milk and meat of the Word so that we may grow in grace and knowledge. We gather together in this family of faith to worship, serve, and minister before Jesus, our High Priest, and to glorify and exalt God the Father with our voices shouting out with everlasting praise.

We proclaim to you what we have seen and heard, so that you also may have fellowship with us. And our fellowship is with the Father and with his Son, Jesus Christ.
(1 John 1:3)

The voices of all children of hope resound with a joyful chorus. Our love of Christ arouses sweet refrains from our hearts so that melodies may flow from our lips like incense. We sing out with words of life and the light of Christ drives back the forces of darkness. The gates of hell will not prevail against us.[8] We make music and play instruments with rejoicing and the strongholds of the enemy crumble before us into ruin.

We once trudged through life as if stuck in dungeons of darkness and gloom. Our eyes were blinded by the shadows of death. There was no light to guide us. We stumbled along, wanting a safe place to rest, but there was only darkness. The night crept into our hearts, filling our lost souls with lifeless despair. Dry bones can't sing mournful dirges. But when these bones are strengthened, they grasp for something to hold onto and a nail-scarred hand reaches out to redeem them. Then the Spirit of Christ breathed the four winds and suddenly, the shadows of death were driven back, and the dry bones came

---
8. Matthew 16:18.

alive.[9] Our souls were restored and found rest in Him. This day is today and we sing of a fruitful vineyard; a place of safety, care, comfort, and eternal rest.[10]

> *We write this to make our joy complete. This is the message we have heard from him and declare to you: God is light; in him there is no darkness at all.*
> (1 John 1:4–5)

Bond servants of Jesus Christ enjoy fellowship with the Father and rejoice in the freedom He gives us. In this bond of fellowship we walk with God in a garden of delights, just as Adam and Eve first walked with their Creator. But if we claim walk in fellowship with the Father while walking according to love, our superficial Christianity is a sin "against the body and blood of the LORD."[11]

As God's sons and daughters, we must continually take an inventory of ourselves to be sure we remain true to our purpose. The measure we use to check up on our walk of faith is God's Word. There is no other standard. Regular examinations are crucial to keep us from slipping into deceiving ourselves.[12] People who mislead themselves become vulnerable to believing a deceiver's lie that leads them to slip back into the dregs of darkness.

> *If we claim to have fellowship with him and yet walk in the darkness, we lie and do not live out the truth.*
> (1 John 1:6)

We delight in assembling because we enter a faithful community where we get caught up in the Spirit's wind. The breath of the Spirit enlivens us to fulfill God's purpose. Indeed, the church began "when they were all together in one place" for a prayer gathering.[13] In our meetings, the Holy Spirit convicts us of our sin and then we confess our sins one to the other and receive God's forgiveness.[14] We delight in gathering where there is an abundance of mercy; more than enough blessings for all who will receive.

Because of God's lovingkindness, we are called, chosen, and then given His name as our family name. We are delivered from the clutches of darkness to walk in the light of Christ. He restores our souls and sets us free from the chains of depravity, want, and infirmity so that we may walk in the light of the fullness of Christ and fulfill our purpose in God's kingdom. As victors in Christ, even when we walk through darkness in the valley of death, we will fear no evil, because Jesus inhabits our every step. His rod and staff are ever-present to comfort us as we suffer with Christ as we proclaim the gospel.

---

9. Ezekiel 37:8–9.
10. Isaiah 27:2.
11. 1 Corinthians 11:27.
12. 2 Corinthians 13:5.
13. Acts 2:1.
14. James 5:16.

But if we walk in the light, as he is in the light, we have fellowship with one another, and the blood of Jesus, his Son, purifies us from all sin. If we claim to be without sin, we deceive ourselves and the truth is not in us. If we confess our sins, he is faithful and just and will forgive us our sins and purify us from all unrighteousness. If we claim we have not sinned, we make him out to be a liar and his word is not in us.
(1 John 1:7–10)

Our purpose in God's kingdom has its roots in the beginning. We are called to worship and serve in a way that affects our lives in the present and builds hope for eternity. The truths of God's Word proclaimed in our gatherings serve to change our worldview by giving us an eternal perspective that drives our purpose. Our worshipful gatherings are empowered by the wind of the Spirit who gives breath to our spirit so we may voice true acclamations of praise to honor our LORD and God.

> "Hallelu Yah![15]
>
> For our LORD God Almighty reigns.
> Let us rejoice and be glad and give him glory!
>
> For the wedding of the Lamb has come, and his bride has made herself ready. Fine linen, bright and clean, was given her to wear." (Revelation 19:6–8)

---

15. When translated from Hebrew, hallelujah is: הַלְלוּ־יָהּ *halәlū-Yāh*. Yah is an abbreviated form of Yahweh.

Chapter 3 Q&A

True to Our Purpose

1. What are the roots of all praise and exaltations that sprout and blossom with shouts of praise?

2. How does true worship affect us in the present and forever?

3. Who are the children of hope? How is it that their hope inspires true worship?

4. Describe the contagious effect of worshipful songs in the assembly.

My Journey's Journal:

Part II
A Repentant Cry

Have mercy on me, O God, according to your unfailing love; according to your great compassion blot out my transgressions. Wash away all my iniquity and cleanse me from my sin. (Psalm 51:1–2)

Let us turn away from self-satisfying worship and praise so we may walk in Jesus' footsteps and cleanse the temple of our lives.

Chapter 4: Cain's Offering

Key Scriptures:

- "For the life of a creature is in the blood, and I have given it to you to make atonement for yourselves on the altar; it is the blood that makes atonement for one's life" (Leviticus 17:11).

- "In fact, the law requires that nearly everything be cleansed with blood, and without the shedding of blood there is no forgiveness" (Hebrews 9:22).

If mom said it once, she said it a thousand times, "Eat your vegetables," and she was right. Carrots, peas, and broccoli are, indeed, healthy food for the body, but they can't save lost souls. True worship has its roots in the Garden of Eden. But many of us unwittingly fall into a Cain kind of worship that forgets what God established in the beginning. This apathetic mindset quickly turns into worshipping to please our own desires. We turn away from God's abundant gifts for the church to seek those who lead us in worship that tickles our ears.[1]

Repenting and turning away from sin is a vital part of preparing our hearts for gathering to be taught and to sing out with praise. It's too easy to listen to voices that seduce us to enter worship in a way we think is best. When we assemble with an attitude of repentance and hear the truths of God's Word rightly taught, we'll realize that human intellect is not a reliable arbiter of truth.

Together we'll discover aspects of real worship that outshine all trivial and meaningless traditions. Our words, our teaching, and our songs that are not true to the gospel must be eliminated. Our worship must reflect Christ and the cross. Our Savior provides the only remedy for sin. As we lift our voices before Christ Jesus, our High Priest, we are shielded and made strong to stand against the fiery darts of the enemy. But when we drift away from what is true and right in our gatherings, we will soon hear discordant voices in the congregation.

---

1. 2 Timothy 4:3.

> A prayer according to Ezekiel 11:19:
>
> Oh Lord, give us undivided hearts and pour your Holy Spirit into us. Remove our hearts of stone so that we may overflow with the Spirit of Christ.

Cain reminds me of the age-old saying, "You can't get blood out of a turnip." He should have known that vegetables were completely insufficient to save a sinner. We don't know all the reasons God rejected his sacrifice, but we do know that it was not offered in faith.[2] We also know that years later many men in Israel followed in his unfaithful footsteps.[3] Cain brought an offering that discounted God's grace. What he offered did not point the way to forgiveness, cleansing, and the hope of a Redeemer. An atoning sacrifice was required of him, and since then, God's nature and purpose have not changed.[4] Cain came with an unrepentant and self-sufficient attitude. Like Balaam, idolatry ruled in his heart.[5] He turned from the truth that without the shedding of blood there is no forgiveness.[6] Indeed, he came to worship for with detestable things according to his own plan.[7]

It's likely that Cain brought the fruits of his harvest thinking they were good enough. After all, they were produced by his sweat and hard labor. But what he brought was commonplace. In later generations, Yahweh, Israel's God, commanded the people to gather for the firstfruits festival of *Shavuot* at the beginning of harvest. They brought the first and best of their harvest to offer before a holy God. But, the firstfruit offering was intended as a thanksgiving offering to be given to the priest in a basket to acknowledge their God for leading them into a land flowing with milk and honey. The gift was to provide for the priests who served in the temple. Our heavenly Father never promised that offerings from our gardens would save us.

> *But on Cain and his offering he did not look with favor. So Cain was very angry, and his face was downcast. Then the LORD said to Cain, "Why are you angry? Why is your face downcast? If you do what is right, will you not be accepted? But if you do not do what is right, sin is crouching at your door; it desires to have you, but you must rule over it."*
> (Genesis 4:5–9)

---

2. Hebrews 11:4.
3. Amos 5:22.
4. Hebrews 6:17.
5. Revelation 2:14.
6. Hebrews 9:22.
7. Deuteronomy 7:26.

The Genesis account doesn't tell us the reason God rejected Cain's sacrifice, but there are clues throughout the Bible. Apparently, he was caught up in sins like those of Balaam. Many years later, the spirit of Cain was manifested in this prophet from Pethor who counseled king Balak to entice the people of Israel into sexual immorality (Revelation 2:14). King Balak couldn't make Balaam curse God's holy nation, but Balaam advised him to draw them into sensual, idolatrous sin. This foreign king lured them into eating pagan sacrificial meals together, bowing down before foreign gods, and participating in sensual orgies.

It is our sin-bent hearts that lead us into idolatrous worship. But such unacceptable worship separates us from the presence of our holy heavenly Father. The God of our salvation is mighty to save, but souls ruled by wanderlust leave the protective covering of His presence and turn a deaf ear to the Father's redemptive call.

Why would anyone turn away? If people understood the truth, no one would reject Christ. In the kingdom of heaven, our boundaries are established in pleasant places.[8] Entering the Good Shepherd's green pastures means that we can kick up our heels in lush meadows.[9] Living according to His commands sets us free to run on His pathway.[10] Dwelling in the house of the LORD means that goodness, love, and mercy follow us all the days of our lives.[11] But sin deceives us into leaving all these good things behind for idolatrous worship.

So Cain went out from the Lord's presence and lived in the land of Nod, east of Eden.[12]
(Genesis 4:16)

We live in a culture steeped in distracting media. Seductive images pop up unsolicited on our cell phone screens. People post selfies on social media that tempt tender souls and foster selfish yearnings. Soon after the opening credits roll across the screen of a movie, the spirit of Balaam tosses out his enticements. But we're so used to these enticements we barely notice them. Movie stars and blockbuster films are all that our friends talk about, so it's okay, right? Such thoughts would drag us down into the pit with them.

They were the ones who followed Balaam's advice and enticed the Israelites to be unfaithful to the LORD in the Peor incident, so that a plague struck the Lord's people.
(Numbers 31:16)

---
8. Psalm 16:6.
9. Malachi 4:2.
10. Psalm 119:32.
11. Psalm 23:6.
12. In Hebrew, "Nod" means "wandering."

Paul's letter to the Philippian church reminds us that we are the true circumcision of God. He teaches that those of us who are baptized into Christ are called to cut ourselves off from the enticements of the flesh. Our human weaknesses and self-centered desires are like cords that entangle us. Human reasoning makes us feel so clever and self-sufficient that we see no need to humble ourselves before a holy God. But we must never allow the world's ideas to override our heavenly Father's reign over our lives. Without the Spirit of Truth, human reasoning cannot establish truth, but in fact, leads us astray. Neither life experience nor personal light bulb moments can serve as the authority that establishes truth. They will inevitably mislead us.

As an example of our tendency to depend on our own understanding,[13] consider what Christians say when discussing Bible truths they don't embrace. They rarely turn to the Scriptures to help them understand what God's Word teaches about the subject. Instead, their conversations are often filled with phrases like, "Well, I think that means…" Or they might say, "That's not the way I was taught." They set themselves up as experts based upon their own thoughts. Before long, they set aside what is true. They reject the truth and justify their position by means of human reasoning.

Some have assumed Paul's teaching means to literally cut themselves off from society, turn to asceticism, and live lives that strictly deny what their bodies need. God's Word instead reminds us we are responsible to keep our physical bodies healthy and strong to accomplish the kingdom work He assigned to us. Extreme self-denial turns into a source of pride and makes us too self-focused.

> *For it is we who are the circumcision, we who serve God by his Spirit, who boast in Christ Jesus, and who put no confidence in the flesh.*
> (Philippians 3:3)

Exalting angels and lifting them up like deities is a deceptive kind of faith.[14] Counterfeit worship encourages a false humility that leads us to think of ourselves as little more than dirt to sweep under the rug. Lifting ourselves up as hyper-spiritual Christians and saying "Praise Jesus" in every other sentence reduces our spiritual life to showmanship.

As Christians, we have no need of such trivialities. We serve an awesome God who is more than able to show His arm strong on our behalf. There is no need to season our words with spiritual sounding talk that quickly becomes meaningless. Talking up our spiritual experiences leads to exalting ourselves, rather than our heavenly Father who is Giver of all good gifts.

---

13. Proverbs 3:5.
14. Colossians 2:18.

> *Do not let anyone who delights in false humility and the worship of angels disqualify you. Such a person also goes into great detail about what they have seen; they are puffed up with idle notions by their unspiritual mind.*
> (Colossians 2:18)

Israel's sin brought a plague among them that killed 24,000 people. The plague finally ended when Phinehas, the son of the high priest, proved that he was zealous for the honor of God's holy name by putting an idolater to death. Indeed, he stood in the gap to save a nation.

Relying on reasoning as our guide can lead us to think that it's okay to satisfy the desires of our flesh because we'll be forgiven. But such cheap grace cannot make us impervious to the consequences of our sin. Balaam earned his wages by counseling Balak to seduce God's holy nation into idolatrous sin. In their moments of sensual pleasure, Israel's people forgot that the "wages of sin is death."[1] They neglected the truth that our heavenly Father provides the only remedy for sin through His Son, Jesus Christ.

> *They have left the straight way and wandered off to follow the way of Balaam son of Bezer, who loved the wages of wickedness.*
> (2 Peter 2:15)

It's an amazing truth that those who are caught up in the clutches of sin always desire for you to join them and be bound in chains of addiction with them. They aim for the best of God's people and attempt to entice them into the pit with them. They stand against Christ and walk in the footsteps of Balaam.

> *Do not be like Cain, who belonged to the evil one and murdered his brother. And why did he murder him? Because his own actions were evil and his brother's were righteous.*
> (1 John 3:12)

Like Balaam, Cain refused to submit himself to God's requirements. Instead, he allowed his anger to burn so hot he killed his brother Abel who pleased God. Abel was the first prophet in a line of many who would be slain for proclaiming truth and righteousness.[2] When there is sin in the congregation, a discerning worship leader senses the weight of it and calls the people to repentance. The leader may not know the specifics of the sin but they can see the congregation's reverence for God devolve into worship by rote. This doesn't mean they listen to rumors. No, they discern the weight of it by the Holy Spirit's witness in their spirit regarding sin in the camp.

---

1. Romans 6:23.
2. Luke 11:51.

If those who guide us in worship ignore the warnings and continue leading as if nothing is wrong, this eventually leads the Spirit to turn away, saying; "Away with the noise of your songs! I will not listen to the music of your harps."[3] Keeping peace in the congregation at any price opens the way for selfish ambitions to thrive. Love that refuses to right a wrong is an empty love. Indifference to sin leads to great error, shallow ministries of music, and gradually leads to discord in the church. Before long, everyone sings a different tune to the beat of their own drummer. But we are called to sing in harmony with Jesus' new song—hymns, psalms, and spiritual songs that proclaim the Good News.

> *Woe to them! They have taken the way of Cain; they have rushed for profit into Balaam's error; they have been destroyed in Korah's rebellion.*
> (Jude 1:11)

We may try to fool ourselves with false spirituality and self-sufficient attitudes. Instead, we are called to stand on the Rock, Christ Jesus, and stand up as His servants in the power and strength of the Lord. He is more than able to save. This struggle is constant because our minds come up with more and more ways to make ourselves right with God. We need constant reminders that our heavenly Father provided the only remedy for sin through His only Son, Jesus Christ.

Abel is the first prophet who stood up for truth and righteousness, and it cost him his life. Fast forward through the time-line of history and many more prophets walked in his footsteps and paid for it with their lives. In the age of the modern-day church, the Spirit of Christ still raises up servants who will stand up for truth and righteousness and warn the congregation when they slip into self-satisfying worship. We must decide. Will we listen to their warnings or despise them in the way of Cain? We must not. We are called to hear and do what is right in the sight of the Lord. With the heart and attitude of Jesus, we can enter the joy of harmonious, redemptive, and truly worshipful assemblies.

> "Oh, that one of you would shut the temple doors, so that you would not light useless fires on my altar! I am not pleased with you," says the LORD Almighty, "and I will accept no offering from your hands." (Malachi 1:10)

---

3. Amos 5:23.

Chapter 4 Q&A

Cain's Offering

1. What is the result of self-sufficient attitudes in our walk of faith?

   _____
   _____
   _____

2. Can you get blood out of a turnip? Why is this an important question for the modern-day church as we take an account of ourselves?

   _____
   _____
   _____

3. What happens when the glitter and glam of the world creeps into our times of worship?

   _____
   _____
   _____

4. Describe the battle between human reason and the mind of Christ.

   _____
   _____
   _____

My Journey's Journal:

Chapter 5: Out of Focus

Key Scriptures:

- "And when you were eating and drinking, were you not just feasting for yourselves?" (Zechariah 7:6).
- "How can you believe since you accept glory from one another but do not seek the glory that comes from the only God" (John 5:44).

Clouds that give no rain may offer a few moments of shade for parched ground, but soon the wind blows them on their way, leaving the land still dry, thirsty. Such clouds appear to hold a promise of refreshing yet leave the ground dry and unfruitful.[1] This joyful ascent upon God's holy mountain unites us as pilgrims in fellowship with Christ who keeps us focused on what is true. Too many churches are like uprooted trees in the autumn—twice dead.[2] We must not allow our desire for self-expression to distract us from bowing down to worship. Self-inspired worship is, in many ways, like offering prayers with wrong motives. Both echo off the ceiling and go no higher.[3] We are left parched and thirsty.

Let us grieve for coming together like so many bouquets of artificial flowers with no fragrance. To avoid this kind of gathering we must take an account of ourselves with God's Word as our standard of measure. We dare not trust experience to be our teacher, it, like our human nature, tends to mislead us. To avoid these pitfalls, we must make God's Word our standard. When we stand in the truth, we'll realize that we were false worshippers who had no fragrance of Christ.

---

1. Proverbs 25:14.
2. Jude 1:21.
3. Lamentations 3:44, James 4:3.

> A prayer according to Isaiah 5:12:
>
> Change our hearts, oh Lord. Too easily, our musical instruments sound out with pleasing songs that soothe our souls, but our singing shows little regard your mighty acts. By our own words we devalue what you have created—all the work of your hands. Bring our hearts to repentance, for we have sinned against you.

All too often, people go home after church, saying, "I didn't get anything out that today." They came empty and left empty. Christians often come to church with an attitude that says, "What are you going to do for me and my kids today?" But worshipful assemblies are not like the world around us that declares, "Give so you can get."

Our heavenly Father guards us with a tender, jealous love. God's affections toward His children hold us close so that our hearts stay fixed upon Him. Under His protective covering, we can focus our worship on Him alone. Why then would we raise our hands in the air to dance and sing death metal lyrics on Saturday night and then, with the same heart, hands, and voice, sing God's praises in church on Sunday morning? Is this kind of worship acceptable? Can we sing in an all-night party at the pub and then sing God's praises at church with the same voice? No! This is a Cain style of worship.

Here is the heart of the matter. A person's hands, roughened by labor at the construction site, honor God in the work they do as unto the Lord.[4] But hands become something even more when we lift them high to exalt a holy God. The hands you extend in worship are the hands of "a chosen people, a royal priesthood, a holy nation, God's special possession."[5]

The inability of the modern-day church to distinguish between our God-given natural talents and the spiritual gifts leads to unacceptable worship and weakens us in the work of the Great Commission. In their rightful place, common and spiritual gifts are equally good. Both are gifts from the Lord. Common gifts serve to provide for our family and community. Spiritual gifts are for ministry and service in the church and for advancing the Gospel. But they must be kept separate. They are compatible but serve different purposes.[6] We keep them separate because common fire, while good in its place, cannot do the work of the Holy Spirit's fire.[7]

---

4. Colossians 3:23.
5. 1 Peter 2:9.
6. Leviticus 10:10, Ezekiel 44:23.
7. Leviticus 10:1.

> *"The God who made the world and everything in it is the LORD of heaven and earth and does not live in temples built by human hands. And he is not served by human hands, as if he needed anything. Rather, he himself gives everyone life and breath and everything else."*
> (Acts 17:25)

We need Jesus, our High Priest, to keep us focused so we may praise and exalt the LORD God in reverent awe. The wind of the Holy Spirit is the breath that gives our spirit a voice to glorify our heavenly Father who is the focus of our worship. We must beware of others who would distract us with rites that are more about ourselves, our needs, and our personal preferences.

When we come to worship, we are called to humble ourselves in the presence of the Lord. Without contrite hearts, our ears are stopped to God teaching, correcting, and redirecting our lives to walk according to what is right.[8] Can we accept words of admonishment in the pastor's message? If a church leader tactfully corrects us, will we leave in a huff and never return? If that's where we're at, the prophet Micah knows just the right church for us.

> *Suppose a prophet full of lies would say to you, "I'll preach to you the joys of wine and alcohol!" That's just the kind of prophet you would like!*
> (Micah 2:11 NLT)

We come together in Jesus' name where He serves as High Priest to lead us in worship and minister to us according to our need. He gives us His strength to overcome our weaknesses. He lifts us up when we are beaten down. He teaches us so that we may know Him and walk in His footsteps. And then, as overcomers in Christ, we serve and minister to those who gather with us. In the light of Christ and by means of the Spirit of Christ we are anointed, gifted, and empowered to speak what Jesus is saying in the moment. We extend our hands to offer a ministering touch. Indeed, we come to serve in the same way as our Savior who gathers us to care for us as the sheep of His pasture.

> *The greatest among you will be your servant. For those who exalt themselves will be humbled, and those who humble themselves will be exalted.*
> (Matthew 23:11–12)

Silk flowers are always attractive and they stay pretty for a long time. They don't turn brown around the edges and shed petals that need to be cleaned up. There's no need to water them. Faux flowers don't get old and moldy. They only require an occasional dusting. But all that they offer is artificial, an imitation of real beauty.

---

8. 2 Timothy 3:16.

It's important to regularly examine ourselves and our worship. It's like checking every item in our backpack to be sure it's what we need for our ascent and then throwing out the excess. A checkup keeps our prayer time, teaching, and praises uncluttered and real. Taking an inventory of ourselves prepares us so we can belt out worship songs without making a show of great spirituality. We need to ask ourselves, is our praise genuine, does it spring up from a grateful and contrite heart? True and real worship requires us to prepare our hearts with care. True hearts exalt our Father alone. We are urged to stop imagining ourselves to be like David on his harp.[9] It's important to know the difference between songs we improvise to tickle our ears and spiritual songs inspired by the Holy Spirit. Our songs of praise must be continually watered from the spring of living water. Then the wind of the Spirit spreads the sweet fragrance of our worshipful songs.

> *And when you pray, do not be like the hypocrites, for they love to pray standing in the synagogues and on the street corners to be seen by others. Truly I tell you, they have received their reward in full. But when you pray, go into your room, close the door and pray to your Father, who is unseen. Then your Father, who sees what is done in secret, will reward you.*
> (Matthew 6:5–6)

Personal experience can't teach us how to worship in spirit and in truth. Minds that depend completely on reason rather than godly wisdom lead us in the wrong direction. Experience and reasoning minds limit us to the power of human nature. Because of our nature, we have a high need to take charge and try to look reverent by our own means. But genuine worship can only arise when the Holy Spirit supernaturally flows through the spirit of worshippers who stand on the truth of God's Word. By our own means, our gatherings often become syrupy, emotional, and sentimental. Adoration for our heavenly Father soon turns into a feel-good religious practice that is self-serving.

The teachers of the Law in Jesus' day offer us examples of using human reasoning to deny the truth. They denied that Jesus had the authority to forgive sins and heal a paralytic. They reasoned in their minds and hearts that His words were blasphemous according to their teaching.[10] We must not be like them and reduce our worship to the limited resources of the common realm and our man-made rules.

> *Can you fathom the mysteries of God? Can you probe the limits of the Almighty? They are higher than the heavens above–what can you do? They are deeper than the depths below–what can you know?*
> (Job 11:7–8)

---

9. Amos 6:5.
10. Mark 2:5–7.

The vacuum caused by spiritual ignorance could not be filled by natural man even if the collective powers of all earth-bound mental genius came together.[11] The void created by lack of true knowledge can never be filled by reasoning intellectuals.[12] The only standard for truth, wisdom, and knowledge is God's Word. The holy Scriptures are opened to us by means of the Holy Spirit. Its precious truths serve as the only light for our pathway. They appoint our steps and guide our plans.

Christ Jesus is the head of the church and He raises up prophets, pastors, teachers, and evangelists to teach us and lead us to His throne of grace. They teach us so that our feet remain on the firm foundation of truth and righteousness. Christians are called to be faithful, seeking to know our Savior who is revealed in God's Word. True worshipers remain faithful to all truth so we may continue to walk in its light.[13]

> *For the lips of a priest ought to preserve knowledge, because he is the messenger of the LORD Almighty and people seek instruction from his mouth.*
> (Malachi 2:7)

American individualism is a character trait we carry to an extreme, allowing it to infect our even times of worship. Rather than worshipping in harmony, we blaze our own trail while singing our own tune. It's as if we all sing at the same time in various keys, accompanied by different music. Every Bible teaching gets filtered according to the path we've mark out for ourselves.

This maverick mentality is opposed to what Paul teaches about submitting ourselves to serve as useful, working parts of the body of Christ. This is one of the American church's most destructive weaknesses. We must turn from this and serve as our part in the body, working in conjunction with all other parts of the body. It doesn't work when one person tries to do all the jobs that other parts of the body are gifted to do. In Christ we are called to come together, united in spirit to work together as a united body.

> *Just as a body, though one, has many parts, but all its many parts form one body, so it is with Christ.*
> (1 Corinthians 12:12)

It's too easy for mortals to be distracted from God's Word and think His blessings are never enough.[14] When this happens, church gatherings leave us

---

11. 1 Corinthians 2:14.
12. Luke 5:21-22.
13. 3 John 3.
14. 2 Samuel 12:8-9.

feeling empty. Our unrepentant hearts and spiritual duplicity take our eyes off of Jesus. Before long, we think that our own righteousness is good enough. We end up like wanderers who dance along with whatever song we hear. We are like wayfarers who set their sails to every wind of doctrine that comes our way. We breeze into whatever church we feel like on a whim, or decide to skip church entirely.

Contrite hearts are sure to hear God's call to spread their wings to soar upon the wind of the Spirit. The Spirit's breath gives us voices to exalt the LORD Almighty in a way that is spiritual and real. Focusing on the Spirit of Christ brings us into showers of blessings. When we gather to truly glorify God, we can open the windows and throw open the doors to let the aromas of Christ waft out to permeate the world all around.

> "Hallelu Yah!
>
> Salvation and glory and power belong to our God, for true and just are his judgments."(Revelation 19:1–2)

Chapter 5 Q&A

Out of Focus

1. If both holy and common are good, why do we need to focus on what is holy as we minister and serve in the church?

___

2. What are the hazards of depending on personal experience to help us know what is true?

___

3. How does individualism distract us in times of corporate worship?

___

4. How does the wind of the Spirit keep us focused on true worship?

___

My Journey's Journal:

Chapter 6: It's in the Bulletin

Key Scriptures:

- "Come near to God and he will come near to you. Wash your hands, you sinners, and purify your hearts, you double-minded" (James 4:8).
- "Having a form of godliness but denying its power" (2 Timothy 3:5).

It's a good idea to have a navigational app so you don't get lost along the way. Staying on a familiar road can give us a sense of security, but when traveling somewhere new, it's good to know the best way to our destination. Our heavenly Father established the means for orderly worship that rises above external regulations or man-made guidelines. In the full light of Christ, the shadows of a religious system cannot limit us. God enables us to overcome our human nature that desires what is familiar and comfortable. We see the way into true exaltations that flow out from us as we gather before our High Priest who leads us to exalt the LORD Almighty.

God's established order for the church is not a structure built with man-made methods or earthen stones. True worshippers are seated with Christ in his Father's presence. So, let us enter the way of peace our heavenly Father prepared for us so we may ascend to the heights to glorify Him with true and acceptable worship.

> A prayer according to Hebrews 9:10:
>
> O LORD Jesus, lead us to rise above matters of external regulations and ceremonial acts. Lift us up from outward rules that no longer apply to a New Covenant people.

Putting on rock climbing shoes, taking an ice axe in hand, hoisting a climbing pack, and throwing rope over our shoulder only makes us look like a mountain climber. Looking right doesn't get us up the mountain. We must repent of our pretenses, humble ourselves, and let Jesus' servant attitude appoint our footsteps. A broad, well-worn path is not a reliable guide for what is true and right. Instead, we prepare our hearts and humble ourselves to sing out in harmony with our Savior's new song. We must throw off worthless baggage that weighs us down. Instead, we come to Christ and continually abide in Him whose burden is light so that we produce the good fruit of the vine.

External forms of worship are attractive because they appeal to our human nature. But we can't go back to the shadow of Christ in the Old Covenant. The true object of our worship is now revealed in the Christ of the New Covenant church. Our Redeemer sings a new song. Old Covenant external rituals offered a covering for sin. A man-made system of worship is like Adam's fig leaf saying to us, "If I do this, that, and the other, I have worshipped." It's human nature to want a formula that tells me that when I bow my head and fold my hands to pray, sing with uplifted hands, and take notes during the sermon, I'm a good person and have fulfilled my duty to worship. Now I can do my own thing until next Sunday when I'll prove I'm a good person again." This kind of attitude serves a false image of God by means of self-satisfying rituals.

> *Therefore do not let anyone judge you by what you eat or drink, or with regard to a religious festival, a New Moon celebration or a Sabbath day. These are a shadow of the things that were to come; the reality, however, is found in Christ.*
> (Colossians 2:16–17)

How then can we be lifted out of this self-made trap and go up to Mount Zion, the mountain of the Lord? How is it possible to enter in and worship with the "church of the firstborn, whose names are written in heaven."[1] The Apostle Paul shows us the way: "God raised us up with Christ and seated us with him in the heavenly realms in Christ Jesus."[2]

The author of James makes it clear and simple. We must humble ourselves in the sight of the LORD and He will lift us up.[3] We are called to stand upon the Rock, Christ Jesus, and in Him we are raised up to the heights. He makes our feet as sure as a deer's footing on the cliffs. He preserves our lives and keeps our feet from slipping so that we may go up with singing. He cleanses and washes us so our hearts may rejoice as we trek on to the sound of flutes, ascending upon the mountain of the LORD to the Rock of Israel.[4]

> *Who may ascend the mountain of the Lord? Who may stand in his holy place? The one who has clean hands and a pure heart, who does not trust in an idol or swear by a false god.*
> (Psalm 24:3–4)

---

1. Hebrews 12:22–23.
2. Ephesians 2:6.
3. James 4:10.
4. Psalm 66:9–10, Isaiah 30:29.

We must not be like the Pharisees who ceremonially washed their hands, and then came to the table with their hands soiled by greed and corruption. They wore flowing robes, prayer shawls, and phylacteries, but murdered blood dripped from their hands. They came to the temple to pray their extensive and flowery prayers in public view, but covered up the fact that they just evicted a widow from her home and threw her hungry children out into the street. They defended themselves, saying, "Business is business. I serve the bottom line." After all, if their income is reduced because of a widow who can't pay rent, they have less to give in their tithes and offerings, right?

We must ask ourselves if we are any different. All too often we weigh other people's faith by their house, cars, and fashionable clothes. We raise an eyebrow and wonder, "If they're so sick, do they really have faith?" Our big check goes into the collection plate with a flourish and then we look at the guy next to us thinking, "What's wrong with him. He's only putting in a dollar?" We point an accusing finger at other people and then march right up to the communion table with proud, unrepentant hearts as if we truly remained in Christ. All the self-inspired things we do, motivated by prideful thoughts serve as barriers to entering true and real worship.

> *These people come near to me with their mouth and honor me with their lips, but their hearts are far from me. Their worship of me is based on merely human rules they have been taught.*
> (Isaiah 29:13)

Imagine a beautiful kitchen mixer sitting with its sparkling stainless-steel bowl on your countertop. But what if you still mixed ingredients by hand because that's the way your family always did it. You just have the electric mixer for show. Some people in ancient Israel looked forward to Christ as they came to worship in the temple. But too many were stuck in powerless worship that was a matter of external traditions and regulations. We can learn from them and exalt God in the light of Christ by the power of the Spirit.

The Law still teaches us good spiritual truths. As an example: Old Testament priests were not to wear wool when ministering because it would make them perspire.[5] Then they were to leave their linen ministry garments behind when they went into the outer courts.[6] This teaches those who minister in the church that we must only serve when clothed with power from on high and not by our own strength.[7] God's work cannot be accomplished by our own sweat. We need to be plugged into the Holy Spirit, who is the source of power. Laboring sweat is the curse of Adam's sin.[8]

---
5. Ezekiel 44:17–18.
6. Ezekiel 42:14.
7. Luke 24:49.
8. Genesis 3:17–18.

An outwardly applied command may make a person look good, but it can only satisfy the fleshly nature. What good is it to proudly declare, "I didn't tell a single lie today," while our hearts are filled with deceit? When we focus only on outward appearances, our worship is limited, serving merely as a veneer to cover a rotten core. Our heavenly Father established the way of orderly worship for the church through His Son, who serves as our High Priest. Those who serve under Christ's authority by leading people into true worship must be clothed from on high.

For God is not a God of disorder but of peace.
(1 Corinthians 14:33)

Solomon built the temple with ascending steps, massive walls, gates, special courtyards, and thresholds. It was designed as a place to offer acceptable worship within the bounds of Yahweh's commands. But God's established order for worship under the New Covenant is not a structure built by human hands. Instead, the gates, walls, and stairways of the New Covenant leads us to ascend to the heights where Jesus our High Priest ministers before us. Indeed, there is a gate the glory of the LORD enters to fill the sanctuary built for His holy name.[9] The gates of righteousness are everlasting doors,[10] and the gates of hell will not prevail against it.[11] Our Father set out a way of peace from which acceptable worship can blossom. As our worship heightens into harmonious exaltations, we'll soon learn that it goes way beyond what can be printed in a Sunday morning bulletin that provides an order of service.

Old Testament regulations, feasts, sacrifices, and offerings could not work from the inside out to cleanse the conscience. They only offered a temporary covering for sin—a shadow of Christ.

We must learn from the mistakes of Israel as a nation. They slid into idolatry again and again. Rather than looking forward to Messiah's perfect redemptive sacrifice, they soothed their guilty consciences with man-made rules and regulations. Strict personal observance of Talmudic rules made them feel as if they were upright. They could proudly declare, "I'm right before God because I only walked one kilometer on the Sabbath." Twenty-first century Jews who remain under the law don't push elevator buttons on the seventh day, but do they feel superior when their elevator stops automatically at every floor? Man-made rules defeat God's true purpose. Today, Christians can push elevator buttons and walk a mile to church because all the requirements of the Law and the feasts are fulfilled in Christ.

---

9. Ezekiel 43:5.
10. Psalm 118:19, Psalm 24:7–9.
11. Matthew 16:18.

These people honor me with their lips, but their hearts are far from me. They worship me in vain; their teachings are merely human rules.
(Matthew 15:8–9)

Money is a useful means of trade. The workings of worldwide commerce that serves to feed and clothe us depends on exchanges of currency. We all need it, and it grows in importance when we don't have enough. But while useful, we must not let our assets own us. Money is a cruel taskmaster. Many of us work and slave and save so we can buy that second home and get away to relax a bit. But then we spend our vacation time breaking our back to do the cleaning, repairs, and upgrades our vacation home requires. In reality, our money owns us.

There is a much better way to find rest. First, God calls us to the realization that all we have—every button, lug nut, retirement account, dollar bill, and credit card—it's all the property of our LORD God. He is our best financial planner. We give back a portion to Him because we are wise stewards over a small part of His vast estate. We manage it according to His instructions.

When our money no longer owns us, we can be heartily generous. When our pocket books no longer weigh us down, we are liberated so we can give freely. Now our wallets can open to cheerfully support the poor and our local church.[12] Indeed, we love the One who is Master over our all we have more than the nickels and dimes that once weighed us down and enslaved us.

No one can serve two masters. Either you will hate the one and love the other, or you will be devoted to the one and despise the other. You cannot serve both God and money.
(Luke 16:13)

We live in a culture that constantly assaults us with sensual attractions. But children of the Most High God are countercultural. We are called to deny self and live in Christ. His kingdom cannot be reached by means of external restrictions on self-indulgence. We may choose to limit ourselves to stay in compliance with biblical precepts, but rules themselves are not the pathway to righteousness. Jesus showed us the way to live. He said, "I am the way and the truth and the life. No one come to the Father except through me."[13] We abide in Christ, who is our righteousness. God's sons and daughters are forgiven, cleansed, and made whole as they partake of Christ's body and blood. Then we are free to walk in the light of our Savior, who gives us hearts that seek first the kingdom of God and His righteousness.[14]

---

12. 2 Corinthians 9:6–7.
13. John 14:6.
14. Matthew 6:33.

The gospel of Jesus Christ calls us to a higher standard than Old Testament Law. We are compelled to live by the law of love, and its measure is deeper, wider, and higher. Jesus' teaching makes this truth clear. First, he reminded the people about the law that says, "You shall not murder." Then He raised the standard higher. He taught that spewing out contempt and slanderous words upon another person makes you subject to judgment.

> *Such regulations indeed have an appearance of wisdom, with their self-imposed worship, their false humility and their harsh treatment of the body, but they lack any value in restraining sensual indulgence.*
> (Colossians 2:23)

God's people come before the LORD to worship with contrite hearts. We submit ourselves before Christ Jesus, our High Priest, and He lifts us up to the heights of Mount Zion. We leave behind man-made forms of godliness to sing in accord with Christ Jesus' new song: songs of freedom, psalms of joy, hymns of exaltation, refrains of saving grace, and choruses of gospel truth.[15]

God's sons and daughters are led by the Spirit of Christ into genuine worship. Bulletins and overhead projectors must not be allowed to limit the power of true worship. Instead, our hearts sing out and speak out with all the delights of God's bountiful blessings and mercies and they are more than enough to satisfy our every need.

> Trust in the LORD with all your heart and lean not on your own understanding; in all your ways submit to him, and he will make your paths straight.
> (Proverbs 3:5–6)

---

15. James 4:10.

Chapter 6 Q&A

It's in the Bulletin

1. What is Jesus' new song and what is our part in His song?

___

2. How do you prepare yourself to make your ascent?

___

3. Do the credit cards or the green stuff your wallet own you?

___

4. What does it mean to live victorious in Christ as an overcomer?

___

My Journey's Journal:

Chapter 7: The Reality of Experience

Key Scriptures:

- "So, if you think you are standing firm, be careful that you don't fall!" (1 Corinthians 10:12).
- "I declare to you, brothers and sisters, that flesh and blood cannot inherit the kingdom of God, nor does the perishable inherit the imperishable" (1 Corinthians 15:50).

The past is not a reliable arbiter of truth. We don't need to go back to the worship experiences our mom, dad, or grandparents had. Our job is to build on all that they did that was right and true. Staying true and walking in the Spirit is not possible when we're stuck with rigid rituals and paradigms. God's Word calls us to godly order. Another person's past experiences are not an accurate predictor of what God will do in our times of worship.

Often, just when we feel like we've got it made in life and we're unshakeable, God stirs things up to shake us out of our complacency. Is godly wisdom within our reach? True wisdom doesn't come from our own experience, but by standing in the Lord's counsel in reverence and awe.

Many signposts are placed along our pathway to redirect our footsteps. Scripture by Scripture, we walk in the light of the Spirit who appoints our path and lights the way to true fellowship with our Savior in a community of faith.

> A prayer according to 2 Corinthians 13:5:
>
> Help me to examine myself to be sure I am true to the faith. Let true gospel precepts be the standard for me to test my worship. Show me my folly. Help me see how I have turned from Christ's indwelling presence so I may return to a faith that will not fail the test.

Statements like, "I thought," "I felt," and "I supposed," get us in a lot of trouble when it comes to worship, teaching, and ministry in the church. The prophet Samuel's interactions with King Saul offer an example of this. Samuel instructed Saul to wait seven days for him to arrive so they could sacrifice to the LORD before going into battle. Samuel planned to pass on battle instructions from the LORD after making an offering. But when Saul and his men saw the vast, well-equipped army of the Philistines draw battle lines against them, his men scattered. As his troops disappeared into the trees, Saul gave in to what he thought might be a better plan. He saw himself as wise enough to deal with troubles like this.[1]

When Samuel finally arrived, Saul was full of excuses for going ahead and making a sacrifice without him. His foolish error offers an excellent lesson for us. In matters of the kingdom of heaven we can't rely on what we think is right. Personal intuition and our own opinions rarely help us do what is right.[2] When fearsome horrors lurk in front of our eyes, we must not make choices based on our fears.

When we do mess up, and we all do, we are called to confess our sin and failures so we may be forgiven and restored. Making excuses for ourselves doesn't work, even in the world, and certainly not in God's kingdom. We can learn from Saul's mistakes. He tried to cover up his error, pretending concern for God's help against the Philistines. But the Almighty was not pleased with an offering presented in disobedience. Samuel told him, "Obedience is better than sacrifice."[3] The lesson for us is that we are called to worship and serve in accordance with love, mercy, truth, and righteousness, not according our own intuitions, thoughts and fears.

> *I thought, "Now the Philistines will come down against me at Gilgal, and I have not sought the Lord's favor." So I felt compelled to offer the burnt offering.* (1 Samuel 13:12)

There may be times in our lives when everything seems to be going our way. Perhaps our career is off to a good start, we have a beautiful family, two cars and a quad in the garage, and no weeds in the yard. We've got it made. In such times it's easy to think that we're set up to skate through a few more years and then retire early to surf in Hawaii. It's human nature to begin depending on our own resources and forget the source for all our good stuff. It's easy to disregard the One who provided all these good things.

When we begin to worship what God supplies, forgetting to thank to Him, and worship the gift more than the Giver, we drift away from God who provides. Instead, we must constantly bathe ourselves in God's Word and walk in concord with the Spirit of Christ to keep our feet from slipping from the pathway of righteousness.

1. Proverbs 3:7.
2. Jeremiah 7:24.
3. 1 Samuel 15:22.

When I felt secure, I said, "I will never be shaken." Lord, when you favored me, you made my royal mountain stand firm; but when you hid your face, I was dismayed.
(Psalm 30:6–7)

Is true wisdom within our reach? How can we become wise—not just streetwise, but a heaven kind of wise? Supernatural understanding is rooted in the fear of the Lord, not in what we learn from our friends. But what is the fear of the LORD and how do we get there? The fear of the LORD is reverence, awe, and delighted obedience.[4] This reverent awe comes by means of God's holy Word and by the work of the Holy Spirit. A wise and godly person will no longer conform to the ways of the world. With Christ as our light, we begin to train ourselves in the Word so our minds can be renewed.

Now, with wisdom guiding us, we may enter true, real, and blessed worship. If you lack wisdom, just ask and it will be generously given to you.[5] Wisdom is the foundation of all creation and the catalyst for all teaching, preaching, and songs of praise. But when we become wise in our own eyes our worship quickly turns into foolishness that must try to duplicate what the Holy Spirit did in the past. If we expect God to part the water of the Jordan River in the same way He did at the Red Sea, we miss our opportunity to cross over to all God has promised. try to depend on what the Spirit of Jesus did through us in years gone by, we're in danger of claiming it as our own work and we become presumptuous.

Those who trust their own insight are foolish, but anyone who walks in wisdom is safe.
(Proverbs 28:26 NLT)

A roof doesn't cave in with the first few snowflakes. It takes many days of snowfall until the weight of snow is more than the roof was designed to hold. A person's downfall doesn't happen in a day, it occurs by giving up one inch at a time. In the same way, a church erodes into apostasy after years of spiritual compromise until it finally it collapses under the weight of its past.

Every church needs a faithful watchman who cries out against the erosion caused by prevailing tides of social pressure. The shifting sand under our feet erodes in the wind of our desire to be like the world around us.[6] We need a voice to speak up and warn us because our silence quickly turns into acquiescence, then into apologies for being such a peculiar people, and finally we become ashamed of the cross and try to sanitize it. Now we're on the defen-

---
4. This is the opposite of servile fear which is the fear of punishment.
5. James 1:5.
6. 1 Samuel 8:20, Romans 12:2.

sive and this leads to self-justification. The world beats us into compromise and before long we're despised because our faith is meaningless. Then all we have left are worn out experiences that turn away from Christ's living and active presence.

> *The prophets prophesy lies, the priests rule by their own authority, and my people love it this way. But what will you do in the end?*
> (Jeremiah 5:31)

At some point, every child says to the person trying to help them, "I can do it." They push away mom's helping hand so they can grasp the spoon on their own. It can get a bit messy. In the same way, Christians who are not yet mature in the faith may refuse direction from God's Word and try to worship in their own way. When the whole church rejects good instruction, demands sermons that make light of the truth, and refuse teaching that confronts sin, they're on a slippery slope. Worship and ministry turn into common inspirational thoughts and motivational platitudes. Instead of directing the congregation in true worship the people are led to worship for themselves in a way they find pleasing. In place of the true gospel of Jesus Christ and the fountain of living water, people are offered water with a church's private label on it.[7] In essence, we push away the hand of God and say, "I can do it."

In the end, when we sing the words of our own song, we end up with shame on our face. Our own song has no eternal value. Words that we conjure up are like water on the ground can't change anyone's eternal destiny. It is a severe and arrogant misuse God's holy name to claim to speak in Jesus' name, but speak our own words.[8]

> *And your prophets cover up for them by announcing false visions and making lying predictions. They say, "My message is from the Sovereign Lord," when the LORD hasn't spoken a single word to them.*
> (Ezekiel 22:28 NLT)

Imagine you're out West and see a sign posted beside the path warning all hikers: "Please stay on trail. Beware of rattlesnakes." But then, after a mile or so one hiker starts to feel safe and wanders off the trail to snap a close-up of a patch of wildflowers. With his feet shuffling in the underbrush, he doesn't hear the rattle—until the diamondback strikes. The trail sign's warning was clear, but he didn't pay attention. When his friends dialed 911, they were too far out to have any signal.

God's Word warns us in many ways. Our heavenly Father sends many messengers to warn us of the perils of wandering from His narrow pathway.

---
7. Jeremiah 2:13.
8. Exodus 20:7, Jeremiah 23:25.

Friends offer words of caution about the choices we make, but sometimes we refuse to listen. Jesus, our High Priest, leads us in worship. The holy Scriptures warn us away from those who might lead us away from true worship. Will we ignore the warning signs, or will we listen?

> *I warned you when you felt secure, but you said, "I will not listen!" This has been your way from your youth; you have not obeyed me.*
> (Jeremiah 22:21)

When spelunkers leave the bright morning sunshine and crawl into a dark cave they are as good as blind at first. They cautiously feel their way until they turn on their headlamps. But there is greater darkness than a cavern in the depths of the earth. Shadows of spiritual blindness permeate the deep recesses of the soul. Without Jesus, the Light of the World, we stumble on every obstacle in our way. Apart from Christ, even at high noon we grope about to find our way. Yet, the deepest spiritual darkness envelops the man who once walked in the light and then turned his back to the light. He soon falls into a pit of destruction.[9]

We become spiritually blind when we overlook God's power revealed in Jesus Christ's living and active presence in the moment. Our eyes are so darkened that we can only admire the good things that happened in the past. We're fallible and tend to fall back on the past instead of building on the faith of those who have gone before us. We strengthen our faith when we search the Scriptures to test the teachings of Luther, Calvin, Wesley, and other church leaders who taught by searching God's Word with the Spirit's help. If we get stuck in human tradition, we're in danger of missing Christ's living and active presence at work among us today.

> *Like the blind we grope along the wall, feeling our way like people without eyes. At midday we stumble as if it were twilight; among the strong, we are like the dead.*
> (Isaiah 59:10)

One of the first things Army recruits learn in bootcamp is to stand tall and march in step. The drill sergeant hollers out to set the pace, "Left, right, left, right." If a man falls out of step with his platoon, he'll have to do a lot of pushups to remind him to always keep in stride.

Before Jesus ascended to heaven, He promised to send a teacher who would keep us walking in harmony with the Christ. Of course, the Spirit doesn't call a cadence or punish with pushups. Instead, He instructs us so we may walk by faith and not by means of natural eyesight.[10] The Spirit of Christ teaches us to deny our selfish, corrupt desires and walk in agreement with

---
9. 2 Peter 2:20–22.
10. 2 Corinthians 5:7.

Him.[11] He appoints our footsteps so we may walk in the light and keep in step with our community of faith, because our Savior has purified us from all sin by the power of His blood.[12] The Spirit's leading, and the call of our heavenly Father's name, lead us worship in tempo with the full glory of His name.

Since we live by the Spirit, let us keep in step with the Spirit.
(Galatians 5:25)

The Great Awakening inspired deep devotion. Spiritual fervor stormed America during the Second Great Awakening, and the Azusa Street Revival brought blessings to the church. They were great moments in Christianity that reshaped people's lives and the course of the nation for many years. But that was then, and this is now. We are called to live, serve, and worship in the light of Christ with God's Word to light our pathway right now.

When we're stuck in the past, we tend to overlook the fact that our job is to build on the faith of those who have gone before us. We learn from our forefathers and then build on the foundations of faith they established. We continue to build the church in our generation. This great work will not be finished until we all come into the unity of faith and attain the whole measure and the fullness of Christ?[13]

> Then I looked and heard the voice of many angels, numbering thousands upon thousands, and ten thousand times ten thousand. They encircled the throne and the living creatures and the elders. In a loud voice they were saying: "Worthy is the Lamb, who was slain, to receive power and wealth and wisdom and strength and honor and glory and praise!" (Revelation 5:11–12)

---

11. Galatians 5:16.
12. 1 John 1:7.
13. Ephesians 4:13.

Chapter 7 Q&A

The Reality of Experience

1. What great turning points in church history have changed people's lives and the course of nations for years?

2. Does our unchanging God always do the same things in the same way throughout time?

3. What dangers do we face when we're fully satisfied and all it going well for us?

4. How do we build on the faithful work of people who built the church throughout the centuries, and keep ourselves from getting stuck in the past?

My Journey's Journal:

Chapter 8: Testimony Time

Key Scriptures:

- "For we did not follow cleverly devised stories when we told you about the coming of our LORD Jesus Christ in power, but we were eyewitnesses of his majesty. he received honor and glory from God the Father when the voice came to him from the Majestic Glory, saying, 'This is my Son, whom I love; with him I am well pleased.' We ourselves heard this voice that came from heaven when we were with him on the sacred mountain" (2 Peter 1:16–18).

- "You are witnesses of these things. I am going to send you what my Father has promised; but stay in the city until you have been clothed with power from on high" (Luke 24:48–49).

When a politician speaks to a cheering crowd, he may exaggerate to make a point or to enhance his credentials so you'll vote for him. A commissioned sales associate at an upscale department store may embellish how beautiful you look in that expensive new outfit to convince you to buy it. But when giving testimony of Christ and the cross, there is no need to exaggerate what is already far above what anyone could ask or imagine.

True worshippers become Spirit-empowered witnesses of our living and actively present Savior. In His presence we have come to know the life changing power of His saving grace. The Word of God dramatically changes our lives, causes us to see our heavenly Father's love, justice, and mercy. With this life-changing miracle the Holy Spirit seals us and then ignites a fire in our spirit to tell others, "Look what God has done." We are hungry for the Word that strengthens us and compels us to speak out to our co-workers, friends, family, and neighbors.

A real testimony is not about ourselves or our personal experiences. Instead, we proclaim the power of the Word that burns in our hearts. Every testimony of Christ is valuable. God has specially prepared each of us so we may speak out to someone who could only hear the good news in the way we tell it. Our Savior has given miraculous proofs of His power and might to save. Then He sends the redeemed to give testimony of Christ and the cross and give off the fragrance of Christ.

> A prayer according to Acts 26:22–23:
>
> May the Holy Spirit empower us to testify to small and great alike. May our words speak only what is right and in keeping with the true gospel message. Give us opportunity to give testimony of Christ Jesus' resurrection power. Pour out your Spirit upon us so we may speak out the message of light and life to all people.

God's saving grace is beyond awesome and totally sufficient. Exaggerating what Jesus has accomplished dishonors His name. Overstatements are deceitful fabrications that destroy our testimony. Expanding on the truth is a lie. Truth, and nothing but the truth, is what sets people free. But embellishing what God has done misleads people into a false spirituality and empty expectations rather than leading them to saving faith in Jesus Christ. People who expand on the truth do so because they speak without power from on high.[1] But true witnesses gain their value in Christ and proclaim the gospel by means of the empowering work of the indwelling Holy Spirit. So, let's toss out all self-aggrandizing witness methods, stop adding to God's promises, and declare pure and simple good news in the power of the Spirit.

When we gather together in Jesus' name to worship and exalt the great I AM, it is a time of preparation to go out and serve as witnesses of what He has done in our lives. Jesus' disciples are eager to come together to worship where we are armored up with the full armor of God to make us fearless in spiritual battles. Prayerfully waiting upon the Spirit who empowers us, makes us effective present-day witnesses of our Savior's living and active ministries among His people.

When new people join us in church, we become firsthand witnesses of people who, by the power of the Word and the Holy Spirit, have their chains of sin and addiction broken. Discipling them makes us eyewitnesses of a newborn Christian's hunger for God's Word. The joy of watching them grow in grace and knowledge encourages us to proclaim the good news. We have seen Christ's hand extended and know he can truly redeem lost souls.

> *"You are my witnesses," declares the Lord, "and my servant whom I have chosen, so that you may know and believe me and understand that I am he. Before me no god was formed, nor will there be one after me."*
> (Isaiah 43:10)

---

1. Luke 24:48–49.

When we see our heavenly Father as He has revealed Himself in the Scriptures and acknowledge His awesome nature, we rise up as true worshipers who offer a true and powerful testimony of His power and might to save. But if we think the Almighty asks too much of us, we easily create a god in our own image who requires less. Does the God of glory ask too much when He claims all our possessions and assets? Our heavenly Father only asks for a portion to acknowledge that we serve as stewards of what He has given us. Is this too much to ask? Maybe we can create a custom-made god who demands less and offers more. Then we'll have something to talk about, right?

When we act deceitfully toward our Father in heaven it touches all our relationships. When our wallets are sealed tight against heaven it affects our spouse, children, neighbors, community, and our work. A tight fist can neither give nor receive. An open hand unites us in the grace of our LORD Jesus Christ, the love of God, and the fellowship of the Holy Spirit.[2] He is a witness-worthy Redeemer. Our custom-made gods are the only one who need a lot of embellishments.

As for the man who does this, whoever he may be, may the LORD remove him from the tents of Jacob–even though he brings an offering to the LORD Almighty. (Malachi 2:12)

What kingdom will you serve? Does it feel like a stab in the heart when you read the human resources booklet that prohibits any "religious discussions" on your job? You have the fire of Christ burning in your bones and it feels like you'll burst if you don't let it out.[3] You're a witness of God's power to save lost souls, but how will you reach out to those in need of Christ when your workplace forbids it?

Your employer deserves your full efforts while paying your wages or salary. Doing your job as unto the LORD is a powerful witness that creates opportunities for you to testify of Christ at the right time. Your coworkers will notice the words you speak and the expletives you don't speak. They'll see the Spirit of Christ in your attitude and may find themselves compelled to ask, "What makes you so different?" This could be your opportunity to say, "Let's go out for lunch."

This is church in the real world—a testimony that is very real and powerfully effective.

We are witnesses of these things, and so is the Holy Spirit, whom God has given to those who obey him.
(Acts 5:32)

---
2. Proverbs 19:17, Galatians 6:2.
3. Jeremiah 20:9.

A testimony is effective when we are empowered in the Spirit and fearlessly speak out true gospel words. It is effective when it's backed up by what we do. We don't talk about ourselves or our personal spiritual experiences. Bragging about what a great catch God made when He found us isn't a worthy testimony. Instead, we speak words that the Holy Spirit breathes through us. The testimony we proclaim is first kindled as a fire in our heart and soul. Then by the power of the Word, the Spirit of Christ overflows with words of saving grace to those who will hear.

As we serve as God's messengers, we're covered in the shadow of His wings,[4] protected with God's armor,[5] and sheltered in the hallow of our Father's hands. Whom shall we fear? We are empowered by the Holy Spirit and sent out as His witnesses. We are as bold as lions and gentle as lambs because we stand firm and proclaim the power of Christ to save lost souls.

> *One night the LORD spoke to Paul in a vision: "Do not be afraid; keep on speaking, do not be silent. For I am with you, and no one is going to attack and harm you, because I have many people in this city."*
> (Acts 18:9–10)

We may ask ourselves, "What do I know? What have I witnessed? What have I seen that's worth talking about?" But giving testimony of God's saving grace is not about ourselves or our experiences. Few of us have seen fire come down from heaven so we can talk about our great spiritual encounter. But when our spiritual eyes are opened to see the workings of God's kingdom, we'll have more than enough to share.

A beautiful example is when we witness a baptism of a once lost and wandering soul and then see how dying with Christ and being raised in Him changes a person's life. When someone takes this step of faith, we see a profound, witness-worthy miracle. What we saw in a baptism was Jesus' living water at work to give new life. With our own eyes we caught the moment when someone died with Christ, was buried with Him, and then raised up in the power of resurrection. The person we see dripping with the water of baptism is a whole new creation in Christ, and that's worth shouting about.

When we gather to worship, Jesus' living, and active presence is manifested. As the Scriptures are taught and the true gospel is preached, we become witnesses of the powerful effect of saving grace. That is something worth proclaiming. In our assemblies, Jesus extends His loving hands through His servants to touch, strengthen, and minister to God's people in their moment of need. When the prayers of the people are lifted up, miraculous answers are

---
4. Psalm 17:8.
5. Isaiah 59:17, Ephesians 6:11.

poured out from heaven. Now we have a cornucopia of miracles to declare to our friends and family.

You will be his witness to all people of what you have seen and heard.
(Acts 22:15)

When the true gospel is preached by the power of the Spirit, and is heard and believed, the great I AM confirms the message with signs, wonders, and miracles. The Holy Spirit blesses God's people with spiritual gifts for ministry as further testimony of the power of His saving grace. These manifestations of the Spirit through His gifts are especially needed in our day to confirm the power of the gospel to save.

We live in a world that is blind to the light of Christ. There are people all around us who can't shake off the chains of sin and depravity by themselves. They're enslaved by the kingdom of darkness. People have lost hope because they have no anchor for their lives. How will they believe except that they hear the gospel and see living proofs that Jesus' message is powerfully and presently effective?[6]

We must go beyond holding up a banner at the ballgame that says, "John 3:16." The Spirit of Christ empowers us to live, obey, and preach a true gospel that reveals our LORD and Savior and is confirmed with spiritual gifts for God's people.

How shall we escape if we ignore so great a salvation? This salvation, which was first announced by the Lord, was confirmed to us by those who heard him. God also testified to it by signs, wonders and various miracles, and by gifts of the Holy Spirit distributed according to his will.
(Hebrews 2:3–4)

Paul wrote his letter to Titus by the inspiration of the Holy Spirit. His words may seem to be focused on an external law until we realize he isn't just saying, "You must," or "Thou shalt not." His letter was sent to a true son in their common faith who sought to live with godly morals, values, and disciplines of the Christian faith that please the God he loved. Paul's purpose was to open people's understanding to the fruit that comes by being grafted into Christ and serving as a branch of the vine. His words describe the love inspired obedience of true worshippers. He teaches correct doctrine and right living that offers a genuine testimony of the work of Christ in our lives.

Look at the fragrant fruit on the vine's branches and you'll see elements of temperance, submission, self-control, and good work ethics. Pluck the fruit from the vine and you'll breathe in the aromas of prudence, sound speech,

---
6. Romans 10:14, Romans 15:19.

and honesty. Taste the fruit from the season's new growth and you'll enjoy the sweetness of fidelity, uprightness, godliness, hope, compassion, generosity, and zeal for good deeds. All these attributes send out a beautiful fragrance that draws others to Christ and His saving grace.

> *These, then, are the things you should teach. Encourage and rebuke with all authority. Do not let anyone despise you.*
> (Titus 2:15)

When you're walking behind someone who had splashed themselves with cologne, the scent trails them like a fine mist. This gives us a picture of the fragrance of Christ that flows out everywhere the gospel is proclaimed.[7] This sweet aroma gives us hope and strengthens us to press on as we wait for Christ's ultimate victory over sin, Satan, death. In Jesus' final victory, choirs of angels shout out with voices like the roar of rushing waters and peals of thunder, "Hallelu Yah! For our LORD God Almighty reigns."[8]

We look forward with great hope to the wedding supper of the Lamb of God and seeing our promised Bridegroom. We will be dressed in wedding garments of the finest linen, so bright and clean. We will stand together with our brothers and sisters who have been faithful to the testimony of Jesus, revealed to us in the Scriptures. We will bow down with the elders who lay their crowns before Him who sits on the throne.[9]

> *At this I fell at his feet to worship him. But he said to me, "Don't do that! I am a fellow servant with you and with your brothers and sisters who hold to the testimony of Jesus. Worship God! For it is the Spirit of prophecy who bears testimony to Jesus."*
> (Revelation 19:10)

The Scriptures teach us to keep our witness clear, simple, and true. We know there's no need to embellish what is greater than anyone can express. But when we walk on this narrow pathway it's easy to start feeling like it cramps our natural style. Then human nature kicks in, and we try to change God. This leads to creating our own god that we think is *really* witness-worthy. But our witness of this custom-made god needs a lot of embellishment, and this puts our feet on a slippery path.

An empowered and faithful testimony is dynamic and effective even in real-world circumstances. When this redemptive message is heard, believed,

---

7. Matthew 26:13.
8. Revelation 19:6.
9. Revelation 4:10.

and embraced, signs, wonders, and the ministries of spiritual gifts prove it is true and real. Then, right living continues to confirm our witness of the cross of Christ and His saving grace. Our testimony of Jesus, our Savior, is like a fragrance that follows us as we share the good news and look forward to Christ's final victory over sin, Satan, and death. May our voices be strong and sure as we proclaim Christ and His saving grace.

> Then I heard every creature in heaven and on earth and under the earth and on the sea, and all that is in them, saying: "To him who sits on the throne and to the Lamb be praise and honor and glory and power, for ever and ever!"
> (Revelation 5:13)

Chapter 8 Q&A

Testimony Time

1. Why do people exaggerate their witness? Why is this kind of testimony pointless?

   _____
   _____
   _____

2. How can a Christian become fearless in their testimony of God's saving grace?

   _____
   _____
   _____

3. What is the most powerful miracle you've ever witnessed?

   _____
   _____
   _____

4. How does the Holy Spirit confirm that the true gospel message has been proclaimed, believed, and truthfully embraced?

   _____
   _____
   _____

My Journey's Journal:

Chapter 9: Cleanse the Temple

Key Scriptures:

- "Jesus entered the temple courts and drove out all who were buying and selling there. he overturned the tables of the money changers and the benches of those selling doves. 'It is written,' he said to them, 'My house will be called a house of prayer,' but you are making it a den of robbers'" (Matthew 21:12–13).

- "I am the true vine, and my Father is the gardener. He cuts off every branch in me that bears no fruit, while every branch that does bear fruit he prunes so that it will be even more fruitful" (John 15:1–2).

Every gardener knows that she must trim those thorny bushes harshly to grow the best roses. Viticulturalists know that vines need deep pruning to produce the best grapes. If Jesus taught techies, He might say, "You need to reboot your life." This teaching is vital because it's easy for fallible people to build strongholds of pride. We like the wild branches we've grown and want to tie our swing to them. Our affections get distracted by the ways of the world and we turn our eyes away from the God of glory.

Let's get real. Worship isn't a matter of saying ten "amens," twelve "praise the Lord's," and singing one psalm, one hymn, and one praise song while raising our hands seven times. Doing church by the numbers may make us feel good about ourselves, but it's not genuine.

A gathering to exalt our LORD and God is cause for rejoicing. As we come together in Jesus' name, we see the powerful effect of His living and active presence in the congregation. It's important for us to get ourselves out of the way so that we may minister and serve in the power, strength, and authority of our Savior's holy name. Allowing our selfish ambitions or traditions to rule stifles the work of the Spirit and the power of the Word that changes lives for eternity.

It's time to rid ourselves of the things that weigh us down and submit our "branches" to pruning so that we can bear abundant fruit for the kingdom of heaven. If we refuse pruning, we defeat our true calling and purpose in Christ.

> A prayer according to Malachi 3:1–3:
>
> Oh Lord, raise up messengers among us who will lead your people into true worship in your holy temple. Bring our hearts to repentance and then refine us like gold and silver so we will not come empty handed to worship but bring offerings in righteousness.

When you have a fitness app on your cell phone it's easy to get trapped into exercising only for points. The app requires a certain number of heart points and step counts before affirming that you've done enough to keep healthy. It's easy to slip into only doing what counts on your smartphone. Instead of using the app as a tracker for healthy exercise, it turns into little more than, "if I reach that number, I'm healthy."

When we gather to worship, it's easy to slip into doing what pleases people and leave real worship behind.[1] We develop certain words in our praise songs that serve as cues to raise our hands. Special words in a leader's prayer always prompt an "amen." If we go through the motions of worship, we can tell ourselves, "I worshipped." Then we feel good about ourselves. Every church has its rules and patterns for their gatherings. "No suits or ties allowed." "You're being real if you come in your Harley gear." "You're very spiritual if you carry a big Bible tucked under your arm." "It's real worship when we sing five-hundred-year-old hymns of the church."

We need to get rid of all the man-made rules, humble ourselves and repent so that Christ, our High Priest, may be present with us and lead us to truly bow our hearts in worship. We must not get caught up in the winds of vain doctrines so that true worship can be breathed through us by the Holy Spirit.

> *These people come near to me with their mouth and honor me with their lips, but their hearts are far from me. Their worship of me is based on merely human rules they have been taught.*
> (Isaiah 29:13)

Look at what God has done. Consider the power and might of His Holy Spirit who teaches us truth and righteousness. Reflect on the work of our Savior's grace that changes the hearts and minds of all those who hear and believe the gospel's message. We serve an awesome God who is mighty to save, forgive, and heal the wounds of His people. He lovingly shepherds us and guards us jealously. He is patient with us as He leads us to run free on paths of righteousness.[2]

---

1. 1 Thessalonians 1:4–6.
2. Psalm 119:32.

We are encompassed with grace upon grace so that we may see His mighty works and give glory and honor to His holy name. He opens our eyes to see the wonderful things in His commands.[3] Let us rejoice, for our LORD and God has given us His holy name. We are His sons and daughters who make known the beauty and majesty of His holiness. Our love for our heavenly Father, His Son, and the Holy Spirit inspires us to honor His name in worship, and then reflect this reverent awe in the way we live our lives. We rejoice to gather for instruction that enlightens us so we may cleanse the temple to prepare us for spiritual and real worship.

> *When they see among them their children, the work of my hands, they will keep my name holy; they will acknowledge the holiness of the Holy One of Jacob, and will stand in awe of the God of Israel. Those who are wayward in spirit will gain understanding; those who complain will accept instruction.*
> (Isaiah 29:23–24)

We're a fallible people who prefer to show ourselves strong. It makes us feel good to use our personal competencies and skills to accomplish the task before us. It's self-satisfying to apply our common talents to complete the work and then stand back to see what a great job we've done. In our committee meetings we pray a quick prayer and read a devotional with a Bible verse to give it a Christian touch, and then work out our own plans by our own devices.

The work of the church and dynamic of worship are not accomplished by common means. The church began in a gathering with fasting and prayer. Why have we abandoned the origins of our first love? Why do we attempt to do the work of God's kingdom by mortal strength and human might when this impossible task can only be accomplished by the power of the Holy Spirit?[4] Why are prayers limited to one person for few minutes in church and a quick thank you over dinner? Can we forget the power of fasting and prayer and attempt to solve our problems with lengthy deliberations?

> *"Woe to the obstinate children," declares the Lord, "to those who carry out plans that are not mine, forming an alliance, but not by my Spirit, heaping sin upon sin."*
> (Isaiah 30:1)

Visitors who come to our church gaze at our beautifully decorated sanctuary, and then delightfully comment on the way out, "what a beautiful church." But the beauty of church is not in material things, it's in the worship of our hearts. A church that truly worships is beautiful even if they meet in Joe's garage and sing psalms, hymns, and spiritual songs accompanied by his garage band. There is nothing wrong with a beautifully adorned chapel with

---

3. Psalm 119:18.
4. Zechariah 4:6.

a grand piano. Well-practiced and orchestrated music can honor God, but this must not become a stronghold that we delight in while putting genuine worship aside. The real temple of God's delight is the joining of people exalting the LORD Almighty in the presence of Christ Jesus, our High Priest. If we give our honor to anything less, his presence will be taken from us.

> *Say to the people of Israel, "This is what the Sovereign LORD says: I am about to desecrate my sanctuary–the stronghold in which you take pride, the delight of your eyes, the object of your affection."*
> (Ezekiel 24:21)

The Apostle Paul instructs us how to decorate and adorn a church. First, we need to clean and sanitize our hearts by prayer and God's Word. We cast our concerns upon the Lord. Our personal rubbish, selfish ambitions, and our need for control get thrown out. The windows get washed inside and out so we can embrace the light of Christ. Then, by the power of the Word and the work of the Holy Spirit, our lamp is filled with oil to keep the fire of the Spirit burning in our hearts. These are all necessary steps to keep us unburdened as we continue on our ascent to true worship.

The next job is to paint everything with holiness. We hang chandeliers of praise, with reverence and awe. We cover the floor with a carpet of submission so we may bow down and worship a holy and awesome God. Once the environment is prepared we ascend into an aura of God's splendor and majesty.

> *Therefore, since we have these promises, dear friends, let us purify ourselves from everything that contaminates body and spirit, perfecting holiness out of reverence for God.*
> (2 Corinthians 7:1)

The true temple is a place where we must stop depending on common strength, talents, and man-made rules. We are called to repent of our reliance on our own means to do the work of the church. With contrite hearts, we reject the ways of the world so we may serve our heavenly Father in the power and strength of the Spirit of Christ. We put aside all pride, because our boast is in Christ alone who ministers and serves before us as High Priest. Our confidence is not in our own worth, but in God who is worthy of all praise, glory, and honor.

There is nothing left of us to boast about except our weaknesses. Knowing that God's grace is more than sufficient and that His power is greatly manifested in weak vessels is enough for us.[5] Our confidence in not in our own abilities, but in our heavenly Father, who fulfills all that He has promised.

---

5. 2 Corinthians 12:9.

> *For it is we who are the circumcision, we who serve God by his Spirit, who boast in Christ Jesus, and who put no confidence in the flesh.*
> (Philippians 3:3)

That backpack full of useless tools is breaking your back. It's weighing you down, bending you over, and wearing you out. You're getting burned out from trying to do God's work in your own strength rather than His strength.[6] Confess your self-gratifying ways for getting the job done so that the load can be lifted from your shoulders and the basket of burden from your hands.[7] At the end of the day you'll no longer say, "Look what I did," instead, you'll declare, "Look what God has done."[8]

Now you're ready for the Potter to form you into a useful vessel.[9] Without the load on your back, you can be equipped to do the work prepared for you from before the beginning of time.[10] Your heavenly Father has a place that only you can fill in the workings of His kingdom. He gives us the Holy Spirit to anoint, gift, and empower us so that we may serve with the very heart and mind of Christ and work by means of a power not our own.

> *Those who cleanse themselves from the latter will be instruments for special purposes, made holy, useful to the Master and prepared to do any good work.*
> (2 Timothy 2:21)

We tend to get stuck in our own ways and grow comfortable in our own nest. Too often, when we check up on ourselves, we tend to adjust our interpretations, theology, and doctrines so we can justify what we're doing. Before we know it, we're spinning our wheels and doing nothing of eternal value. Indeed, we abandoned our first love for affections that leads us astray.

The dead branches on Christ's vine get cut off and burned. Living branches still need to get pruned back to make them more productive.[11] Indeed, God's just and righteous judgments begin in the church so we may bear abundant fruit. When we're in the middle of getting pruned, it's painful but fruitful.

> *For it is time for judgment to begin with God's household; and if it begins with us, what will the outcome be for those who do not obey the gospel of God?*
> (1 Peter 4:17)

---

6. Colossians 1:29.
7. Psalm 81:6, Isaiah 10:27.
8. Psalm 46:8.
9. Isaiah 64:8.
10. Ephesians 2:10.
11. John 15:1–2.

The Spirit of Christ still cleanses temples. Church leaders may say, "I've got the numbers to prove we're doing it right. We got well over a two hundred 'likes' on our worship survey." Our church techie creates an app that tracks what we do and declares, "The numbers add up. We worshipped." Fulfilling man-made rules and tracking external actions may serve to make us feel good even though we miss the true mark and need a temple cleansing.

To start the cleaning job, let's put our complaining aside and get rid of our selfish ambitions. Then, with our sanctuaries cleaned up we can continue our ascent to exalt the LORD with true hearts.

Christians tend to get stuck in a rut and then hang tinsel on the dead branches to make them look alive. That may seem to work, because when we wander from the path of truth, we simply adjust our Bible interpretations. Instead, we are called to truly examine ourselves and cleanse our temples. We do this in the fear of the Lord, knowing that God's just and righteous judgments begin in the church.

> But if we walk in the light, as he is in the light, we have fellowship with one another, and the blood of Jesus, his Son, purifies us from all sin. (1 John 1:7)

Chapter 9 Q&A

Cleanse the Temple

1. Can true worship be proven by the numbers, statistics, or surveys?

_____
_____
_____

2. Where do we start when we clean our churches?

_____
_____
_____

3. What treasures has the modern-day church left behind?

_____
_____
_____

4. Does Jesus still cleanse temples?

_____
_____
_____

My Journey's Journal:

Part III
Children of Zion

"Let Israel rejoice in their Maker; let the people of Zion be glad in their King."
Psalm 149:2

This part of our ascent leads God's sons and daughters into the abundant blessings to true worship and praise.

Chapter 10: Abel's Sacrifice

Key Scriptures:

- "And Abel also brought an offering—fat portions from some of the firstborn of his flock. The LORD looked with favor on Abel and his offering" (Genesis 4:4).

- "In fact, the law requires that nearly everything be cleansed with blood, and without the shedding of blood there is no forgiveness" (Hebrews 9:22).

Abundant blessings pour over God's people when we gather to worship the great I AM who is worthy of all praise, glory, and honor. We are a people set apart to lift our voices in praise to our heavenly Father who is exalted among the nations. We sing His praises because of His great love and faithfulness that reaches to the heavens. With our hearts bowed to worship, and our hands lifted up, His glory shines out to encompass all the earth.[1] In this study we'll leave behind Old Covenant traditions, no longer worshipping in the shadow of Christ. We are led forward to see Christ, the all-sufficient sacrifice, the Lamb of God who takes away the sin of the world.

We'll learn how important it is to know that our bodies are living sacrifices in Christ so that He may be exalted in our bodies.[2] We know we are a temple where the Holy Spirit dwells. From this temple we make true and acceptable offerings of praise like Abel's. All such offerings are presented to the LORD in righteousness.[3]

Those who gather as a New Covenant church are called to a higher standard of worship than those who remain under the law. All that we do and say in our assemblies acknowledges Christ who has set us free to live in accord with the Holy Spirit.[4] Abel worshipped from the heart, not under the demands of the law. Neither does the church offer sacrifices of praise under the

---

1. Psalm 57:10.
2. 2 Corinthians 4:10.
3. Malachi 3:3.
4. Galatians 3:13, Colossians 2:17.

law that only casts a shadow of our Savior.[5] Children of hope come to partake of the fullness of Christ, the once-and-for-all-time sacrifice.[6] We come to the Lord's table and partake of visible signs[7] of an invisible reality—His living and active presence with us and in us.

> A prayer according to Psalm 19:14:
>
> Oh LORD Almighty, may the words our mouths sing and our hearts meditate on be pleasing in your sight, for you are our Rock and our Redeemer.

We look up to where we will plant our banner on the top of a mountain. Will we look for a taller peak to conquer when we get there? There is no higher place for God's people to worship than God's holy mountain where we are called to worship Him in all His glory and majesty. True worship serves to enlarge God's kingdom and is a blessing to all who come to dwell within its pleasant boundaries.[8] The Scriptures instruct us so we may know what honors God who is worthy of all praise.

The Old Testament details strict ceremonial laws for worship. The law was established and based on God's love for His holy people. Their worship set them apart from the nations around them, but they defiled themselves by doing whatever they thought was right. New Testament worshippers have a higher calling than those who served under Old Testament law. We can meet this higher standard because God's grace is sufficient for those whom the Holy Spirit indwells.[9]

God established blood sacrifice in the beginning to cover Adam and Eve's sin. Our Creator God knew Eve would be deceived and that Adam would knowingly disobey God's covenant command. He had a plan of grace and mercy prepared to redeem their lives. The blood of an animal sacrifice provided a covering for their sin. Then, under the law, God required the death of sacrificial animals. The butchered fat was offered as a burnt offering to honor God, who provides from the "fat of the land."[10] The blood of the sacrifices provided atonement for sin but could not clear the conscience. This showed the way forward to the Lamb of God who would come in the flesh to offer His body and blood as a once-and-for-all-time sacrifice for the sins of the world—for all who would believe and receive.

---

5. Hebrews 10:1.
6. Hebrews 10:14.
7. The bread and the cup are true signs. Example: The Sabbath was given as a sign to Israel so that they "will know that I am the LORD your God" (Ezekiel 20:20).
8. Psalm 16:5–6.
9. John 14:17.
10. Psalm 36:8, Philippians 4:19.

Those who gather as the church offer true worship to acknowledge Christ as our all-sufficient sacrifice to cleanse us of our sin. We are blood-bought servants of the Most High God who enter into the fullness of Jesus Christ so we may lift up holy hands to worship the King of Glory who has redeemed us. We come together as His holy nation, a royal priesthood to worship, serve, and minister before Jesus Christ.

> *For the life of a creature is in the blood, and I have given it to you to make atonement for yourselves on the altar; it is the blood that makes atonement for one's life.*
> (Leviticus 17:11)

The tribes of Israel worshipped in the shadow of Christ. They were called together to celebrate holy feasts and holy fasts in every season of the year. The festivals served to open their eyes to see the way forward to the promised Messiah. Noah, Abraham, Moses, and David are just a few of those whose eyes looked forward to Christ. They stepped out of the shadow and loved the light. Their deeds proved their love and their faith in the Lamb of God.

The power of the blood of Christ is beyond awesome. We were once far from Christ. Church was meaningless. God's promises meant nothing. Now we are brought near to God through the blood of Jesus.[11] We are blood-bought souls, purchased from slavery to sin. By Jesus' shed blood we are covered, protected from God's just and righteous wrath. The blood of Christ cleanses us and justifies us before our heavenly Father. The God we serve is worthy of all praise, glory, and honor.

> *Since we have now been justified by his blood, how much more shall we be saved from God's wrath through him!*
> (Romans 5:9)

We do our children an injustice if we teach them that their bodies are their own. When they believe that they hold the power to decide what is right for their own bodies, they might injure themselves on a whim. We must not encourage them to act as their own gods, using, or harming their bodies as they wish. The truth is that our bodies belong to Christ. As Christians, we are called keep our bodies pure and clean as a holy temple where the Spirit of Christ may dwell. Christ Jesus is the true master all his people, including our believing children.

> *Do you not know that your bodies are temples of the Holy Spirit, who is in you, whom you have received from God? You are not your own; you were bought at a price. Therefore honor God with your bodies.*
> (1 Corinthians 6:19–20)

---

11. Ephesians 2:13.

A blood sacrifice like Abel's was later instituted as lawful worship for God's holy nation. Year after year on Yom Kippur, the Day of Atonement, the high priest offered a sacrifice for his own sins before carrying the atoning blood of a bullock into the Most Holy Place for the sins of the people. This system of worship was in the shadow of Christ as they looked forward to His final redemptive sacrifice.

In the church today, we worship in the light of Christ. By faith we receive the full benefits of His vicarious sacrifice. Jesus gave His body to be broken and offered His own blood to be shed on a cruel Roman cross to pay the debt for all sin. Yeshua HaMashiach[12] now serves as our forever High Priest in the order of Melchizedek, the king and priest of Salem.[13] Like Abel, we enter true and acceptable worship by honoring and exalting Christ Jesus who offered a once-and-for-all-time blood sacrifice for the sins of the whole world. We enter the Most Holy Place, cleansed of sin and sealed from God's just and righteous wrath by the blood of the Lamb of God.

> *But only the high priest entered the inner room, and that only once a year, and never without blood, which he offered for himself and for the sins the people had committed in ignorance.*
> (Hebrews 9:7)

Worship in the New Covenant church calls us to a higher standard than worship under the law. Their ceremonial sacrifices only served as a covering for sin, but Christ Jesus' sacrifice is timeless and cleanses from the inside out. We no longer need to tie Scripture ribbons on our hands or attach them to our foreheads[14] because they are written on our hearts. Jesus' sacrifices cleanses our conscience to the depths of our soul. This cleansing comes as the Good Shepherd gathers us as a flock to restore our souls.[15]

There is no other acceptable offering or sacrifice for sin's death penalty.[16] Giving one hundred percent of our wealth to the church won't save us. Donating our new Mercedes SUV to the pastor can't redeem our lost souls. Giving up self-indulgent party nights with friends is a good thing to do, but it doesn't even come close to saving us. Self-inflicted wounds serve no redemptive purpose. Our heavenly Father sent His only Son as an all-sufficient sacrifice. It is only by faith in Christ and His atoning sacrifice that we are saved; and for a good purpose. We are called to serve as holy priests in the priesthood of all believers.[17] We serve in a priesthood that worships, serves, and ministers before Jesus, in a way that is spiritual and real.

---
12. Hebrew for "Jesus, The Anointed One."
13. Genesis 14:17–20, Hebrews 7:4, 6–7.
14. Deuteronomy 6:8.
15. Psalm 23:3.
16. Romans 6:23.
17. 1 Peter 2:5.

How much more, then, will the blood of Christ, who through the eternal Spirit offered himself unblemished to God, cleanse our consciences from acts that lead to death, so that we may serve the living God!
(Hebrews 9:14)

The consequence of sin is death.[18] The reason is clear. When our self-indulgent passions conceive and come to term, they "give birth to death."[19] The dark shadow of the law serves to drive us to Christ, who paid the full price of our redemption to save us from its curse. There is no redemptive sacrifice apart from Christ that is sufficient to give us right standing before our Father who is seated on His throne in glory.

In Christ we are separated from our sin as far as the east is from the west. We are wrapped in His robe of righteousness, and He ushers us into the presence of God our Father who sees us as perfect in Christ. We have nothing to offer, no further sacrifice is necessary to make us right with the LORD of Glory. No lesser sacrifice than God's one and only Son is acceptable. This thread of truth must be interwoven with every note and word spoken and sung in our gatherings.

"Their sins and lawless acts I will remember no more." And where these have been forgiven, sacrifice for sin is no longer necessary.
(Hebrews 10:17–18)

Have you noticed that our Savior most often gathers His sheep from among those the world looks down on? Has it ever come to mind that few converts to the faith come with the world's treasures to offer? We come poor in spirit, with nothing to offer of our own. The reality is, that paupers are willing to fully depend on Christ for redemption. It's too easy for those who are wealthy to think that the church is lucky to have them on their membership role and serving as president of the board. Jesus' words ring true for the disadvantaged, "Blessed are the poor in spirit, for theirs is the kingdom of heaven."[20]

Abel's parents had witnessed God's grace as He provided a covering from an animal that had been slain. The Creator covered their sin with the skin of a sacrificed animal.[21] Abel came to the altar and offered a blood sacrifice. Now, we have come to Christ who is the perfect Lamb of God whom the Father sent as an atoning sacrifice to redeem all who will believe on Him and receive Him as Lord.

---

18. Romans 6:23.
19. James 1:15.
20. Matthew 5:3.
21. Genesis 3:21.

> *For you know that it was not with perishable things such as silver or gold that you were redeemed from the empty way of life handed down to you from your ancestors, but with the precious blood of Christ, a lamb without blemish or defect. He was chosen before the creation of the world but was revealed in these last times for your sake.*
> (1 Peter 1:18–20)

We have a new and better covenant sealed with the blood of Christ. He gathers us to His table of remembrance, together with His blood-bought sons and daughters. When we come together at the Lord's table, we are reminded of His perfect sacrifice and receive His forgiveness. We come to His table where He is actively present, indwelling all who rightly partake of the cup of His blood and the bread that is His broken body. Jesus' blood is life to us, given to make atonement for our lives.[22] Jesus' broken body makes His body, the church, whole. In the church there is healing for our body, soul, and spirit.

When we come to the communion table to partake of Christ, we, the branches, feed from the Vine. This strengthens us in the Spirit of Christ so we may bear abundant fruit. At His table we are partakers of the Bread of Life, who is the fulfillment of the bread of the presence in Israel's tabernacle.[23] The shewbread was presented as twelve loaves of unleavened bread in the holy place. It offered a visible sign to declare God's presence. On the Lord's table, our Savior's living and active presence is affirmed in the bread and cup. When we partake of the bread our eyes are opened to see Christ who is present with us.[24] Those who are in Christ come to drink of the cup and they are forgiven, cleansed, and united in a covenant of grace. Our mutual participation is a sign of the union that joins us together in sweet fellowship in Christ.

> *Then he took a cup, and when he had given thanks, he gave it to them, saying, "Drink from it, all of you. This is my blood of the covenant, which is poured out for many for the forgiveness of sins."*
> (Matthew 26:27–28)

New Testament worshippers are called to a higher standard than the requirements of Levitical law. The festivals and sacrifices practiced by the tribes Israel opened their eyes so they could look forward to Christ who is the final and all-sufficient sacrifice for sin. Abel offered an acceptable sacrifice that kept faith with the mercies the Creator shown to his parents, Adam and Eve.

---

22. Leviticus 17:11.
23. Exodus 25:30.
24. Luke 24:30–31.

His burnt offering also looked forward to Christ, the Lamb of God who takes away the sins of the world.

Why would we go back to a ceremonial system of worship that only offers external regulations that veil our eyes? Remember that our Savior loves us with a radical love. Will we love Him any less? He brought us into a new and better covenant that cleanses us from the inside out so that we may minister and serve before Him for His glory and honor.

> I rejoiced with those who said to me, "Let us go to the house of the Lord." Our feet are standing in your gates, Jerusalem. (Psalm 122:1–2)

Chapter 10 Q&A

Abel's Sacrifice

1. How did Old Testament worship show the way forward to Christ?

2. What is the higher standard that Jesus established for the New Covenant church?

3. Does the Old Testament law continue to serve a good purpose for Christians today?

4. Describe the powerful effect of partaking of Christ at the Lord's Table.

My Journey's Journal:

Chapter 11: Dressed and Ready For Battle

Key Scriptures:

- "Your troops will be willing on your day of battle. Arrayed in holy splendor, your young men will come to you like dew from the morning's womb." (Psalm 110:3)
- "Therefore I want the men everywhere to pray, lifting up holy hands without anger or disputing." (1 Timothy 2:8)

Come join us in the ascent to Mount Zion. With every step, we fight to overcome the obstacles in our way. But we band together in the Spirit who strengthens us. In this tour through the Scriptures, we'll see the Spirit of Christ who prepares us through worship to do battle as soldiers of the cross. The Scriptures inspire us to gather to Mount Zion where we are equipped as a mighty army to carry the gospel of Jesus Christ to neighbors and nations. We'll learn battle tactics that are not of this world. Instead, we'll rise above the world's system, holding out the sword of the Spirit, which is the Word of God.

We hear a voice crying out to "prepare the way of the Lord." With Christ's banner in hand we look to the goal. Every pilgrim on this journey listens to the call to be awake, alert, and clothed with Christ. We rise up and step out as a mighty choir to sing out with praises that drive back the forces of darkness. Our weaknesses fall away so we may serve by means of the empowering work of the Holy Spirit. The Word readies soldiers of the cross to go from strength to strength, equipped to speak of Zion with victorious songs of praise.

> A prayer according to Luke 24:49:
>
> Give us hearts that wait for the Holy Spirit to cloth us with power so we may lift up Christ to the nations.

Those who enter true worship are equipped and ready to go out and do battle. Like the choir that preceded Israel's armies, worshipful songs drive back for forces of darkness. We are made strong in the Lord's presence. Our strength comes by means of his mighty power. The saints are equipped with weapons of the Spirit. We put on the armor He provides, and it serves as a sign of His covenant with us.[1]

The sword of the Spirit, which is the Word of God, is a vital weapon against dark principalities and powers in spiritual realms. We need this effective weapon because no armament of our own can battle against the kingdom of darkness. Putting on every piece of God's armor and learning to wield our sword prepares us to serve as ready warriors on the day of battle. We face an enemy who knows our failings and tries to exploit our weaknesses. In our weakest moments, Satan comes to knock us off our feet. But he cannot overpower those who are made strong in the power of God's might. We stand strong because we are shielded against our adversary's fiery arrows.[2]

> *Finally, be strong in the LORD and in his mighty power. Put on the full armor of God, so that you can take your stand against the devil's schemes.*
> (Ephesians 6:10–11)

The foot soldier twists and turns in his bedroll, tossing with anticipation of the morning's march to the frontline. He cleaned and reassembled his rifle. He checked and rechecked his ammunition and his body armor. His helmet, camouflage gear, and bayonet are ready. All the training and practice flash before his eyes again and again through the night. Then, before the crack of dawn, he fortifies himself with field rations and gears up to join the ranks with his buddies to march out at the sergeant's command.

The Holy Spirit equips us for battle by opening our understanding to God's Word. Apart from the truth of God's Word we can never be prepared to worship, serve, and minister before Him as soldiers of Jesus Christ.[3] The Spirit gives our spirits a voice to sing out with exaltations as we gather. He enables us to teach the Holy Scriptures and preach the gospel to shield the children of Zion with God's armor to go out and do battle.

We realize the strength that is ours at bountiful feast at the Lord's table. In holy worship we come face to face with our Savior. He anoints our heads with healing oil and fills us to overflow with springs of living water.

> *You prepare a table before me in the presence of my enemies. You anoint my head with oil; my cup overflows.*
> (Psalm 23:5)

Soldiers of light ascend to the mountain of the LORD where we are strengthened for battle with a bountiful feast. We march out in His strength to see the adversary's strongholds destroyed. We defeat our foe, who advanc-

---

1. 1 Samuel 18:4. Jonathan gave David his robe, weapons, and belt as signs of a covenant between them.
2. Ephesians 6:16.
3. 2 Timothy 2:3.

es by deceit and treachery. We speak out God's Word to shatter the enemy's cloak of deception that blinds the people of every land and chains them in darkness. We search for lost and wandering sheep and call them to come back into the Good Shepherd's fold. In Christ, we know that death is defeated, and souls are forever restored.

Our weapons are the sword of the Spirit, which is the Word of God. We march out, refreshed by the bounty of the Lord's table and empowered with the message of the gospel's grace. A mighty army marches out from Mount Zion to carry the good news that death is forever swallowed up in victory.[4]

On this mountain the LORD Almighty will prepare a feast of rich food for all peoples, a banquet of aged wine–the best of meats and the finest of wines.
(Isaiah 25:6)

The battle we fight is not won by mortal strength nor by human power but by the Spirit of Christ in us.[5] Our battle tactics are not those of the world, instead, the battle is won in the same way our Savior gained His great victory. In an attitude of submissive obedience, we arm ourselves. The attack plan is to turn the other cheek by doing good to those who persecute us. There is victory in Christ for all who hunger and thirst for righteousness for His name's sake.[6] The kingdom of heaven advances its cause through forgiveness and mercy. The battle against darkness is won by peacemakers.[7] Victorious soldiers suffer through persecution and insults for the sake of Jesus' holy name. Indeed, joining together with Christ in His sufferings prepares us to serve as a great army of saints who will be dressed in fine linen.[8] Christ's victorious troop goes out with singing; their praises ring out with shouts of exaltation as they overcome the enemy.

Get ready; be prepared! Keep all the armies around you mobilized, and take command of them.
(Ezekiel 38:7 NLT)

Consider the disgrace of pride versus the humility that comes with wisdom.[9] Those who exalt themselves are thrown down. The finest fashions that cover them with pride are torn away like rags. Proud and contemptuous words are silenced forever. All idolatry—the work of human hands—is brought to shame. The violence and deceit they used to gain their wealth comes back to condemn them. Seekers of self-indulgent pleasures open their hands to see that all they have left is nothing but dust that blows away.

---

4. 1 Corinthians 15:54.
5. Zechariah 4:6.
6. Matthew 5:6.
7. Matthew 5:9.
8. Revelation 19:14.
9. Proverbs 11:2.

Those who are wise come and stand silent before the Lord, who is the just and righteous Judge. We come with repentant hearts and humble ourselves in the sight of the Lord. We are called to Christ Jesus who is the Lamb of God who takes away the sins of the world. He forgives those who approach with contrite hearts to receive His forgiveness and saving grace. Our grieving hearts turn to joy as we are forgiven. The burden of guilt is lifted from us. In the light of God's mercy we are prepared to joyfully lift up our voices to the great I AM who is worthy of all praise, glory, and honor.

> *Be silent before the Sovereign Lord, for the day of the LORD is near.*
> *The LORD has prepared a sacrifice; he has consecrated those he has invited.*
> (Zephaniah 1:7)

The pure in heart will see God in all His glory.[10] But how are sin-stained hearts made pure and presentable before the Lord, our Maker? Only through Jesus Christ—the Lamb of God who is the unblemished sacrifice who washes away sin, cleansing us to the depths of our soul. As our eyes overflow with repentant tears, all superfluous, man-made religious baggage that weighs us down is washed away in the mighty flow of Jesus' cleansing blood.

We are mortally wounded by our sin and depravities, but we come with contrite hearts to have the burden of our sin lifted. When our sin crushes us, the Spirit of Christ is grieved, and He feels the pain of our ruin. Listen to the voice of the prophet as he cries out in despair, "Is there no balm in Gilead? Why is there no healing for the wound of my people?"[11]

But we have a great hope. Our Savior rises up with healing in His wings. We are forgiven and cleansed so we may serve the LORD Almighty in spirit and in all truth.

> *Who may ascend the mountain of the Lord? Who may stand in his holy place?*
> *The one who has clean hands and a pure heart, who does not trust in an idol or swear by a false god.*
> (Psalm 24:3–4)

The life path we once chose was like getting our feet bogged down in quicksand. Our Savior lifts us out of this mess. In Christ we turn around and answer the call to come to the fountain, to the spring of living water. In this cleansing fountain we are washed so we may press on to victory. Soldiers of the cross are cleansed by water and by fire.[12] The furnace of affliction refines us like gold and silver to get rid of the dross so we may be pure vessels for God's special purpose. By the power of the Word and the work of the Holy

---

10. Matthew 5:8.
11. Jeremiah 8:22.
12. Numbers 31:23.

Spirit we are strengthened as soldiers who march on to the heights and exalt the LORD our God.

We accomplish the good work of our calling and finish all we are commissioned to do by putting away what is unholy and what is common so we may press on in our ascent in the strength, power, and anointing of the Holy Spirit. We march out when we see His banner unfurled. He raises His flagstaff to rally the royal priesthood of the redeemed for battle.

> *Pass through, pass through the gates! Prepare the way for the people. Build up, build up the highway! Remove the stones. Raise a banner for the nations. The LORD has made proclamation to the ends of the earth: "Say to Daughter Zion, 'See, your Savior comes! See, his reward is with him, and his recompense accompanies him.'" They will be called the Holy People, the Redeemed of the Lord; and you will be called Sought After, the City No Longer Deserted.*
> (Isaiah 62:10–12)

Bitterness in the ranks can defeat a whole army. The apostle Paul admonished the church to root out all bitterness, anger, and wrath."[13] Instead, we are commanded to be Christ-like.[14] This is a very real but impossible command. In the strength of our flesh, we constantly fail to live in accord with God's love. There is no way we can be holy by our own means. How then will we ever see the Lord? We're fallible and we constantly trip up on our life's journey. Bitterness sticks to our pant legs like cockleburs. Someone gets in our way and makes us stumble, and resentments stick like seeds in our socks.

Only by grace through faith in our LORD and Savior, Jesus Christ, can we overcome bitterness and resentments. We are abundantly forgiven for our sin and wrongdoing and in this we are shown the way to forgive those who have offended us. We are made victors in Christ. We have overcome by the blood of the Lamb.

> *Make every effort to live in peace with everyone and to be holy; without holiness no one will see the Lord. See to it that no one falls short of the grace of God and that no bitter root grows up to cause trouble and defile many.*
> (Hebrews 12:14–15)

Hear the voice crying out in the wilderness, "Prepare the way of the Lord."[15] Raise up a banner for the nations for them to see the way prepared for the remnant of God's people.[16] What an awesome God we serve. He sent His only Son to give His body to be broken and His blood shed to redeem a

---

13. Ephesians 4:31.
14. Philippians 2:5.
15. Isaiah 40:3.
16. Isaiah 11:12, 16.

people as His own. He made a "Way of Holiness" for all who are cleansed to walk on it.[17]

"Awake, awake, Zion, clothe yourself with strength!"[18] Put on your gospel shoes, for all beautiful feet ascend to the mountain to proclaim the gospel that makes peace with the Father. Beautiful feet declare God's salvation and speak to Zion, "Your God reigns!"[19] Announce glad tidings of wonderous things the LORD has done to gather a holy nation as His own. Come, walk in the way so that we may be raised up in resurrection power to see our victorious LORD Jesus Christ when He is fully revealed on the day of the LORD.

Therefore, with minds that are alert and fully sober, set your hope on the grace to be brought to you when Jesus Christ is revealed at his coming.
(1 Peter 1:13)

When our heavenly Father's sons and daughters gather, the wind of the Spirit lifts us up to worship in our Savior's holy presence. By the power of the Word, we are prepared and equipped as a mighty army that presses on to do the work of the kingdom. We are sent out to proclaim the good news of Christ victorious to every nation. Our weapons and our battle tactics are not those of the world. No, we follow Christ and His example of obedient submission. We are united with Christ in His sufferings. We are one with Christ in His victory on the cross.

Listen and hear the voice of the One who calls out in the wilderness to make straight the way of the Lord. He's calling us to wake up, put on our gospel shoes, and ascend to true worship that strengthens us for battle. We go up with great joy because "our God reigns." We step up to the battle line because we are a holy nation called out of darkness. We march out in resurrection power, dressed and prepared as a bride for His coming.

You heavens above, rain down my righteousness; let the clouds shower it down. Let the earth open wide, let salvation spring up, let righteousness flourish with it; I, the Lord, have created it. (Isaiah 45:8)

---

17. Isaiah 35:8.
18. Isaiah 52:1.
19. Isaiah 52:7.

Chapter 11 Q&A

Dressed and Ready For Battle

1. Describe how soldiers of the cross are clothed for battle.

   _____

   _____

   _____

2. What are the best ways to prepare ourselves for the battle?

   _____

   _____

   _____

3. How does bowing down in worship and singing songs of praise prepare us to be victors in Christ?

   _____

   _____

   _____

4. What effect does bitterness have on God's army?

   _____

   _____

   _____

My Journey's Journal:

Chapter 12: Crossing the Threshold

Key Scriptures:
- "At the sound of their voices the doorposts and thresholds shook and the temple was filled with smoke" (Isaiah 6:4).
- "Then the glory of the LORD rose from above the cherubim and moved to the threshold of the temple. The cloud filled the temple, and the court was full of the radiance of the glory of the Lord" (Ezekiel 10:4).

The guide for our ascent has charted a path that leads his climbers to their goal. He reviews the plan with everyone to be sure they all stay together. Then he warns them that anyone wanders from the guide's directions puts themselves at risk.

In the twenty-fifth year of Israel's exile, the LORD took Ezekiel by the hand and led him to a very high mountain in a vision. God showed the prophet every detail of the temple. He watched as it was carefully measured to show that it conformed to the Designer's plan. Ezekiel's detailed records reveal many thresholds in the temple. The detailed measurements show God's plan for His sanctuary. The Lord's design teaches us that we must not place any man-made thresholds next to the Great I AM's threshold. God will not share His glory with any other god that we make in our own image and to our liking.

Don't hesitate to cross over the threshold and join Christ Jesus, who made a way for us to come into true worship. We are called to rise above ourselves and allow the Holy Spirit to thrust us into the realm of the Spirit. With contrite hearts we'll come to see the temple's plan and design so we may be faithful as true worshippers.

The guide on our ascent leads you to the crossing point. Will you cross the threshold? Will you come to worship in our High Priest's living and active presence? Come now and enter into the holy assembly to be refreshed like the dew of the morning.

> A prayer according to Psalm 119:133:
>
> Oh Lord, appoint our footsteps according to your Word so that no sin may rule over us.

Little children seated at a kitchen table are always eager to learn. First, they learn how to hold a spoon. Then, after a lot of spilled peas and carrots, they finally get enough food in their mouths. They imitate mom and dad as they learn table manners. When they get older we teach them how to make spaghetti with meatballs so they can eat more than Ramen when they go off on their own. Hunger compels them to eat and grow so they can enter adulthood healthy and strong.

What about people who come to church with their own ideas about worship? In their arrogance, they mutter through worship, criticize the musicians, and then yawn at the leaders who try to direct the service. Such people do the one-hour church thing to convince themselves that they've done their duty and are good people. Their kids did Sunday School and learned about David and Goliath, so now they can put a "good kid" label on. This kind of worship is empty and amounts to nothing but dust that blows away in the wind. Their contrary hearts reveal an unwillingness to enter worship that is right and good. Their refusal to grow and mature as Christians shows their willful ignorance of God's design and plan for worship.

But children who believe in the name of God's one and only Son come hungry for real spiritual food. They gather in Jesus' name and the Spirit of Christ leads them into nourishing spiritual and real worship. We must set our common abilities aside so we may step into the realm of the spirit.[1] Depending on our flesh to worship is unacceptable.[2] We ascend to Mount Zion where the Holy Spirit leads us over the threshold into worship that is true to God's design and plan for the temple.

> *Like newborn babies, crave pure spiritual milk, so that by it you may grow up in your salvation, now that you have tasted that the LORD is good.*
> (1 Peter 2:2–3)

There is a threshold in front of us and we must decide. Will we leave behind the limitations of this common realm to enter the kingdom of heaven's

---

[1] Common abilities are God-given natural gifts used for the work we do to provide for our family. Spiritual gifts are empowered in Christians by the Holy Spirit for the work of the church and Great Commission. They may work together, but they are not interchangeable. The author's book, *Great Separations*, offers an in-depth study on this topic.

[2] Jeremiah 17:5, Zechariah 4:6, John 6:63.

realm? Our High Priest leads us to break out of self-serving worship so we may enter what is spiritual and real. We let the Spirit of Christ carry us over the threshold with the wind of the Spirit so we may stand upon God's holy mountain. Entering the true glory of worship to effectively serve and minister in the Spirit begins with repentance. We must turn away from worshipping for ourselves and cross over from darkness into the full light of Christ. Worship by our own plan is not faithful to the design of God's temple. Man-made worship never measures up to the standard that is God's Word.

> *Then the glory of the LORD departed from over the threshold of the templae and stopped above the cherubim.*
> (Ezekiel 10:18)

We are called to take an account of our worship, to measure our praise, exaltations, preaching, and teaching by the standard of the Word. We must ask ourselves if our paradigms of worship are no more than manmade traditions that deny God's power.[3] Are we singing words of beautiful five-hundred-year-old hymns to rapturous organ music but refusing to live out what we sing? Does the worship team lead us in singing choruses and praise songs accompanied by great stringed and percussion instruments, but they're just tunes we forget to live by come Monday morning?

When empty kinds of worship continue on without repenting and turning back to our first love, we're in danger of God's glory departing from our gatherings. Before we know what happened we end up worshipping to serve our own needs. Our only purpose is to fulfill our traditions.

> *Then he went to the east gate. he climbed its steps and measured the threshold of the gate; it was one rod deep. The alcoves for the guards were one rod long and one rod wide, and the projecting walls between the alcoves were five cubits thick. And the threshold of the gate next to the portico facing the temple was one rod deep.*
> (Ezekiel 40:6–7)

True worship echoes from the walls of God's holy temple—a sanctuary that measures up to His standard of holiness. His standard is perfection.[4] When you stand at the threshold and realize that stepping over is impossible on your own you're ready to be brought over, lifted by the wind of the Spirit. We stand in awe as we observe the measuring of the temple that shows it is perfect according to God's design.

---

3. 1 Timothy 3:5.
4. Matthew 5:48.

> *The alcoves for the guards were one rod long and one rod wide, and the projecting walls between the alcoves were five cubits thick. And the threshold of the gate next to the portico facing the temple was one rod deep.*
> (Ezekiel 43:8)

Let living water flow like a river, flowing from the temple accompanied by songs of praise and thanksgiving as the Spirit gives a voice to God's holy people. May His holy fountain of life-giving water flow as God's people sing, "All my fountains are in you."[5] As we gather and sing out, the desert around us is turned into pools of fresh water and the parched ground is turned into flowing springs.[6]

> *The man brought me back to the entrance to the temple, and I saw water coming out from under the threshold of the temple toward the east (for the temple faced east). The water was coming down from under the south side of the temple, south of the altar.*
> (Ezekiel 47:1)

Will you cross the threshold? Will you ascend upon God's holy mountain and come up to Mount Zion? Will you express your own song or step over the threshold into God's holy sanctuary to worship in a way that is spiritual and real?

Take an account of your worship. Then you will see where you stand and come with a contrite heart to enter through the gates of the temple to join with the congregation in jubilant songs of thanksgiving and praise. Cross over as a diligent hearer of the Word who will obey the gospel's commands. In God's holy sanctuary the Spirit of Christ gives wind to our spirit, giving us a voice for true worship. Our songs waft out from the depths of our soul and spirit to confirm that the LORD our God dwells with us in Zion, on His holy hill.[7] In the ministries of the church, our Savior's living and active presence becomes wonderfully evident. We will go out from the assembly saying; "God is truly among us."[8]

> *Multitudes, multitudes in the valley of decision! For the day of the LORD is near in the valley of decision.*
> (Joel 3:14)

The power of the Word and the Holy Spirit compels us to worship in accord with all truth. In the Spirit, true worshippers are not like the early morning dew that disappears. We are established on the foundation of God's holy mountain and inside the gates of Zion, which the LORD loves.[9] Real worship

---
5. Psalm 87:7.
6. Psalm 107:35.
7. Joel 3:17.
8. 1 Corinthians 14:25.
9. Psalm 87:1.

is like refreshing rain upon desert wastelands and the dew of the morning that enlivens green leaves and budding blossoms. Songs of praise are like gentle rain that waters our gardens.[10]

Congregating in Jesus' name makes us glad because we are the people of Zion. As we stand in Christ's presence, we make music and sing, "All my foundations are in you."[11] We rejoice in the LORD God whose Spirit comes like faithful autumn rains to refresh fallow ground.[12] The spring rains come to make the seeds of faith grow and flourish.

> *In that day the mountains will drip new wine, and the hills will flow with milk; all the ravines of Judah will run with water. A fountain will flow out of the Lord's house and will water the valley of acacias.*
> (Joel 3:18)

We live in a generation that has no time for fruitless and hollow worship. They see through our efforts to make our gatherings attractive to them. Focusing on things like community service is good, but it doesn't make our meetings fulfilling and relevant. Serving our neighbors is only one element of church. Getting rid of the pulpit and altering the sanctuary to serve only as a food bank to feed poor accelerates the decline of real church. Serving espresso instead of communion causes further damage to genuine worship. A barista's work cannot replace the ministries of an elder. Doing yoga and kimchi instead of prayer time is destructive to true spirituality.

To restore true worship, we must step over the threshold into a temple that measures up to God's standards. We can't design our own worship for our gatherings. We are called to put ourselves aside, put on Christ, and be wrapped in His robe of righteousness. We must quiet our own perfect soprano and tenor voices and wait for the breath of the Spirit to give wind to our voice so we may sing out from our spirit with psalms, hymns, and spiritual songs. The preacher must give up his own words so he can speak the Word by the inspiration of the Holy Spirit.

We are called to take stock of our worship and ask ourselves: will we give in to cultural pressures to attract a crowd or step through the gateway into what is real, eternal, and truly spiritual? People pleasing plans are an offense to God's perfect design and plan for His sanctuary.

> *On the day of the Lord's sacrifice I will punish the officials and the king's sons and all those clad in foreign clothes. On that day I will punish all who avoid stepping on the threshold, who fill the temple of their gods with violence and deceit.*
> (Zephaniah 1:8–9)

---
10. Joel 2:23.
11. Psalm 87:7.
12. Hosea 10:12.

God's people are called to repent and enter true worship that is as pure and simple as the gospel. The good news of Jesus Christ is the only true inspiration for worship. We were sinners in need of a Savior. Now we hear God's Word and believe in Jesus Christ who was sent by the Father to die in our place and for our sins. We are baptized into the name of the Father, Son, and Holy Spirit. The Spirit and the Word compel us to answer Jesus who is knocking on our heart's door, knowing that He is the way, the truth, and the life, and there is no other way to the heavenly Father. We believe and declare that Jesus is our LORD and believe in our hearts that God raised Jesus from the dead and He has saved us.[1] We put our trust in God, for it is by faith that we are saved and not by anything we have done—it is a gift from God.[2] All that is left is for us to we call on the name of the LORD and He redeems us.[3] We listen to the precious words of the gospel, receive them as life-giving, and now our love compels us to act according to God's calling.

By the grace and mercies of our LORD and Savior we are washed cleaner and whiter than freshly fallen snow.[4] So, we lift up pure hands in praise and thanksgiving to the LORD our Maker. In our gatherings we exalt the LORD who is Creator of all the heavens and the earth. By the breath of the Spirit we sing out with joy from our spirit to the God of your salvation and then proclaim His holy name to the nations.

> *Very truly I tell you, whoever hears my word and believes him who sent me has eternal life and will not be judged but has crossed over from death to life.* (John 5:24)

When God's people come into the knowledge of the Christ, they leave behind man-made rules and traditions and cross the threshold into the realm of true worship. He calls us to worship with a renewed mind and refreshed spirit, accompanied by "thousands upon thousands of angels in joyful assembly" and "the church of the firstborn, whose names are written in heaven."[5]

We've come to an intersection and must decide. Will this valley of weeping we are passing through be blessed with refreshing pools of water? God's people are called to leave the world's distractions behind and cross the threshold into the holy sanctuary where true praises ring out.

---

1. Romans 10:9–10.
2. Ephesians 2:8–10.
3. Romans 10:12–13.
4. Isaiah 1:18.
5. Hebrews 12:22.

No longer do we lead our congregations into people-pleasing worship that invites idolatry. We don't try to be relevant to an irreverent world. We flourish like the garden of God that sprouts and blossoms with heaven's refreshing rain showers. Now revived, we rise as a people of faith to sing out and live out the true gospel of Jesus Christ. We are true worshippers who stand before Christ at the gates of Zion to worship His holy name before all the nations.

> How great are his signs, how mighty his wonders! His kingdom is an eternal kingdom; his dominion endures from generation to generation. (Daniel 4:3)

Chapter 12 Q&A

Crossing the Threshold

1. Why is it important to know God's plan for His sanctuary?

_____

2. What is the standard we use to measure our worship?

_____

3. Describe the point of decision that faces the postmodern church.

_____

4. What is the result of worship that pleases people rather than our heavenly Father?

_____

My Journey's Journal:

Part IV
Awaken the Dawn

*Your troops will be willing
on your day of battle.
Arrayed in holy splendor,
your young men will come to you
like dew from the morning's womb.
(Psalm 110:3)*

The Scriptures in this section are like steps up the mountain that bring us into the presence of Christ. We'll come to know our purpose and focus on the one true God. When we join the daily grind or pass through life's storms, our worship will remain anchored in Christ.

Chapter 13: Where We Gather

Key Scriptures:

- "How lovely is your dwelling place, LORD Almighty! My soul yearns, even faints, for the courts of the Lord; my heart and my flesh cry out for the living God" (Psalm 84:1–2).

- "Exalt the LORD our God and worship at his holy mountain, for the LORD our God is holy" (Psalm 99:9).

Children of resurrection worship their holy God on every island and continent in culturally relevant ways. Every local church has a special worship quality and unique voice. Churches around the world have distinctive teaching and preaching styles. Whether entering a Presbyterian, Methodist, Lutheran, Orthodox, Pentecostal, Charismatic, or Baptist church, we join in worship according to their unique manners. But the Holy Spirit is the universal means of worship.

The place we gather to worship is a house with pleasant boundaries where we enter God's garden of delights. We come into God's presence through Christ who has thrown open the gates so we may enter to worship. This kind of worship begins at home and then unites our family with other families in the delights of fellowship and worship. This is a sanctuary where everyone is offered a place.

> A prayer according to Ephesians 4:16:
>
> Heavenly Father, join us together to strengthen each other. By the power of your Word and the Holy Spirit, cause us grow in grace and knowledge so we may build your church in the love of Christ with each one doing our part.

When it comes to true worship, our boundaries are set in pleasant places.[1] Sons and daughters who belong to the LORD grow as they are nurtured by the Word at home. Our daughters become strong like pillars to adorn

---
1. Psalm 16:6.

our dwelling place.² In a worshipping home, mom thrives like a fruitful vine caring for children who flourish like olive shoots around the family table.³ A home that is centered on and constantly washed in the Word is a worshipful home. Dad and mom serve to instruct and train up their children in the way they should go.⁴

A gathering of worshipping families is a beautiful assembly where great and glorious exaltations ring out. Children who are nurtured in the LORD and taught to practice the disciplines of Christian faith at home are often eager to come to church and soak up more truths from God's Word. A well-taught congregation is primed to learn at home. This preparation for worship leads them to lift up God's holy name with voices that proclaim His majesty. Then they carry these blessings to their workplaces, classrooms, and community.

> *Ascribe to the LORD the glory due his name; worship the LORD in the splendor of his holiness.*
> (Psalm 29:2)

God's house is not located in Jerusalem or Rome. The door of temple for worship cannot be reached by taking a pilgrimage along the stations of the cross on the Via Dolorosa. It's not even possible to enter this gate by ascending the 11,674 steps up Mount Niesen in the Swiss Alps. Instead, we are called to ascend to the heavenly Mount Zion where we enter His holy gates with thanksgiving.⁵ We can make this ascent to worship even from the solitary confinement of a hospital bed or prison cell. We can lift up holy hands in this place while on our knees in our prayer closet. Even better, God's people enter this mount of worship as they gather to exalt our Almighty God.

Stand at the gate and sound a trumpet to call God's people to worship. Call to those who got lost along the way. Cry out to the wanderer on hill and mountainside driven by wicked shepherds from their resting place.⁶ Gather God's people into the happy crowd who dwells in His house, ever singing His praise.⁷

> *Stand at the gate of the Lord's house and there proclaim this message: "Hear the word of the Lord, all you people of Judah who come through these gates to worship the Lord."*
> (Jeremiah 7:2)

It's important to include all elements of worship in our Holy Spirit inspired gatherings. We celebrate the sacraments of the Lord's Table and

---

2. Psalm 144:12.
3. Psalm 128:3.
4. Proverbs 22:6.
5. Hebrews 12:22.
6. Jeremiah 50:6.
7. Psalm 84:2.

rejoice in the miracle of baptism. The five-fold teaching ministries God ordained for the church provide an enduring vitality.[8] Each prepares God's people for "works of service, so that the body of Christ may be built up."[9] But Christ, the Head of the church, has even more blessings for us. Worshipers are satisfied with the richest of heaven's foods, and they burst out with spiritual songs as they minister their spiritual gifts.[10] Without the ministries of the entire priesthood of believers,[11] the church becomes spiritually impoverished and worship devolves into an hour of self-focus.

There were separate courtyards in Solomon's temple and even more in the Herodian temple of Jesus' day. A special place was provided for priests, men, women, Nazarites, lepers, and Gentiles. Gathering places were provided for everyone who was called by Yahweh's holy name. The courtyards were not discriminatory. They were designed to be sure everyone who came to worship the Great I AM was included in a way that honored and glorified God. The design of the temple prefigured worship for our assemblies that bring us all together as one in Christ. But the design of the Old Testament temple still teaches us the value of orderly gatherings in the church. No one who seeks the LORD will be turned away. All those whom our Savior has called and chosen are invited to honor and exalt God in His holy presence.

> *This is what the LORD says: Stand in the courtyard of the Lord's house and speak to all the people of the towns of Judah who come to worship in the house of the Lord. Tell them everything I command you; do not omit a word.*
> (Jeremiah 26:2)

Families are the building blocks of the church. Because of this, the church ought to focus on encouraging godly homes. As this is lived out, husbands worshipfully and humbly serve by nurturing and tenderly admonishing their children. Mom and dad strengthen each other as they teach the children. The structure of a family is held together in a bond of love, nurturing affection around the dinner table. Parents use moments of family life to provide teaching opportunities.[12] Mom and dad demonstrate the security God provides by their faithful love to each other.

We have to give up our own self-centered wants to serve the family. Dad can't just plant himself in his recliner with a beer and his Xbox while his kids run wild. Love requires work. Love compels us to give up our rights and be present in every challenging family moment. In our homes as in our church-

---

8. Ephesians 4:11. Apostles, prophets, evangelists, pastors, and teachers.
9. Ephesians 4:12.
10. Psalm 63:5.
11. 1 Peter 2:9.
12. Deuteronomy 6:7, 11:19.

es, we are called to do the hard work of ministry because home is where true worship begins.

> *Husbands, love your wives, just as Christ loved the church and gave himself up for her.*
> (Ephesians 5:25)

A tall, handsome, and charismatic preacher, with a resonate voice and great oratorical skills, isn't what we need to lead us in worship. This is not the way of the God's kingdom. A stellar résumé doesn't always reflect the condition of a person's heart. What we need are leaders who are first godly parents who nurture and care for their own families faithfully.[13]

As we come to worship, it's imperative to know where our feet are planted and what our hearts yearn for. We need leaders and friends who provide good examples for us to follow. A man whose heart is bound up in the flesh isn't going to be able to help lead us into real worship. Are our feet stuck in earthen clay? Do our trendy fashions outshine Christ's robes of righteousness? Yes, we sing with our minds, but this is a renewed mind, the mind of Christ.[14] The things the world values must be cut away. There is no place for the stuff this world cherishes when we gather to worship in a way that is spiritual and real. Instead, we are provided with church leaders who are led by the Spirit to lead us as true worshippers.

> *For it is we who are the circumcision, we who serve God by his Spirit, who boast in Christ Jesus, and who put no confidence in the flesh.*
> (Philippians 3:3)

It is possible to regulate, establish paradigms, create traditions, and impose ourselves upon every word and song in our gatherings, but this self-serving control soon turns into selfish ambition and idolatrous worship. Our own agenda produces an unwelcoming atmosphere that drives away the breath of the Spirit. Bowing our heads and folding our hands may look like worship, but external appearances are not always a true reflection of our hearts. We must give up on our own way of doing things so we may cross the threshold into what is spiritual and real.

By the teaching of the Word and power of the Holy Spirit our hearts and minds are renewed and refocused on obeying Christ and His gospel's command to love one another.[15] When God's Word is declared, we must test what is taught, agree if it is the truth, and then do what we have heard. By doing this, we walk in the light of godly wisdom and live in agreement with our songs of praise and worship.

---

13. 1 Timothy 3:4–5.
14. Ephesians 4:20–24.
15. John 13:34.

Such regulations indeed have an appearance of wisdom, with their self-imposed worship, their false humility and their harsh treatment of the body, but they lack any value in restraining sensual indulgence.
(Colossians 3:23)

New covenant members of the body of Christ are like tents cleansed in the blood of Christ. As we come together, every word and note, every hand extended to minister, and all prayers and intercessions must be awash in the blood of the Lamb of God who takes away the sins of the world.[16] All Christians who gather in Jesus' name are the tabernacle tent that is established for worship. This is the holy place where we exalt our LORD and God.

We teach, preach, minister in our spiritual gifts, serve others, and sing songs of exaltation in a gathering of where all are welcomed into the church family. We carry this devotion to our homes where we strengthen one another to thrive in a hostile world. True worship begins at home and leads to a strong church. This kind of worship pours out like a pent-up flood that the breath of the LORD drives along.[17] All this is possible because we have a better covenant with Jesus Christ serving as our Prince and High Priest. We serve in a sanctuary washed in the blood of Christ where there is forgiveness of sin and cleansings to the depths of our conscious.

In the same way, he sprinkled with the blood both the tabernacle and everything used in its ceremonies.
(Hebrews 9:21)

How do we know that we worship a holy God? Are God's sons and daughters holy? When we gather, is it a holy place for worship? The Creator revealed that He is holy when He rested from the work of creation on the seventh day. God has made us a holy people by separating us to Himself and giving us His holy name as our own. An assembly of the saints is holy because we separate ourselves from the world's distractions and our common work. We cast off life's burdens and enter God's rest. By faith in Jesus Christ people from every nation obey the gospel's command to gather in Jesus' name to worship for the glory and onor of God's holy name.

Who will not fear you, Lord, and bring glory to your name? For you alone are holy. All nations will come and worship before you, for your righteous acts have been revealed.
(Revelation 15:4)

---

16. John 1:29.
17. Isaiah 59:19.

The exaltations we offer up to our heavenly Father in public assembly start at home with family. It begins as we prepare ourselves and our children from the rising of the sun until it sets, and through the watches of the night. This loving preparation is a path that leads us into the splendor of His holiness.

We, the church, have a new and better covenant that encompasses every moment of family life. Whether we gather by the river, around a campfire, on a mountain top, or in a building, we gather as a saints set apart for praise. We are gathered together as a people of saving faith in every nation to exalt the Lord, our Maker—for He is holy.

> Shout for joy to God, all the earth! Sing the glory of his name; make his praise glorious. (Psalm 66:1–2)

Chapter 13 Q&A

Where We Gather

1. Where does true worship begin? What are the steps that lead us to ascend into joyful praise?

2. What are the benefits of preparing ourselves at home before coming together as one family to worship?

3. Why are the ministries of spiritual gifts by the priesthood of all believers so vital to true worship in our assemblies?

4. What attributes are necessary for those who lead us as we worship?

My Journey's Journal:

Chapter 14: Come Together With Purpose

Key Scriptures:

- "To him who is able to keep you from stumbling and to present you before his glorious presence without fault and with great joy—to the only God our Savior be glory, majesty, power and authority, through Jesus Christ our Lord, before all ages, now and forevermore! Amen" (Jude 1:24–25).

- "I have seen you in the sanctuary and beheld your power and your glory. Because your love is better than life, my lips will glorify you. I will praise you as long as I live, and in your name I will lift up my hands. I will be fully satisfied as with the richest of foods; with singing lips my mouth will praise you" (Psalm 63:2–5).

Can you hear the great harmony of worship? God's people are strengthened in a bond that unites us with the Father, Son, and Holy Spirit. Together, we enter His glorious presence with singing and come to know God's purpose for our lives.

In this glorious fellowship, we are instructed to serve our brothers and sisters in Christ and prepared to be sent as ambassadors for the good news. In this holy sanctuary we wait and pray for the Holy Spirit to empower us. Then we go as pilgrims to bring the light of Christ to people isolated in darkness and hopelessness. We go up with singing, knowing that we are servants who are honored to answer this high calling.

Every Scripture for this topic leads us into His presence where we rejoice, pray, and offer up our thanksgiving. In our worship gatherings we are woven together like threads that strengthen the fabric of the church. The Creator prepared a work for us from the beginning of time, and we rejoice to bless others by means of the anointing and empowering work of the Holy Spirit.

For you make me glad by your deeds, Lord; I sing for joy at what your hands have done.
(Psalm 92:4)

> A prayer according to 1 John 1:3:
>
> Oh Lord, may your Spirit give wind to our voices so we may proclaim before you all your mighty works that we have seen and heard. May we gather in your holy presence, joined in sweet fellowship with the Father, and with your Son, Jesus Christ.

We press on together, unified in purpose, girded with praise, and sheltered by the Almighty's wings. The light of Christ shines on our faces as we continue this great ascent. We press on, looking forward to the day when the Lion of Judah, the Root of David, rises triumphant with all things subject to him.[1] We magnify our Savior whose Spirit comes like a cleansing fire.

We are ambassadors of Christ, commissioned to carry this good news to the farthest reaches of the earth. The authority in our hands is the sword of the Spirit which is the Word of God.[2]

For Zion's sake I will not keep silent, for Jerusalem's sake I will not remain quiet, till her vindication shines out like the dawn, her salvation like a blazing torch.
(Isaiah 62:1)

The Master Builder prepares a place for His bride, the church. She waits for His return, rejoicing with great expectation. Christ's betrothed keeps the flame burning with the oil of joy—the joy of salvation. In her waiting hours she speaks His words of comfort to those who mourn and to lift the burden of those who grieve. She was brought up from the ashes of ruin and bestowed with a crown of beauty. The Bridegroom adorns her with garments of praise. She is strengthened with songs of rejoicing. She is strong like a mighty oak tree—an oak of righteousness the LORD has planted to display His splendor.[3]

As a young man marries a young woman, so will your Builder marry you; as a bridegroom rejoices over his bride, so will your God rejoice over you.
(Isaiah 62:5)

When true knowledge of the gospel of Jesus Christ is proclaimed, the people break out with praise, rejoicing in the message of the true gospel message of the cross. The power of the good news, when rightly spoken, awakens us to the living and active presence of our LORD and Savior. Then He proves His Word true with signs and wonders performed among the people.[4]

---
1. Revelation 5:5
2. Ephesians 6:17.
3. Paraphrased from Isaiah 61:2–3.
4. Romans 15:19.

A powerful harmony of faith is created when both the speakers and the listeners long for Christ's truth. The church prevails against the gates of hell when God's people are united in purpose and stand on their Rock, Christ Jesus.[5]

For the lips of a priest ought to preserve knowledge, because he is the messenger of the LORD Almighty and people seek instruction from his mouth.
(Malachi 2:7)

The desire of a true worshipper's heart is to be at peace with their Creator. We desire to dwell in the shelter of the Most High God and worship in His presence. When we pray and sing with exultations, we sing words worthy of heaven's throne room. This is only possible because of Jesus Christ's victory on the cross. He gave His life, dying in our place and for our sin so that we may be made right with the Father. Now, all those who have come to saving faith in Christ and remain in Him are justified before the great I AM, and prepared as ambassadors of God's kingdom.

Those who partake of Christ come into peace and favor with our heavenly Father. All who come to saving faith and abide in Christ are called "friends" by the LORD Almighty.[6] We remain in Christ, who is our peacemaker, the mediator between God and man.[7] We abide in Christ because He is our only hope of glory and favor with the heavenly Father. Jesus wraps us in His robe of righteousness and presents us to the Father so we may stand in the wisdom of His counsel.[8] In His awesome presence, we are enlightened in the hope of our salvation. In God's glorious presence we are confident that every prayer and song of praise is received in the heavenly realm as sweet incense.[9] This is something worth boasting about as we take the good news to our neighbors and then to the rest of the world.

Therefore, since we have been justified through faith, we have peace with God through our LORD Jesus Christ, through whom we have gained access by faith into this grace in which we now stand. And we boast in the hope of the glory of God.
(Romans 5:1–2)

The inhabitants of the far-flung corners of the earth rise up with a new song. They sing aloud as they triumph over the chains of sin. Christ's disciples venture to every island and continent to proclaim the good news and sing our Savior's new song. He infuses His ambassadors with zeal and they shout from the mountaintops with a battle cry as they join the church to march out to see the LORD Almighty conquer every continent on the face of the earth.[10]

---

5. Matthew 16:18.
6. James 2:23.
7. 1 Timothy 2:5.
8. Psalm 32:8, 73:24.
9. Psalm 141:2.
10. Revelation 11:15.

Hear the Redeemer's call to prepare ourselves and make ready for His day of battle.[11] Ambassadors of the cross put on gospel shoes, take up shields of faith, grip the sword of the Spirit in their hands, fasten on His breastplate of righteousness, and put on His helmet of salvation to be equipped and ready to step out as peacemakers. We come together with fasting and prayer and then wait for the Holy Spirit to empower us before we go out to do the work of the Great Commission.

Where are His ambassadors sent? There are too many islands of darkness and hopelessness where people are isolated from hearing God's Word. Christ sends out His disciples with words of saving grace. He is more than able to send an ambassador to be sure that the gospel's triumphant new song is heard on every isle.

> *Sing to the LORD a new song, his praise from the ends of the earth, you who go down to the sea, and all that is in it, you islands, and all who live in them.... The LORD will march out like a champion, like a warrior he will stir up his zeal; with a shout he will raise the battle cry and will triumph over his enemies.* (Isaiah 42: 10, 13)

"For unto us a child is born, to us a son is given."[12] Jesus came as a babe, born of the virgin, Mary laid him in a manger. He grew up in Nazareth, apprenticed by Joseph as a carpenter. Then He walked among us as Immanuel, taught the crowds beside the lake, fed multitudes from just a few loaves and fish, and healed the sick with His powerful loving touch. When His time came to be fulfilled, Jesus made His triumphant entrance into Jerusalem, "gentle and riding on a donkey."[13] In this great city, He was crucified, died, buried, and then rose again from the dead on the third day, just as the prophets foretold. He ascended to the right hand of the Father and sent His Holy Spirit with a mighty wind and tongues of fire to establish His church.

God's people gather in Jesus' name and then go out as ambassadors. With every step we take and word we speak, His living and active presence is continually manifested. We constantly abide in His presence. In our place of worship there is no room for a custom-made Jesus, made in our own image. We sing words of faith and then go out with life-giving words. Venomous words have no place.[14] In moments of weakness and temptation, it's easy to forget that the Spirit of Christ is ever-present with us. We ignore Him and do what pleases us. We are brought back into sweet fellowship when we turn away from these self-focused attitudes and repent. When the heart attitude of Christ is in us, He

---
11. Psalm 110:3.
12. Isaiah 9:6.
13. Matthew 21:5.
14. James 3:10.

draws near and we have great cause to rejoice in the joy of His salvation. We are weak vessels who have every reason to break out with worship and praise as we are forgiven and strengthened to serve in God's kingdom.

> *Rejoice in the LORD always. I will say it again: Rejoice! Let your gentleness be evident to all. The LORD is near.*
> (Philippians 4:4–5)

When you heard the precious words of the gospel message, the seed of faith was planted in your heart. You were given faith to believe and received words of saving grace with rejoicing. You were baptized into the Father, Son, and Holy Spirit. The plan for God's holy sanctuary shows God's sons or daughters how to honor His holy name. The design of His temple then compels us to step out as ambassadors of Christ. As Jesus' disciples, it's important to remain anchored, because we are sent like sheep among wolves.[15] Witnesses of the cross stay secure by rejoicing in the Lord, delighting in His salvation, and being constant in prayer.

These things are good markers to keep us fixed on the goal of our ascent. The prophet Micah teaches us the way of love's commands. He wrote in his book, "What does the LORD require of you? To act justly and to love mercy and to walk humbly with your God."[16] With your feet on this pathway, you may ask, "Does my Father have a job for me to do?" Yes, a custom designed job created just for you. He planned ahead and prepared a mission for you to accomplish in your lifetime. Paul wrote to the Ephesian church to answer this question; "For we are God's handiwork, created in Christ Jesus to do good works, which God has prepared in advance for us to do."[17] This is something worth rejoicing about and a great encouragement to put on gospel shoes.

> *Rejoice always, pray continually, give thanks in all circumstances; for this is God's will for you in Christ Jesus.*
> (1 Thessalonians 5:16–17)

Caring for the fatherless and poor is one vital element of Christian service. Keeping ourselves focused on the essentials and not getting drawn into the glitter, glamor, and self-serving pleasures of the world around us is vital to the well-being of every member of Christ's body, the church. Our personal lack of focus tends to distract the whole church and defeat our mission. Because of this, contrite hearts are a vital for true worship that prepares us to disciple others.

---

15. Matthew 10:16.
16. Micah 6:8.
17. Ephesians 2:10.

Serving the poor is one essential thread in the fabric of true worship. Jesus rebuked Judas for scolding the woman who poured expensive perfume over Jesus' feet. He made it clear that she had done a good thing. Then He said, "You will always have the poor among you, but you will not always have me."[18] Worshipping in the living and active presence of our LORD and Savior is like a silver thread that strengthens the church.

> *Religion that God our Father accepts as pure and faultless is this: to look after orphans and widows in their distress and to keep oneself from being polluted by the world.*
> (James 1:27)

As we begin serving, we soon realize it's impossible to affect people's lives for eternity in our own strength. We must look to the Spirit of Christ who is greater than ourselves and clothes us with power from on high. Before we begin our work we must wait to receive the anointing, gifting, and empowering work of the Holy Spirit who makes it possible to complete our work. Carried by the wind of Spirit, our souls lift up the name of the LORD Almighty. We sing and applaud with shouts of joy to glorify the great I AM.

> *You are worthy, our LORD and God, to receive glory and honor and power, for you created all things, and by your will they were created and have their being.*
> (Revelation 4:11)

We lift our eyes to see an awesome banner raised on the mountain top and waving in the wind. Our Savior raises His flagstaff to gather the saints as a mighty army. We rise as a choir whose voices ring out to the far reaches of the earth. Great mountains turn into plateaus as the LORD makes the way straight before Christ our King.[19]

Jesus came in weakness and "made Himself nothing, taking on the nature of a servant."[20] He gave up His glory in heaven to come down and serve among us. He descended so that He may ascend "higher than all the heavens."[21] At the climax of His ministry, Jesus rode into Jerusalem humbly on the colt of a donkey. Then, on that rugged wooden cross He suffered to win a mighty victory over sin, Satan, and death. What appeared to men as the ultimate weakness was the ultimate demonstration of God's power. Then our Redeemer rose again to reign on high, where He ministers to His church with

---
18. John 12:8.
19. Zechariah 4:7.
20. Philippians 2:7.
21. Ephesians 4:9–10.

His active presence. We gather in His name so that we may go out as ambassadors with the mind and attitude of Christ and the anointing of the Spirit of Christ so that God's power will be manifested in and through us.

Every good work is from above. The strength, power, and authority we need to spread the good news comes from above. We must wait to receive the Spirit's empowering work before we step out to fulfill our calling and purpose in Christ.

> In the last days the mountain of the Lord's temple will be established as the highest of the mountains; it will be exalted above the hills, and all nations will stream to it. (Isaiah 2:2)

Chapter 15: Exalting God in a Storm

Key Scriptures:

- "Though the fig tree does not bud and there are no grapes on the vines, though the olive crop fails and the fields produce no food, though there are no sheep in the pen and no cattle in the stalls, yet I will rejoice in the Lord, I will be joyful in God my Savior" (Habakkuk 3:17–18).

- "These [trials] have come so that the proven genuineness of your faith—of greater worth than gold, which perishes even though refined by fire—may result in praise, glory and honor when Jesus Christ is revealed" (1 Peter 1:7).

Martin Luther King Jr. spoke powerful words that gripped the heart of a troubled nation when he voiced with unwavering certainty, "I have a dream." Winston Churchill stiffened a nation's resolve during WWII when he boldly declared, "Victory. Victory at all costs. Victory in spite of all terror. Victory however long and hard the road may be. For without victory there is no survival." John F. Kennedy rallied a nation to work together, saying; "And so, my fellow Americans: ask not what your country can do for you—ask what you can do for your country." Desmond Tutu inspired a nation to heal its wounds with his oratorical skill. He brought them together, proclaiming; "Without forgiveness, without reconciliation, we have no future."[1]

Words are powerful agents of change in troubled times; they can alter the course of history. And yet the greatest of man's words fall to the ground like spent blossoms compared to the words of the great I AM. History began in the shadow of the cross and reached its apex as the full light of the cross was revealed. The word of life is powerful to change a heart, heal a body, restore a soul, and strengthen a spirit through life's storms.

Psalm 29 reveals the voice of the Lord's awesome resonance. There is no fortress too thick, no mine shaft too deep, no forest so dense that His voice will not be heard. Indeed, His voice shakes the foundations of the earth.

---

1. Desmond Tutu, *No Future Without Forgiveness*, p. 165.

Hebrew tradition teaches that David wrote this psalm while meditating on the LORD during a massive storm. The skies filled with gloomy clouds, claps of thunder, bolts of lightning, and torrents of rain inspired him to worship of the Almighty. In later years, Israel's priests read Psalm 29 to the congregation during the Feast of Trumpets. God still speaks like a whisper that is heard even through claps of lightning and thunder.

> A prayer according to Psalm 89:8–9:
>
> Oh Lord, give us hearts that overflow with worship, for you are mighty. You surround us with your faithfulness as you rule over the raging seas. When troubles come against us like mighty waves, you still the storms.

Children of resurrection worship their Almighty Creator even during life's raging storms. Continents shake, and the oceans roar, yet we continue to lift holy hands to God who created the heavens and earth. At the presence of the Lord, the mountains leap like rams and the hills like lambs.[2] The sound of His voice is like rushing waters.[3] By His awesome word, all things were created: "For he spoke, and it came to be; he commanded, and it stood firm."[4] Through His Word we come to know Him so that we may attribute to Him all the glory due Him by proclaiming His word, with songs of praise, and uplifted hands.

Ascribe to the Lord, you heavenly beings, ascribe to the LORD glory and strength.
(Psalm 29:1)

When you're battered in a storm and feeling too troubled to worship or pray, stop and remember the honor due our Father's holy name. When you're scratching out a living and trying your best to get ahead in the game, take a break from your hard work to rest in the Lord, knowing that God is your Provider who is worthy of all praise. When you have no place to go, no one to turn to, and no place to lay your head, take the time to exalt the LORD God in all His grandeur and glory. We enter our Father's rest knowing that He satisfies us in this dry and thirsty land where we must dwell until He calls us home.

Ascribe to the LORD the glory due his name; worship the LORD in the splendor of his holiness.
(Psalm 29:2)

The awesome voice of the LORD Almighty awakens us to His might and power. Children of resurrection are awakened to worship the Creator of all the heavens and earth. The Father's sons and daughters are stirred to worship

---
2. Psalm 114:6–7.
3. Revelation 1:15.
4. Psalm 33:9.

Him who is mighty in battle. All children of light hear this awesome call, turn from their fears, and raise their voices in a mighty chorus to glorify God who is high and lifted up.

Servants of the Most High God offer our hands, voices, and hearts to proclaim the good news no matter the circumstances. Our God shields His messengers through all of life's raging storms. We are like those who are forced to hunker down when a storm stops them on their ascent. We are simple pilgrims who bow to the One who is greater than any furious wind. We worship Him who is more than able to calm raging seas.

The voice of the LORD is over the waters; the God of glory thunders,
the LORD thunders over the mighty waters.
(Psalm 29:3)

The Creator of all things is sovereign over all creation. He is God Most High who has dominion over all kingdoms and nations on earth.[5] He reigns as King over all the heavens and earth. The sound of our Father's holy name penetrates the depths of our soul. His mighty voice penetrates to cleanse the deepest recesses of our hearts. Hearing His awesome voice compels us to come as living sacrifices ready to serve and spread the light of Christ. We speak God's holy name, knowing that at the name of Jesus every knee will buckle and every head bow down.[6] The mighty of this earth are humbled in His awesome presence, for He is the LORD Almighty who is worthy of all our worship, glory, and adoration.

The voice of the LORD is powerful; the voice of the LORD is majestic.
(Psalm 29:4)

Lightning strikes and shatters a majestic cedar tree with an earsplitting clash. There is no mortal power that can stop the powerful flashes of the storm. The world's power brokers delight in their sway over the affairs of humankind, but they must bow down to God who established them to serve. They must remember that God throws down those who exalt themselves, toppling them from their high pedestals. At God's command, the tallest cedars and the finest cypress trees in the forest are brought to nothing.[7] But those who humble themselves before the LORD need not fear because the woodcutter can no longer cut them down.[8]

---

5. Daniel 4:17.
6. Revelation 2:10–11.
7. Isaiah 37:24.
8. Isaiah 14:8.

The voice of the LORD breaks the cedars; the LORD breaks in pieces the cedars of Lebanon.
(Psalm 29:5)

"The sea looked and fled, the Jordan turned back; the mountains skipped like rams, the hills like lambs."[9] The psalmist asks why the sea fled, why the Jordan River turned back its flowing waters. What caused the mountains to shake and the hills to tremble? The answer leads us to see the Red Sea and the Jordan River as great thresholds God's people crossed by His guiding hand and outstretched arm.

Habakkuk saw a similar vision and asked why God was angry with the rivers.[10] Yahweh unleashed his anger against those who enslaved His people. The Almighty rose up to battle against those who carved wooden idols and called them "father." His wrath burned hot against those who chiseled images in stone and then said, "You gave me birth."[11]

But God's holy nation walked safely through the water that stood high on each side of them like a wall. They reached the other side of the Red Sea and raised their voices in praise: "I will sing to the Lord, for he is highly exalted. Both horse and driver he has hurled into the sea." Our God has not changed; He still delivers His people from their oppressors. He is worthy of all praise, glory, and honor as He leads us through the raging waters that surround us.

He makes Lebanon leap like a calf, Sirion like a young wild ox.
(Psalm 29:6)

A trumpet sounds out to gather God's people into His sanctuary. In this holy place we behold Him in all His power and glory. He whispers and we hear Him even in the thunder. His voice resounds with love that is better than life. Our hearts overflow with songs to glorify our LORD and Master as He showers us with His lovingkindness. Hearing His voice leads us to take an account of our days[12] and we lift up the name of the LORD who sustains us. His voice calls us to come to the Lord's table, where Christ is present to feed us with the richest of foods. Then we go out with songs of great praise for the blessings, strength, and forgiveness His table provides even in the presence of our enemies.[13]

The voice of the LORD strikes with flashes of lightning.
(Psalm 29:7)

---

9. Psalm 114:3–4.
10. Habakkuk 3:8.
11. Jeremiah 2:27.
12. Psalm 90:12.
13. Inspired by Psalm 63:1–5 and Psalm 23:5.

Parched wastelands shake and the sands of time shift, but sojourners continue on their way through barren deserts to God's safe oasis of refreshment and strength. Pilgrims of faith get exhausted, parched, and faint, but they lift holy hands to the God who fortifies them as they continue on their journey.

When everything around us is shaken we soon learn that we have no strength of our own to endure. We try to stay strong, but we are not. We try to stay strong with every bit of grit we can muster, but it is never enough. Now, in weakness we seek the LORD God who is our strength—an all-sufficient strength. Our Father is strong and mighty and He dwells in us. This truth is for all who walk in the light of Christ. "They go from strength to strength, till each appears before God in Zion."[14] Let us lift holy hands and bless the LORD in this dry and thirsty land.

The voice of the LORD shakes the desert; the LORD shakes the Desert of Kadesh.
(Psalm 29:8)

The house shakes with every flash of lightning and thunder. The trees around us are tossed about, first one way and then another. In the morning they are nothing but torn stumps in the ground. The mighty oak tree is uprooted and thrown down. The wind roars and whistles, shaking the foundations of everything we hold dear. We watch helpless as all the stuff we've worked so hard to get is blown away.

But we stand secure in the place of our habitation, in the sanctuary of the LORD Most High. He is our fortress. In this holy place we are shielded. We are held safe because Jesus has taken captivity captive and given us many good gifts.[15] In His holy temple we escape any lasting harm, holding onto God's sure and precious promises.[16] We are comforted by the light of His holy presence and lift our voices with songs of exaltation to God who delivers us.

The voice of the LORD twists the oaks and strips the forests bare. And in his temple all cry, "Glory!"
(Psalm 29:9)

Flood waters rage against your home. Minute by minute you watch the muddy waters spoil your fresh painted walls swirling with devouring shards of rock. As the waters rise, you step up another step, wondering when it will stop, and if your family will be safe. Your thoughts race fearfully through your mind. Then you feel the whole house shift under your feet. It's time to get everyone out to keep them safe.

---

14. Psalm 84:7.
15. Psalm 68:18, Ephesians 4:8.
16. Psalm 68:20.

Murky waters roil under your inflatable boat as you huddle together. Then the finally clouds part, revealing a ray of sunshine, and you're reminded where your hope comes from.[1] You're safe together, not one of you is lost, and you know beyond doubt that together you will be strengthened for each challenge that lies ahead. You're mindful that in the light of Christ you have an eternal hope to carry you through every storm. You look up with praise from your heart because "your redemption is drawing near."[2]

The LORD sits enthroned over the flood; the LORD is enthroned as King forever. (Psalm 29:10)

As the raging waters recede, like Noah, we reach out our hands to receive the dove that returns with an olive branch in its beak. A rainbow appears in the sky and our hearts are strengthened in God's promise. Our trust is in the Lord, and He never leaves us in a lurch—He never forsakes us.[3] Our hearts were torn with fear for our little ones. Confusion roiled our minds as we watched all we own wash away in the flood. We try to remind ourselves that they were all temporal things provided for us to care for our family. We recall precious verses reminding us that our God is still the God who provides.

Suddenly, as we contemplate these unseen realities, God's glory comes like a flash of light. Even in the darkest moment of our suffering our hearts are filled with God's glory. We start to feel solid in faith once again, knowing that suffering produces perseverance, and perseverance produces strong and godly character. We know that a tried and tested character produces hope, "Because God's love has been poured out into our hearts through the Holy Spirit, who has been given to us" to comfort us.[4] From our hearts flow these precious words: "Praise the Lord, O my soul."[5]

The LORD gives strength to his people; the LORD blesses his people with peace. (Psalm 29:11)

David's stormy psalm helps us to live in a world that constantly shakes. Nothing on earth can offer a safe refuge from storms that batter us. But we serve an awesome God, the Sustainer of all things. He leads us to the Rock that rises above the chaos, no matter how high the crushing waves.

---

1. Psalm 121:2.
2. Luke 21:28.
3. Hebrews 13:5.
4. Romans 5:3–5.
5. Psalm 103:1.

Our own strength isn't enough to help us press on through trouble and trials. We exhaust ourselves trying, until we're ready to give up. Then we turn to the Lord, where we find the One who leads us from strength to strength. Though everything gets torn from our hands, we lift our hands and give praise to the Lord. He is our habitation, our sanctuary, our fortress. When our world shifts under our feet, we have a Rock where we can anchor. Finally, when there's is a break in the murky storm clouds, rays of sunshine remind us of the eternal hope we hold in our hearts. When the storms have passed, we realize that the strength we needed to help us endure was not our own. Our strength comes from above and it comes in abundance in our time of need.

> Come, let us sing for joy to the LORD; let us shout aloud to the Rock of our salvation. (Psalm 95:1)

Chapter 15 Q&A

Exalting God in a Storm

1. When life's storms buffet you, what song will you sing?

_____

_____

_____

2. Where can you find refuge when storms rage all around you?

_____

_____

_____

3. Is it possible to hear God's whisper even in the middle of rush hour traffic?

_____

_____

_____

4. What do you do when it feels like everything in your life is shifting under your feet?

_____

_____

_____

My Journey's Journal:

Chapter 16: The Object of Our Worship

Key Scriptures:

- "They will come and shout for joy on the heights of Zion; they will rejoice in the bounty of the Lord" (Jeremiah 31:12).

- "Come, let us bow down in worship, let us kneel before the LORD our Maker; for he is our God and we are the people of his pasture, the flock under his care. Today, if only you would hear his voice" (Psalm 95:6–7).

If you gush over a beautiful quilt, admiring its perfect stitching and intricate patterns while ignoring the person who created it, you've missed the most important part of the design. In the same way, exalting only what God has created misses His whole purpose. Moving our focus from Christ onto His good gifts turns them into distractions. God's Word leads us to focus on worshipping Him, who is the source all these good things.

God is the one who guides us at every intersection of life. He helps us sift through our motives and take an account of our attitudes and actions. Cleansed hearts can center their worship on God, who is our refuge. In His holy sanctuary, we delight in the fear of the Lord.[1] We put aside our selfish ambitions and submit to Christ alone. We are forgiven, cleansed, and unburdened so we may focus our worship on the Most High God. It is vitally important to walk humbly before our LORD, and keep our eyes fixed on Him.

> A prayer according to James 1:17:
>
> Give us hearts to receive every good and perfect gift you give us from above. May we overflow with thankfulness for the blessings that come down from you, the Father of heavenly lights.

When we come to the end of ourselves and place no trust in what the world values, we find ourselves compelled to look up to the One our hearts eternally desire. We realize that this world is not our home; we are just pilgrims in a dry and thirsty land. Then, as the days of life's journey grow

---
1. Isaiah 11:13.

long, our body starts to fail and the pilgrimage becomes even more challenging. The doctor tells us our heart needs a pacemaker. Living our daily lives requires assistance. Our eyes get cataracts, our glasses get thicker, and it hurts when we bend over to pull on our socks.

Look up! There is a Father in heaven who sustains us even when we grow old and our hair turns gray.[2] In our lifetime we built houses or developed start-up businesses. We made a profit and then sold for a gain. But all this quickly fades into obscurity in the light of eternity because our LORD and Savior is ours forever and it is Him whom we exalt.

> *Whom have I in heaven but you? And earth has nothing I desire besides you. My flesh and my heart may fail, but God is the strength of my heart and my portion forever.*
> (Psalm 73:25–26)

You're feeling on the top of the world because the company offered you that good paying dream job. You worked hard to get that diploma, carefully built your resumé, and made sure to get the certifications required. Now it all paid off in a great job. You can buy that new house and in three years get the luxury car you always wanted. This is a good time to stop and take an account of your life and your eternity. And the most important question? Who or what will you worship?

Have your career goals driven you so hard that you have no time for what is most important in life and little energy to think about your eternal destiny? Are you so worn out from working that there's nothing left to nurture and train up your children? Have you tossed aside the desire God gave you to serve as a teacher in your church?

Stop a moment and listen. Before you sign the contract on a new red sports car, wait and listen. You'll hear Joshua's words echo in your ears. "Choose for yourselves this day whom you will serve."[3] Of course, there's nothing wrong with having a cool sports car, but we must only worship God, the One who provides our wheels.

> *"You are my witnesses," declares the Lord, "and my servant whom I have chosen, so that you may know and believe me and understand that I am he. Before me no god was formed, nor will there be one after me. I, even I, am the Lord, and apart from me there is no savior. I have revealed and saved and proclaimed–I, and not some foreign god among you. You are my witnesses," declares the Lord, "that I am God. Yes, and from ancient days I am he. No one can deliver out of my hand. When I act, who can reverse it?"*
> (Isaiah 43:10–13)

---

2. Isaiah 46:4.
3. Joshua 24:15.

The big green sign over the interstate tells us where to exit. The voice on our map app tells us how many feet to our turn. There are signs, signals, and warnings all around us, pointing us every direction. So, which way do we go?

First, we must choose a destination. If we're driving along with our eyes on the ditch, it's not hard to predict where we'll end up. But if we look up, there are more than enough signs in the Scriptures to lead us to our journey's end. God's Word puts us on a path to an incredible destination. On the way to our eternal home, God leads us to worship Him as the One who lights our way and directs our steps.

> *This is what the LORD says–your Redeemer, the Holy One of Israel: "I am the LORD your God, who teaches you what is best for you, who directs you in the way you should go."*
> (Isaiah 48:17)

So, what do you do when the boss offers you a new position, promises to double your salary, and fly your family to the company's resort for all expense paid annual vacations? Before answering you sit down with your spouse and write down the pros and cons. You would be away from home all week and some weekends, but you would finally be able pay off the orthodontist's bill. The negative list grows as you note that you'd have to give up coaching the kid's soccer games and teaching the sixth-grade Sunday School class. But you could afford a new family van to replace your old one.

Can we serve God alone and still work a job that requires so much travel? Must we choose between our role in the church and making a decent living? The answers to these questions get personal. We earnestly seek God's counsel because we're faced with the fact that what we decide affects everyone around us. Each of us must prayerfully take account of our motives and weigh them with God's Word as the standard. When we get back to work on Monday and the boss calls us into his office for an answer, we must not fear the boss, but only fear the LORD whom we worship. We are called to walk in our Savior's footsteps. Satan offered Jesus all the "all the kingdoms of the world and their splendor,"[4] but He knew His purpose and His calling. He knew it was a trap.

> *Jesus said to him, "Away from me, Satan! For it is written: 'Worship the LORD your God, and serve him only.'"*
> (Matthew 4:10)[5]

When our feet are firmly planted on Jesus Christ, the Rock, none of life's difficult choices can distract us from focusing on Him alone. He sends us to serve with unshakeable faith. But our flesh is weak. Our hearts grow faint,

---
4. Matthew 4:8.
5. Jesus quoted Deuteronomy 6:13.

and it's easy for our feet slip from the right path. In our distress we cry out with a repentant heart, "Lead me to the Rock that is higher than I." Once again, we come into His refuge. We are lifted up into a high tower so that no foe can come against us.[6]

In this place of refuge, whom will we fear? We know that our God is a consuming fire and He rises up to destroy every enemy who rages against His church. We're secure in His high tower. We look to see God's adversaries flee. Now safe in our Father's love, we come before Him with adoration, glorifying His name for He is worthy of all praise.

> *Therefore, since we are receiving a kingdom that cannot be shaken, let us be thankful, and so worship God acceptably with reverence and awe, for our "God is a consuming fire."*
> (Hebrews 12:28–29)

A vital element of true worship is a church that seeks God and His righteousness above all else. Every true heart of worship submits before the LORD in the fellowship of a community. In His presence, we enter into a mutual submission to one another before the LORD without quarreling.[7] We allow our leaders to lead us. In unity, our hearts are joined in fellowship so that we may minister and serve in harmony with our Savior's new song. When we seek first the kingdom of God, we test what we hear, and then submit to what is true.

Now reflect on the truth that God's children are called to enter worship clothed with the righteousness of Jesus Christ. This isn't a face that just looks down at the floor. In humility we speak out and sing out with a confident voice.

The humblest act in biblical history may have been when Moses stood before the Red Sea with the frightened and angry tribes of Israel pressing in on him. He didn't react on his own, instead, he focused on the Great I AM, obeyed His command and did the impossible. He set aside his own fears, raised his staff, and stretched out his hand over the sea to divide the water so the Israelites could cross the sea on dry ground.[8] This is the heart of a true worshipper who comes in humility to exalt the LORD Almighty and none other.

> *In the same way, you who are younger, submit yourselves to your elders. All of you, clothe yourselves with humility toward one another, because, "God opposes the proud but shows favor to the humble."*
> (1 Peter 5:5)

---

6. Psalm 61:2–3.
7. Romans 14:1.
8. Exodus 14:16.

Life is a turbulent journey in a rough and tumble world. We struggle against mountain-sized obstacles as we build a life for our family. Then, when the kids are grown, we're faced with the challenges of old age—if we make it that far. To get through all this, we must keep our eyes fixed upon Jesus, who is our strength to endure to the end.

Signs are posted along roads and intersections so we can find the right way. But to get anywhere, we must know where we want to go. God's Word lights the only pathway that leads to our forever home; we just need to read and follow the directions. The world offers detours and deceptive traps to get us off course. We must ask ourselves what path we'll take. Whom will we serve?

When Christians join in the fellowship of true worshippers, they become part of an awesome life changing miracle. And yet, it's not the gathering that we treasure, but the One who gathers us. Every eye is focused on Christ. Every voice shouts out in the Spirit. All hands lift high to exalt God our Redeemer.

> For you, Lord, are the Most High over all the earth; you are exalted far above all gods. (Psalm 97:9)

Chapter 16 Q&A

The Object of Our Worship

1. What is the best thing you can co when you finally achieved your dream and found success?

   _____
   _____
   _____

2. When everything is going your way in life, what is the best thing you can do?

   _____
   _____
   _____

3. What does it look like when you clothe yourself with humility?

   _____
   _____
   _____

My Journey's Journal:

Part V
Strengthen the Foundations

They devoted themselves to the apostles' teaching and to fellowship, to the breaking of bread and to prayer.
(Acts 2:42)

This section leads diligent students of the Word to esteem the essential elements of orderly worship. The way of worship is revealed by the Word who spoke and all things were created. Then we come in reverent awe to exalt the LORD our God as we see Christ revealed in Revelation.

Chapter 17: A Call to Order

Key Scriptures:

- "In the beginning you laid the foundations of the earth, and the heavens are the work of your hand" (Psalm 102:25).

- "That which was from the beginning, which we have heard, which we have seen with our eyes, which we have looked at and our hands have touched—this we proclaim concerning the Word of life" (1 John 1:1).

The report from the judge's gavel echoes from the courtroom walls as the marshal calls out, "Order in the court." The teacher picks up a textbook and calls out, "Okay, class, come to order." How does a courtroom or a class transform from mayhem to calm? When was order first established? When did earth's empty darkness cease and harmony take its place? "In the beginning."

Paul wrote his inspired epistles to call us to orderly worship. His teachings still ring with the authority as he takes us back to the beginning, and all the Creator set in place during seven days of creation. It's vital for a church to recognize this because the end of chaos and the genesis of order was set in place by the Word of creation. All praise and exaltations reflect what God set in place in the beginning. Over time, cultures change, fads come and go, and trends sweep the masses along into collective amnesia. But the Rock on whom we stand is the Alpha, the very beginning, the foundation of all order. He is the Omega, who is present with us to the end of time. This is the Spirit of Christ, in whom we rise up to worship God whose name is exalted in all the earth.

God had Paul give the church in Corinth instructions that were culturally relevant to them as well as universal precepts of worship that never change. His teachings present a challenge that requires a teachable spirit and an honest intellect. If we approach his teaching with prejudiced attitudes, we will get sidetracked into religious chaos. Distorting his epistles leads to our own ruin,[1] so we must not ignore anything Paul writes because we don't want to do the hard work to understand it.

---

1. 2 Peter 3:16.

This segment of our ascent to Mount Zion leads us to honor the God of creation in an orderly way during our times of worship, service, and ministry. We'll learn that the parts parents take in worship is explained in the epistles, emphasizing the power of working together in submission to Christ. We'll learn what Paul means when he sealed his instructions for worship by writing, "because if the angels." Scripture by Scripture, we'll learn that our worship gatherings must build on the foundations of truth established in seven days of creation.

> A prayer according to Ephesians 5:18–20:
>
> Our Father in heaven, fill us with your holy Spirit so we may speak to one another with psalms, hymns, and songs from the Spirit. Give us hearts to make music to the Lord, always overflowing with thanks to God the Father in the name of our LORD Jesus Christ.

Before we examine the following verses it's important to understand that Paul is not promoting a patriarchy or establishing a chain of command. He does not elevate men above women, or say men are better leaders. He does not promote egalitarian, elitist, or authoritarian models for family or church. His epistle teaches mutual submission and makes it clear that we all stand equal before a holy God.[2] Paul's instructions teach us that families ought to serve as reflections of our Savior as we gather to worship so the world may see Christ.

A husband honors the Word of creation when he submits to Christ. A wife stands with him in submission to Christ. This harmony shields her as she serves in the church. Mutual submission is only possible as a married couple when each first submit themselves to Christ. This harmony between them then reflects Christ to the world. This is a relationship that mirrors the Trinity. The Father, Son, and Holy Spirit are one God, yet are equal and unique persons. The Father glorifies the Son so that the Son may glorify the Father.[3] The Son does the will of the Father, the Holy Spirit emanates from the Father and the Son. Each person of the Trinity lifts up and glorifies the other. Similarly, a husband and wife seek the best for each other. They strengthen and build each other up.

Paul's letter to the Corinthian church teaches godly order by using public prayer and prophecy as an example. He teaches that a man is held responsible for hearing God's Word, living it out before his family, and teaching them the Scriptures. This is a vital element of true and real worship. Families that gather in Jesus' name must remain true to all that God established in the beginning and for the church. A faithful assembly acknowledges that we, like

---

2. Galatians 3:28.
3. John 17:1.

Adam and Eve, are a fallen race in need of a Redeemer. As a church we recognize our need of Christ because of our human fallibilities and our sin bent inclinations. Remember, even though Eve was deceived and sinned, Adam is rightly charged with original sin. Eve was snared by a lie but Adam knowingly sinned. He didn't live up to his responsibility as head of his family.

Before Eve was created God gave Adam the command not to eat from the Tree of Knowledge of Good and Evil.[4] It was Adam's responsibility to serve his wife by passing on to Eve what God had commanded. This shows us the Creator's intent was to hold men responsible for serving their family. Families who worship together must reflect and honor what the Word of creation set in place in the beginning.

The early church honored what God established using culturally relevant signs. A man prayed and prophesied with his head uncovered to acknowledge Christ as his head. A woman prayed and prophesied with a covering on her head to recognize her husband's or father's headship. Worshipers in our day must also offer a pertinent sign that gives honor and glory to the God of creation, the Word of creation, and the Spirit who moved over the waters.[5] True worship honors the Father as head of Christ, and Christ as the head of man. In this way our gatherings reflect Christ. We honor the Creator when we acknowledge that man was created first, and then God gave him Eve so he would not be alone.

> *I want you to realize that the head of every man is Christ, and the head of the woman is man, and the head of Christ is God. Every man who prays or prophesies with his head covered dishonors his head. But every woman who prays or prophesies with her head uncovered dishonors her head–it is the same as having her head shaved. For if a woman does not cover her head, she might as well have her hair cut off; but if it is a disgrace for a woman to have her hair cut off or her head shaved, then she should cover her head.*
> (1 Corinthians 11:2–6)

Husbands and fathers are called to submit to Christ and the Spirit of Christ. They are to serve their wife and family, to provide, protect, nurture, and teach. A wife, in all her glory, stands with him to serve. In doing this, she submits to Christ and the wisdom of God. Without submission, all the authority we have in Christ's name crumbles into the ruins of fearful timidity.[6]

Paul emphasizes his teaching by writing, "because of the angels." This warning is often overlooked as being too obscure. The best explanation of his

---
4. Genesis 1:16, "The Lord God commanded the man," and v. 18, "It is not good for man to be alone. I will make a helper for him."
5. Genesis 1:2.
6. 2 Timothy 1:7

point is to reference the words of our Savior as revealed to the Apostle John when he wrote, "The seven stars are the angels of the seven churches."[7] We are called to worship in accord with all that God established. In our gatherings we must remember the grace and mercy as shown to Adam and Eve when the LORD provided them with a covering for their sin. We must acknowledge that we too are sinners in need of Christ's forgiveness and mercy.

In the first letter to the angel of a church, we are warned not to forsake our first love. The church of Ephesus was called to return and do the things "you did at first."[8] True worship is proven true by our deeds. A chosen people, a royal priesthood, a holy nation belonging to God, are called to declare His praises,[9] and glorify our heavenly Father and all He set in place. We must not submit to cultural pressures around us. Instead, we enter into God's kingdom realm with the mind of Christ. What Paul teaches is not about hats or no hats, long hair, no hair, or short hair. His message leads us to worship in submission to Christ even when it looks upside down from the world's perspective.

> *A man ought not to cover his head, since he is the image and glory of God; but woman is the glory of man. For man did not come from woman, but woman from man; neither was man created for woman, but woman for man. It is for this reason that a woman ought to have authority over her own head, because of the angels. Nevertheless, in the LORD woman is not independent of man, nor is man independent of woman. For as woman came from man, so also man is born of woman. But everything comes from God.*
> (1 Corinthians 11:7–12)

When Paul says to "judge for yourselves," he is not saying to make up our own minds about this issue. He urges the church to judge rightly with God's Word as its standard of measure. The Scriptures can be properly applied when we sort out what was culturally relevant in Paul's day and what is unchanging and applies to every generation. In essence, Paul says that it is improper for woman to pray without the covering of a "head," that is, a husband or father. With this covering she prays in the image of and with the attitude of Christ.

A man's long hair is part of a Nazarite vow that required a man to let his hair grow. Paul makes it clear that long hair was a disgrace for a man in their churches. He did not establish a rule for all time. We must discern what is only for a time and what is timeless. We can't be sure what Paul would say about the worship team drummer who shows up with shocking pink mohawk hair.

---

7. Revelation 1:20.
8. Revelation 2:4–5.
9. 1 Peter 2:9.

Judge for yourselves: Is it proper for a woman to pray to God with her head uncovered? Does not the very nature of things teach you that if a man has long hair, it is a disgrace to him, but that if a woman has long hair, it is her glory? For long hair is given to her as a covering. If anyone wants to be contentious about this, we have no other practice—nor do the churches of God.
(1 Corinthians 11:13–16)

Jesus Christ is the Word of creation. He serves under authority as He ministers to the church as our High Priest. He provided true witnesses who had seen, heard, and touched Him so that we may hear and believe that which was from the beginning. Now the Word of creation gathers us to worship in a way that honors all that God has set in place. This orderly worship in the congregation affects harmony in our homes, workplace, and communities.

> We pray this so that the name of our LORD Jesus may be glorified in you, and you in him, according to the grace of our God and the LORD Jesus Christ.
> (2 Thessalonians 1:12)

Chapter 17 Q&A

A Call to Order

1. Why is it important for our worship to honor what God set in place in the beginning?

   _____
   _____
   _____

2. How can we discern between what was culturally relevant in the early church and what are universal precepts of worship?

   _____
   _____
   _____

3. What standard do we use to be sure our worship is true and orderly?

   _____
   _____
   _____

4. Godly order in worship is not hierarchical, nor is it a democracy. So, what is the order of true worship?

   _____
   _____
   _____

My Journey's Journal:

Chapter 18: A House of Prayer

Key Scriptures:

- "And as he taught them, he said, 'Is it not written: "My house will be called a house of prayer for all nations"?'" (Mark 11:17).

- "Therefore confess your sins to each other and pray for each other so that you may be healed. The prayer of a righteous person is powerful and effective" (James 5:16).

A church without prayer is like a fighter jet with no fuel—it can't join the battle. The prayers of the saints are like fuel for heaven's fire.[1] A praying church is an overcoming church. We become effective in the work of the Great Commission when we begin with prayer. It's a joy to pray, knowing that our petitions are received as fragrant incense in heaven and collected as treasure in golden bowls.[2]

The era of the New Testament church began in a meeting of 120 people who gathered during the Feast of Pentecost to earnestly pray. Today, as always, faithful saints who pray in the Spirit serve to sustain and strengthen the church. An interceding church is an empowered church. Prayers fuel the fire that empowers us to complete the work of the church. Intercessions of God's sons and daughters have kept the church strong from all assaults throughout the centuries.

Consider the result of working Americans who gathered to pray in 1857. They sparked a Great Awakening that overflowed to almost every part of the nation from the Atlantic to the Pacific. On bended knees they changed the nation for good and for the benefit of future generations.

---

1. 2 Chronicles 7:1.
2. Revelation 5:6–8.

> A prayer according to Isaiah 56:6–8:
>
> May all those who bind themselves to you to minister be brought to your holy mountain to pray with joyful petitions. Oh Lord, gather all those who have wandered from your dwelling place and make us into a house of prayer for all nations.

Eve gave birth to a son whom she named Seth, because "God has granted me another child in place of Abel."[3] When Seth was 105 years old, he became a father to Enosh, and then lived another 807 years. During his lifetime, people began to call on the name of the Lord.

From this Genesis account we know that during Adam's own lifetime people learned the value of prayers and intercessions lifted up to Yahweh, God of creation. They realized the power of His name and called on Him. Our heavenly Father received their prayers in heaven, where they filled heaven's bowls with sweet incense.[4] The prayers of God's people began at the beginning and will continue through to the full revelation of Jesus Christ.

Seth also had a son, and he named him Enosh. At that time people began to call on the name of the Lord.
(Genesis 4:26)

When God's people come together to pray in agreement with Jesus' name, the earth shakes. A gathering of voices lifted in harmonious petitions, calling on God's holy name, can move God's hand.[5] Our intercessions presented in agreement with all that is in Jesus' name changes our hearts and minds, and changes the world around us.

Consider the beauty of our prayers as they are sent up in Jesus' name. When the saints pray, and especially when they intercede in agreement, their petitions are received as fragrant incense in golden bowls. When we live and pray together in unity, it is like precious oil poured on our heads. Lifting holy hands in prayer is like stepping into a whirlwind of blessings. When we send up our prayers in agreement with Jesus' name, they are the very essence of the anointing oil that the Spirit pours out upon His church. He pours this fragrant ointment upon us and it flows down over our whole being and saturates every fiber of our mind and body. On our knees we come into a powerful circle of blessings that is like the dew from Mount Hermon[6] that the wind of

---
3. Genesis 4:25.
4. Revelation 5:8.
5. Psalm 10:12.
6. When Israel's people saw Mount Hermon, its shape reminded them of the breastplate worn by the priest—a breastplate of righteousness.

the Spirit carries down upon the plains. Prayerful people awake in the morning saturated with dew drops of heaven's righteousness.

> *How good and pleasant it is when God's people live together in unity! It is like precious oil poured on the head, running down on the beard, running down on Aaron's beard, down on the collar of his robe. It is as if the dew of Hermon were falling on Mount Zion. For there the LORD bestows his blessing, even life forevermore.*
> (Psalm 133:1–3)

When God's people gather to pray, we come as equals before the throne of grace. The church is a place where all can unite to pray with one voice. The disciple's first worship gatherings were about prayers and petitions that encompassed everyone who came. They prayed the way Jesus taught them to as they stayed in Jerusalem as He commanded. They waited for the gift the Father promised—the empowering gift of the Holy Spirit.

> *They all joined together constantly in prayer, along with the women and Mary the mother of Jesus, and with his brothers.*
> (Acts 1:14)

These gatherings described in Acts show us the genuine church as the people came together as devoted disciples of Christ. They assembled to hear the Apostles proclaim what Jesus taught them during three-and-a-half years of Jesus university. They gathered to enjoy fellowship in the Spirit of Christ with their brothers and sisters who shared in the hope of resurrection. They came as true worshippers to fellowship with Christ. The believers gathered to partake of the bread of Jesus' broken body and the cup of Jesus' shed blood for cleansing sins. Jesus' followers came to lay their petitions before the LORD of glory. They came to plead for mercy and receive God's forgiveness. The faithful gave generously to help the poor and for the work of the Great Commission. They shared meals together in the presence of their LORD and Savior.

Prayer is a vital part of true worship. The secret to genuine meetings in Jesus' name isn't gathering in homes or in grand cathedrals awash in the light of stained-glass windows. Those who desire to worship in a spiritual way begin with prayer. This requires humbling ourselves in the sight of the Lord. When we're on our knees He will lift us up.[7]

> *They devoted themselves to the apostles' teaching and to fellowship, to the breaking of bread and to prayer.*
> (Acts 2:42)

Jesus taught us how to pray to the Father, and the Holy Spirit helps us with our prayers. Praying the Scriptures is powerfully effective. But how do

---
7. James 4:10.

we know what to pray for when there's no verse that directly covers our need? When our children wander and we don't know where they are or what they're doing, how do we pray? The Spirit of Christ helps us to pray. He knows where they are and the best prayers for them. How do we pray for the persecuted church when tyrannies accelerate faster than we can send up petitions? We pray according to what we know and the Spirit always hears and interprets our heart's cry. He listens to the sighs that come from the depths of our soul and He carries our prayers to the throne of grace with groanings greater than human words can utter.

> *In the same way, the Spirit helps us in our weakness. We do not know what we ought to pray for, but the Spirit himself intercedes for us through wordless groans.* (Romans 8:26)

When we're waiting for test results from a biopsy, we tend to get anxious. Worry tries to overwhelm us when the doctor offers no hope. Life is full of anxiety-worthy moments. But we have a great hope in Christ. In moments of anxiety, when things crash in around us, we are called to pray earnestly and cast our anxieties upon the Lord.[8]

Jesus showed signs of agony as He prayed, knowing that His arrest was imminent. "And being in anguish, he prayed more earnestly, and he sweat with drops of blood falling to the ground."[9] In our moments of distress we are called to pray, following Jesus' example. We have a Father who is ever-present with us, especially in time of trouble. We only need to call out to Him as a wandering lamb who is caught in thorn bushes.[10] A house of prayer is the best place for anxious, wandering lambs to find safety again.

> *Do not be anxious about anything, but in every situation, by prayer and petition, with thanksgiving, present your requests to God. And the peace of God, which transcends all understanding, will guard your hearts and your minds in Christ Jesus.* (Philippians 4:6–7)

Too many Christians wonder what part they serve in the work of the church. Some faithful octogenarians think they are no longer useful in the work of the Great Commission. But this only happens when they forget the greatest calling of the church, that is, to pray. Every person who comes to saving faith is called to pray. The perfect preparation for the gifting and empowering work of the Spirit is to pray and ask for His anointing. Then, the Spirit of Jesus, reveals our part in the work given to the body of Christ. The greatest climax to an elderly saint's long service in the church is to continue to pray in earnest.

---

8. 1 Peter 5:7.
9. Luke 22:44.
10. Luke 15:4, Psalm 119:145.

The most effective prayers are those a congregation of believers lifts up together in agreement with Jesus' name. Prayers of the church are more than just one person doing all the praying while everyone else bows their heads, closes their eyes, and falls asleep. We are called to pray together as one body. Our greatest prayers are those that two or more offer up in agreement, asking anything that is in Jesus' name. It will be done because Jesus promised He would be there with us.[11] The Shepherd of the church comes into our gatherings and agrees with us as we intercede for the leaders of nations and all those who work to serve our communities.

Churches that pray in harmony with all that is in Jesus' name will change people's lives for good. Through earnest prayers of faith, the world's chaos is driven back, and God's righteousness, justice, and faithfulness are made known and take effect in every nation. We have come to a crucial turning point in the history of this nation and the battle can only be won by a church on its knees.

I urge, then, first of all, that petitions, prayers, intercession and thanksgiving be made for all people—for kings and all those in authority, that we may live peaceful and quiet lives in all godliness and holiness.
(1 Timothy 2:1–2)

After Jesus cleansed the temple, He made it clear that "My house will be called a house of prayer."[12] Without prayer, a church soon disintegrates into a den of robbers. Gathering together to call on the name of the LORD is an essential part of the design for God's holy sanctuary. As we pray together in agreement with the Word, and in Jesus' name, our faith grows. We see our prayers answered and lives changed for eternity.

> Praying always with all prayer and supplication in the Spirit, being watchful to this end with all perseverance and supplication for all the saints.
> (Ephesians 6:18)

---

11. Matthew 18:19–20.
12. Matthew 21:13.

Chapter 18 Q&A

A House of Prayer

1. When did people first pray to the Lord?

2. Why is it significant that the church began in a time of prayerful waiting?

3. Describe the blessings we enjoy when heaven's answers are poured out upon God's people.

4. How can a church pray with confident assurance?

5. Why are the prayers of the saints the very essence of true worship?

My Journey's Journal:

Chapter 19: Water Baptism

Key Scriptures:

- "Then Jesus came to them and said, 'All authority in heaven and on earth has been given to me. Therefore, go and make disciples of all the nations, baptizing them in the name of the Father and the Son and the Holy Spirit'" (Matthew 28:18–19).

- "As they traveled along the road, they came to some water and the eunuch said, 'Look, here is water. What can stand in the way of my being baptized?' And he gave orders to stop the chariot. Then both Philip and the eunuch went down into the water and Philip baptized him" (Acts 8:36–39).

Baptism has a vital part in true worship. When someone in our assembly hears the Word and believes that Jesus is the Christ, Son of the living God, and that Jesus came in the flesh to die in their place, they are ready to be baptized. When they believe that Jesus gave His life to pay their sin debt, they are ready to be washed in water and the Word. Believing that Jesus Christ is the resurrection and the life is the faith that leads us into this miraculous water. Baptism by water and the Word is a necessary and effective part of salvation. It's an act of obedience and yet so much more. All those who are baptized into the name of the Father, and the Son, and the Holy Spirit are made one with Christ and enter into His suffering, death, and resurrection. In baptismal water, we die with Christ, we're buried with Christ, so we may live in the power of resurrection as new creations in Christ.

We'll learn that baptism in water by the authority of the Word unites us with Christ. What we see with our eyes is a confirming sign that the baptized person is joined as one with Christ through, in and up from the waters of baptism. We'll explore Old Testament history and the original Greek so see what Jesus intended when He commanded us to go and make disciples and baptize them.[1]

---

1. Matthew 28:19–20.

> A prayer according to Acts 22:16:
>
> Compel us by the power of your Word and the Holy Spirit to enter the waters of baptism to wash our sins away and call on Jesus' holy name.

Yahweh gave Abraham the rite of circumcision as a sign of the covenant. This is a cutting away of the flesh to show that they have put off the flesh and separated themselves to a holy God. It was a God ordained rite, but true circumcision was not performed by human hands.[2] In the same way, true baptism is not performed by human hands. Yes, we see someone immersed, or water poured over them in the name of the Father, Son, and Holy Spirit, but their baptism is into Christ who ministers as our High Priest in heaven's realm. We are washed clean to the very core of our being, to the depths of our soul, and every stain is cleansed away even from our conscience.

For in Christ all the fullness of the Deity lives in bodily form, and in Christ you have been brought to fullness. He is the head over every power and authority. In him you were also circumcised with a circumcision not performed by human hands. Your whole self ruled by the flesh was put off when you were circumcised by Christ, having been buried with him in baptism, in which you were also raised with him through your faith in the working of God, who raised him from the dead. (Colossians 2:9–12)

When we are lifted from the waters of baptism we are one with Christ, a working part of the church that serves under our Savior. Our next step is to grow by being taught from God's Word to prepare to serve as effective ambassadors of good news. We must come to know the power and authority we have in Christ's command to teach all nations and baptize those who come to saving faith in Jesus. First, we learn the disciplines of faith for ourselves and then to disciple others, teaching them to be followers of Christ.

Serving under our Redeemer's authority and by His direct command offers us assurance of His ever-present help until the work of the Great Commission is completed. Until every person whose name is written down in heaven is brought to saving faith, the work of the church is unfinished. We minister with confidence, knowing that Jesus' living and active presence is manifested wherever the true gospel message is preached, heard, and believed.

---

2. Colossians 2:11.

Then Jesus came to them and said, "All authority in heaven and on earth has been given to me. Therefore go and make disciples of all nations, baptizing them in the name of the Father and of the Son and of the Holy Spirit, and teaching them to obey everything I have commanded you. And surely I am with you always, to the very end of the age."
(Matthew 28:18–20)

The power of the gospel is clear and simple. When we hear the good news message preached,[3] the Holy Spirit quickens faith in our hearts to believe,[4] we are saved by faith, and obey God's command to be baptized. God's promise that we are sealed by the Holy Spirit by means of the water and the Word offers incredible comfort to new creations in Christ. What a joy to know that an account is opened for us in the heavens so we can make deposits that last forever.[5]

Whoever believes and is baptized will be saved, but whoever does not believe will be condemned.
(Mark 16:16)

For those who hear and reject the gospel message, there's a dark side to this verse. The second "whoever" reminds us of people like those in Noah's day who refused to hear and believe Noah's preaching. They were condemned in the waters of a world-wide flood. There's a clear demarcation here. When the truth is declared, some will hear, believe, and then follow Christ in baptism. Others are like the unrepentant thief crucified beside Jesus who scoffed at Him. The religious leaders mocked at the foot of Jesus' cross, saying, "He saved others, but he can't save himself!"[6] Later, on the day of Pentecost, some ridiculed and sneered, "You must be drunk."[7] Their own words decided their end.[8]

Why is it that people who are brought to saving faith are baptized in water? The easy answer is, because Jesus was baptized in water, and we are called to follow Him in baptism. Our water baptism prepares us to receive a baptism by the Holy Spirit and fire.[9] The Apostle Peter provides a great insight when he wrote that all of creation "was formed out of water and by water."[10] Now, we become new creations in Christ in and through the waters

---

3. Romans 10:17.
4. John 6:63.
5. Matthew 6:20.
6. Matthew 27:42.
7. Acts 2:13.
8. Matthew 12:37.
9. Luke 3:16, Acts 1:5.
10. 2 Peter 3:5.

of baptism.[11] Peter makes it clear that baptism saves us "by the resurrection of Jesus Christ."[12] By the power of the Word of creation and out of the waters of baptism our old sin-bent selves die and we become whole new creations in Christ Jesus our Savior.

But is there only one way to baptize? The Greek word is *baptidzo*, which meant to "dip repeatedly, to immerse, submerge," establishing immersion in water as the means of baptism. In ancient Israel, they performed ritual cleansing, called a Mikvah, by totally immersing in flowing water. The church developed its various means of baptism by considering Mark 7:4 and Luke 11:38, where *baptizō* is interpreted as "to wash by pouring."[13] Immersion is a beautiful sign of being baptized into Christ and His death, burial, and resurrection. Poured and flowing water beautifully pictures the water that flows from the springs of salvation.[14]

The children of Israel were baptized into Moses as they passed through the waters of the Red Sea.[15] Israel's brides, and some grooms, prepared themselves for their weddings by a Mikvah baptism. John the Baptizer called people to a baptism of repentance and pointed the way to Jesus who would baptize them with the Holy Spirit and with fire. Jesus declared that we would join Him in a baptism of suffering.[16] The writings of the prophets foretold of baptism that saves.[17] How can we deny so great a salvation?

Jesus answered, "Very truly I tell you, no one can enter the kingdom of God unless they are born of water and the Spirit. Flesh gives birth to flesh, but the Spirit gives birth to spirit.
(John 3:5–6)

It's possible that one of the greatest wonder we will ever witness is the miracle of baptism. When a person is immersed, they are buried in baptismal waters and their body is no longer enslaved to sin.[18] Truly, those who are baptized die with Christ and are buried with Christ. In the water of baptism we enter Christ's suffering and made whole by resurrection power.

We call out His holy name with rejoicing as we enter the waters of baptism and then call out His wonderful name as we are lifted from the baptismal waters.[19] Those who witness the miracle of a new creation in Christ have

---

11. 2 Corinthians 5:17.
12. 1 Peter 3:21.
13. The "wash by pouring" interpretation may come from the Old Covenant Mikvah bath that required total immersion in a flowing spring water or rain water.
14. Isaiah 12:3.
15. 1 Corinthians 10:1–4.
16. Mark 10:38–39.
17. 1 Peter 3:21.
18. Romans 6:6.
19. Romans 10:13.

"seen and heard" the powerful effect of water and the Word to redeem lost and wandering souls from the binding cords of depravity and chains of sin's addiction. In Christ we are set free, no longer captive to sin.[20]

> *"You will be his witness to all people of what you have seen and heard. And now what are you waiting for? Get up, be baptized and wash your sins away, calling on his name."*
> (Acts 22:15–16)

We are taught to live in keeping with our baptism every day of our lives.[21] For all new creations in Christ, a whole new pathway is marked out for our feet. An attitude of gratitude flows from our heart. But we need constant reminders that our old, sin-bent self has died and is gone for good. We require reassurance that we really are dead to sin because it tries to creep back into our lives.

The enemy of our soul tries to deceive us into thinking that our old self isn't really dead. He tempts us to slip back into the quicksand of our depravities and addictions. Friends and family who liked the way we used to act try to drag us back down. In moments of temptation when old friendships tug at our heart, it's vital that we remember our baptism. God's Word brings our heart and mind back to the miracle that washed us in the water and the Word.[22] We must constantly think back to the day we died to our old self and were raised up in resurrection power as new creations in Christ. He is our anchor when storms of temptation rage against us.

> *We are those who have died to sin; how can we live in it any longer? Or don't you know that all of us who were baptized into Christ Jesus were baptized into his death? We were therefore buried with him through baptism into death in order that, just as Christ was raised from the dead through the glory of the Father, we too may live a new life.*
> (Romans 6:2–4)

In baptismal waters we are made one with Christ in His crucifixion and death on a cruel Roman cross. Now that we have died with Him, we are raised up with Him in the power of resurrection. The power of sin, Satan, and death is broken and no longer masters us. Too often, we underestimate the eternal power of the resurrection that is ours. This is an essential element to living a victorious life in Christ.

---

20. Luke 4:18.
21. Romans 6:4.
22. John 3:3—6, 1 Corinthians 6:11, 1 Peter 3:21.

This resurrection power makes us overcomers who are given the right to eat from the Tree of Life.[23] We will not be harmed by the second death.[24] We are partakers of the hidden manna.[25] We are strengthened to endure to the end when we will be given authority over the nations.[26] In resurrection power we are overcomers dressed in white. Our names will never be erased from the Book of Life.[27] Living in Christ, who was raised from the dead, makes us pillars in the temple of our God.[28] This kind of victorious living gives us the right to sit with Him on His throne.[29] How could we ever deny so great a salvation?

> *For if we have been united with him in a death like his, we will certainly also be united with him in a resurrection like his. For we know that our old self was crucified with him so that the body ruled by sin might be done away with, that we should no longer be slaves to sin—because anyone who has died has been set free from sin.*
> (Romans 6:5–7)

What an awesome miracle that, in the waters of baptism and by the power of God's promises, we are united to serve as living and active members of the body of Christ, the church. We came fatherless, and now we have a Father in heaven who loves us more than we can imagine. No longer are we alone in the world, because we have many brothers and sisters in Christ. We're not abandoned, because we are brought back with deep compassion.[30]

The waters of baptism join us together as vital, functioning parts of the body of Christ. Our nationality, positions, and social status are all set aside as we come to serve before Christ Jesus in the church.

> *Just as a body, though one, has many parts, but all its many parts form one body, so it is with Christ. For we were all baptized by one Spirit so as to form one body—whether Jews or Gentiles, slave or free—and we were all given the one Spirit to drink. Even so the body is not made up of one part but of many.*
> (1 Corinthians 12:12–14)

The Apostle Paul points out that few people who become Christians are wise in the ways of the world. Why would only a small number of men or women who are powerful, influential, turn to Christ? The reason is simple. They have everything they want and see no need of Christ—they have their reward. A superior intellect may lead them to reason that salvation is noth-

---
23. Revelation 2:7.
24. Revelation 2:11.
25. Revelation 2:17.
26. Revelation 2:26.
27. Revelation 3:5.
28. Revelation 3:12.
29. Revelation 3:21.
30. Isaiah 54:7.

ing more than a crutch for weak people. They are blind to the truth that our heavenly Father lifts the weak, the lame, the downcast, the addict, the homeless, and all those who are crushed by the burden of sin. Jesus didn't come to call the religiously self-satisfied and spiritually complacent. No! He came to call sinners to repentance.[31]

You once floundered about, searching for a safe harbor. People you admired and depended on let you down. The job that provided for your family vanished. Life's burdens became too heavy for you to carry. Listen up, because you are offered a great hope. Jesus calls out to you to cast off all these burdens upon Him. Now you can sigh with relief, because He is a Good Shepherd who gently cares for the sheep of His pasture. He gives us assurance that those who are baptized into Christ come into His true and lasting rest.[32]

> *"Come to me, all you who are weary and burdened, and I will give you rest. Take my yoke upon you and learn from me, for I am gentle and humble in heart, and you will find rest for your souls. For my yoke is easy and my burden is light."* (Matthew 11:28–30)

Christian churches have varying beliefs and practices regarding baptism. Some claim that it is not necessary for salvation, while some teach that baptism is salvific. But Noah,[33] Moses,[34] David,[35] Ezekiel,[36] John the Baptizer,[37] Jesus,[38] Paul,[39] and Peter[40] reveal baptism as an undeniable part of faith and worship. Without baptism, the Great Commission work we do is incomplete. Baptism is for all who come to saving faith in Jesus Christ. It unites us with our Savior in His suffering, death, and resurrection.[41]

By faith and through the water baptism in the name of the Father, Son, and Holy Spirit we are made one with the triune God. By faith, the water of baptism makes us new creations in Christ and set apart for a holy purpose.

> "My son," the father said, "you are always with me, and everything I have is yours. But we had to celebrate and be glad, because this brother of yours was dead and is alive again; he was lost and is found." (Luke 15:31–32)

---

31. Luke 5:32.
32. Galatians 3:27, Hebrews 4:10, Romans 6:3–11.
33. 1 Peter 3:20–21.
34. 1 Corinthians 10:2.
35. Psalm 51:2.
36. Ezekiel 36:25.
37. Matthew 3:11.
38. Matthew 3:13–17.
39. Romans 6:3–4.
40. Acts 2:38.
41. Romans 6:5.

Chapter 19 Q&A

Water Baptism

1. Describe the power and effect of being baptized into the Father, Son, and Holy Spirit?

2. Why are those who are given the gift of saving faith baptized in water?

3. How does baptism effect your everyday life?

4. What is one of the greatest miracles you will ever witness?

My Journey's Journal:

Chapter 20: The LORD's Table

Key Scriptures:

- "For as often as you eat this bread and drink the cup, you proclaim the Lord's death until he comes" (1 Corinthians 11:26).
- "You prepare a table before me in the presence of my enemies. You anoint my head with oil; my cup overflows" (Psalm 23:5).

Every culture around the world has its own style of dinner table. Americans sit in chairs with their feet under the table, while the Japanese sit on cushions around a low table. The "table" for our picnic might be a blanket spread out on the grass, where we share lunch with the ants. There are conference tables, game tables, and negotiating tables. But there is one table that is set apart from all others. This segment of our ascent opens our eyes the miraculous mystery of holy communion and brings us into the knowledge of a holy God. This is not a new mystery, but an age-old wonder that began in the Garden of Eden. Open your Bible and join this life changing search through the Scriptures.

Come to the Lord's table and see that it overflows with bounty like honey from the rock.[1] We'll learn that this table's abundance includes the fruit of the winepress and the bread of Christ's presence. Abram, Melchizedek, and Moses serve to instruct us regarding this blessed table.

Come, let us be joined together in a covenantal feast.

> A prayer according to Matthew 5:6 and John 15:11:
>
> Oh Lord, give us hearts that hunger and thirst for righteousness so that your joy may be in us and made complete.

We begin this teaching by answering a pertinent question Why does the Lord's table offer a cup with fruit from the winepress?[2] Moses, the author

---

1. Psalm 81:16.
2. Deuteronomy 16:13.

of Deuteronomy, writes of God's goodness and provision.[3] He proclaims the mercies of our heavenly Father who lifts us up to ride on the "heights of the land."[4] He reveals the One who anoints us with oil from the flinty rock. He opens our eyes to see God who provides. He unveils the LORD Almighty who nourishes us. Then, Moses caps this great revelation with God's merciful goodness. He calls us to God's bountiful table where our hearts are made glad by offering us the "blood of the grape."[5]

Why the fruit of the grape? This is the mystery of the true vine, who is Jesus Christ, and the joy of those who are grafted into the vine and called by His holy name. Now, in great mercy, our heavenly Father sets a bountiful table before us where we partake of fruit of the vine. Moses sang out to proclaim the bounty of God's table. His teaching fell like rain and his words descended like the morning dew. His beautiful verse teaches us great truths; "He made him ride on the heights of the land and fed him with the fruits of the field. He nourished him with honey from the rock."[6] Let us come together in sweet fellowship to partake of Jesus at the Lord's plentiful table.

And you drank wine, the blood of the grapes.
(Deuteronomy 32:14 NKJV).

Put the bread of the Presence on this table to be before me at all times.
(Exodus 25:30).

Why are bread and wine served at the Lord's table? Melchizedek, king of Salem, provides a clue to this mystery. The feast of bread and wine he offered to Abram is the first record of this meal in the Bible. Melchizedek, priest of God Most High, came out to meet Abram after he and his fighting men rescued Lot, his family, and their neighbors. He blessed Abram and offered him bread and wine to refresh him. He offered visible signs of God's promised covenant of grace. For us today, we come to the Lord's table, where we are strengthened and refreshed in our covenant. We partake of Christ who is the bread of life. He gave His body to be broken so that we might be made whole, serving as parts of the body of Christ. We drink from the cup of Jesus' suffering, remembering that Jesus offered His blood for the forgiveness of sins.

We partake of these elements to remember Christ in a joyful covenant meal. We return from the communion table with our sins forgiven and the weight of our transgressions lifted. This is more than enough cause for us to sing out with exaltations, "Sing to the Lord, for He has triumphed gloriously."[7]

---

3. Deuteronomy 28:5.
4. Deuteronomy 32:13.
5. Psalm 104:15.
6. Deuteronomy 32:13
7. Exodus 15:21.

Listen, listen to me, and eat what is good, and you will delight in the richest of fare. (Isaiah 55:2)

A casual "come as you are" invite does not apply to those who step up to the Lord's table. We are the redeemed sons and daughters of the Most High God, dressed in robes of righteousness, and adorned as a bride in waiting. Our hearts are contrite, fully prepared to receive His forgiveness and mercy. We present ourselves in the presence of Jesus, our High Priest, whose holy name is to be feared. We come into His presence with reverent wonder and with the repentant hearts of unworthy servants. Our steps up to the altar are joyful, knowing there is a blessed feast that provides forgiveness and cleansing for all who come.

We come to this table to partake of Christ Jesus. His bread of life and the cup of His shed blood are an all sufficient and bountiful meal. This is so much more than merely agreeing that forgiveness and mercy are extended to humanity by the cross of Jesus Christ. It is entering into His covenantal blessings with our whole being. We hold back nothing of ourselves. If we are unwilling to put our sin behind us, we come in an unworthy manner. We show contempt for the LORD if we approach the table without examining ourselves. Justifying our sinful deeds shows that we despise our LORD and Savior. Without true repentance, we heap judgment upon ourselves by endorsing cheap grace.

We come to our Redeemer in awe to honor His unblemished sacrifice for our sins. We come as blood-bought servants, holding nothing back from Jesus who shed His life's blood on our behalf. We come to the table with great joy to be partakers of Christ, and we are made whole in Him.

While they were eating, Jesus took bread, and when he had given thanks, he broke it and gave it to his disciples, saying, "Take and eat; this is my body." Then he took a cup, and when he had given thanks, he gave it to them, saying, "Drink from it, all of you. This is my blood of the covenant, which is poured out for many for the forgiveness of sins. I tell you, I will not drink from this fruit of the vine from now on until that day when I drink it new with you in my Father's kingdom." (Matthew 26:26–29)

The bread, the blood of the grape, and the cup of Jesus' suffering[8] offer visible signs of an invisible reality—an unseen but living and active presence of Christ. His presence is more real than anything we see with our natural eyes. The bread and wine embody our Savior's promises, grace, and manifest His holy presence. We partake of Jesus who is present as our High Priest. He ministers this covenantal meal to God's sons and daughters. In truth, we

---
8. Matthew 26:39, 42.

partake of our Savior who is present in the bread and cup. Children of hope partake of the elements on the altar, which are Jesus' body that was broken and His blood that was shed. As we receive the bread and wine, we are participants in His grace, sufferings, holiness, promises, and are united as one in His church. The cup of the covenant is His blood that cleanses His church, washing us whiter than freshly fallen snow.[9]

When we see the elements of the Lord's table in light of the incarnation, the bread and cup are not mere bread, or fruit of the vine. They testify to the presence of divine power. Immanuel, who is God with us, teaches His followers that they are to partake of Jesus who suffered in a physical body on our behalf.[10] We need to be reminded that they are visible signs of an invisible reality—Christ's living and active presence. The bread we receive in our hands and the cup we put to our lips strengthens us in our covenant with Christ. As we eat the bread and drink the wine, we partake of Jesus who came in the flesh.

> *While they were eating, Jesus took bread, and when he had given thanks, he broke it and gave it to his disciples, saying, "Take it; this is my body." Then he took a cup, and when he had given thanks, he gave it to them, and they all drank from it. "This is my blood of the covenant, which is poured out for many," he said to them. "Truly I tell you, I will not drink again from the fruit of the vine until that day when I drink it new in the kingdom of God."*
> (Mark 14:22–25)

Every step up to the communion table is a declaration of faith. Each stride is like raising up a banner in our Savior's name.[11] As we come before the Lord's table, we declare that we are true sons and daughters who are called by His name. We present ourselves at the communion table to honor and remember Christ's sacrificial death, acknowledging that we are one with Him in His suffering.

As the disciples gathered around the table for the Last Supper, Jesus took the bread and broke it. His hour of suffering came near. Then, on the day of His crucifixion, His body suffered torments that served to make us whole, working parts in His body, the church. This is a great mystery of God's kingdom. How does Jesus' lashed and broken body make us whole? How does His death give us life? How is it possible that Jesus' innocent blood paid the sin debt of the whole world?[12] We know that God manifests His power in ways that the world sees as weakness.[13] It's His nature. In reality, "the weakness of

---

9. Psalm 51:7.
10. John 6:53–58.
11. Psalm 20:5.
12. 1 John 2:2.
13. 2 Corinthians 12:9.

God is stronger than human strength."[14] What man sees as weakness is mightier than the combined strength of all humankind. God delights to show the redemptive power of the cross in and through weak and broken vessels.[15]

Now all His redeemed sons and daughters come to the Lord's table in remembrance of Christ and His work of the cross. A covenantal meal honoring His body and blood strengthens our body, soul, and spirit and cleanses us of sin.

> *After taking the cup, he gave thanks and said, "Take this and divide it among you. For I tell you I will not drink again from the fruit of the vine until the kingdom of God comes." And he took bread, gave thanks and broke it, and gave it to them, saying, "This is my body given for you; do this in remembrance of me."* (Luke 22:17–19)

Jesus died in our place to wash away our sin so that we might live our lives in the fullness of Christ. He is the fountain that flows out with words of comfort and hope for a sin-bent world. We rejoice in the hope of our salvation as we come to Christ, because He has set us free from the death grip of sin and Satan. Now we live in remembrance of Yeshua, our Savior, who reveals His splendor before us by means of His sacrificial death; an offering sufficient to ransom us from our debt of sin and break the chains of sin. He ransomed us because of His unfailing love.[16]

As we partake of Jesus' body and blood at His table, there is a powerful unifying effect that draws us together in love. Through his Word, we gain the strength to serve our vital purpose as the parts of His body, the church. The fellowship of Christ is the bond that holds us as one in the unity of the faith.

> *For just as each of us has one body with many members, and these members do not all have the same function, so in Christ we, though many, form one body, and each member belongs to all the others.* (Romans 12:4–5)

The reality of the risen Christ is memorialized in us as we come to the communion table. The cup of salvation is provided to all those who call on the name of the Lord.[17] The bread and cup are a proof of fellowship. The word "participation" in Greek is κοινωνία, koinonia, which means intimate fellowship. Those who come to partake at the Lord's table declare their close fellowship with our LORD and Savior. The church is one loaf, united in Christ. Therefore, all who are unrepentant come to the table in an unworthy manner. They drink judgment upon themselves.[18]

---

14. 1 Corinthians 1:25.
15. Psalm 149:4
16. Psalm 44:26.
17. Psalm 116:13.
18. 1 Corinthians 11:29.

> *Is not the cup of thanksgiving for which we give thanks a participation in the blood of Christ? And is not the bread that we break a participation in the body of Christ? Because there is one loaf, we, who are many, are one body, for we all share the one loaf.*
> (1 Corinthians 10:16–17)

All our heavenly Father's sons and daughters are living proof of the power of Jesus' vicarious death and resurrection. We come to the Lord's table as living sacrifices to proclaim His power and might to save lost souls once condemned to death by the curse of law.[19]

The Apostle Paul revealed the power and benefits of partaking of the true body of Jesus in the bread and the cup. The Holy Spirit empowered him to preach and teach God's people. He instructs us about being joined in an intimate fellowship and participating in the body and blood of Christ through the cup of thanksgiving and the bread we break.[20] We, like Paul, are brought into the New Covenant in this covenantal feast. The visible signs of the bread and cup bring Christ to the forefront of our minds, refreshing us in the New Covenant in His blood. Our soul and spirit are restored as we remember we are sealed as true partakers in the blessings of the covenant.

> *For I received from the LORD what I also passed on to you: The LORD Jesus, on the night he was betrayed, took bread, and when he had given thanks, he broke it and said, "This is my body, which is for you; do this in remembrance of me." In the same way, after supper he took the cup, saying, "This cup is the new covenant in my blood; do this, whenever you drink it, in remembrance of me." For whenever you eat this bread and drink this cup, you proclaim the Lord's death until he comes.*
> (1 Corinthians 11:23–26)

It's not wise to take on the role of being our own doctors because we are not qualified experts on the functions and diseases of the body. Serving as our own lawyer isn't a good idea because we don't know every law, legal precedent, or the workings of justice in the courts. In the same way, we need a better judge than ourselves to examine our hearts because we are biased. We tend to minimize and justify our own actions. Comparing ourselves to others doesn't work because we're all fallible mortals.

We need a reliable measuring rod.[21] That standard is Christ, as revealed in the holy Scriptures. We weigh ourselves using the whole council of God's Word. John 3:16 is a good measure for our lives, but we must build upon this

---

19. Galatians 3:13.
20. 1 Corinthians 10:26.
21. Ezekiel 40:3, Revelation 11:1.

truth by applying every word written by the apostles and prophets by the inspiration of the Holy Spirit. We must examine ourselves with the aid of the measure of the tried and tested chief Cornerstone. We are called to hold up Christ as our standard because everyone else falls short. He is the One who searches our hearts and examines our minds and then rewards us according to our conduct—according to what our deeds deserve.[22]

Now that we have taken an inventory of ourselves, we will see the miraculous work of Christ Jesus, who gave His body to be broken so that we might be made whole in His body, the church.

Everyone ought to examine themselves before they eat of the bread and drink from the cup. For those who eat and drink without discerning the body of Christ eat and drink judgment on themselves. That is why many among you are weak and sick, and a number of you have fallen asleep.
(1 Corinthians 11:28–30)

This topic presented a historic view of the Lord's table, Jesus' words that instituted the supper for the church, and the apostle Paul's teaching. There are many ways that Bible scholars interpret Jesus' words and Paul's teaching, but, even with all our differences, we are brought together as one when we gather to partake of Christ in this essential part of worship. As Christians come to the Lord's table, we are forgiven, cleansed, and united in Christ. There is only one table, and no one can put their private label on it. No church or teacher gets it all right, "Not even one."[23] But in Christ there is more than enough grace and forgiveness to join us together as partakers of His divine nature.[24]

We offer God's sons and daughters the means to examine themselves, but we are not to judge and exclude them from partaking with us.[25] Let us come to the table of the LORD and feast upon the fullness of Christ.

> You prepare a table before me in the presence of my enemies. You anoint my head with oil; my cup overflows. (Psalm 23:5)

---

22. Jeremiah 17:9–10.
23. Romans 3:10.
24. 2 Peter 1:4.
25. Romans 14:4

Chapter 20 Q&A
The LORD's Table

1. How do the bread and cup of the covenant affect unity in the church?

2. Give an example of how partaking of the bread and cup of the Lord's table has strengthened your walk of faith.

3. Why is the fruit of the vine served at the Lord's table?

4. What is the standard we use to examine ourselves before we come to the Lord's table?

My Journey's Journal:

Chapter 21: Teaching the True Word

Key Scriptures:

- "In everything set them an example by doing what is good. In your teaching show integrity, seriousness and soundness of speech that cannot be condemned, so that those who oppose you may be ashamed because they have nothing bad to say about us" (Titus 2:7–9).

- "Not many of you should become teachers, my fellow believers, because you know that we who teach will be judged more strictly" (James 3:1).

The bowl on the pottery wheel began to take shape as the potter formed the clay with her hands. But then, when a friend knocked on her door, she decided to take a coffee break. When she returned to the studio, the fruit bowl was trying to wrench itself into the shape of an ash tray. She could almost hear the clay's protests: "What are you doing. I'm not a bowl. Your hands have no talent for this work. I'll do it myself."[1]

The Holy Spirit chooses whom He will gift and empower to teach in the church. If someone presumes to teach God's Word, they're on hazardous duty. James warns us that "not many of you should become teachers." To step into a teaching position in the church without waiting for the anointing power of the Holy Spirit is to presume upon the Lord.

This lesson teaches us that all truth is revealed in a sanctuary where wisdom, truth, love, mercy, justice, and faithfulness are honored in what we teach. We'll see that when we declare truth with authority from above, it is heard and received. It's time to understand the many benefits of wisdom, the fear of the Lord, and the knowledge of God as we prepare to teach.[2] The foundations of true learning become clear as the Holy Spirit opens our understanding and leads us to teach what is right and true.

Isaiah serves as our guide to instruct us as we embark on this segment of our ascent. He shows us the road we must travel that tests, tries, and prepares us to teach.

---
1. Isaiah 45:9.
2. Proverbs 2:5.

> A prayer according to 2 Timothy 3:16:
>
> May we honor all Scripture as God-breathed, useful for teaching, rebuking, correcting, and training in righteousness.

We must not presume upon the Holy Spirit by promoting ourselves as teachers so we can stand in front of a crowd and expound great personal insights. Teaching in the church is an office or a spiritual gift that may only be imparted as determined by the Holy Spirit. Ideally, and historically, this gift is imparted by laying on of hands by a presbyter.[3] Absent this ministry, the Holy Spirit is more than able to impart this gift in various ways. This is a vital talent given to the church so that people will learn to live fruitful lives. Teaching God's Word affects lives for eternity and it is too important to attempt on our own.

Consider the beauty and glory of the Spirit of Christ demonstrated through a teacher who speaks only what he or she hears Him speaking. Their words fall like gentle rain upon those who hear. The message they speak is like the morning dew that refreshes the new blossoms in the garden. What they teach comes like showers that cool the mid-day heat and refresh the lilies flowering in lush green meadows. The Spirit's words wash over the hearer so that those who pass through a valley of weeping will see it turn into a place of refreshing.[4] The seeds planted by the Spirit's inspired words from the Scriptures bear fruit that changes lives forever.

> *Let my teaching fall like rain and my words descend like dew, like showers on new grass, like abundant rain on tender plants.*
> (Deuteronomy 32:2)

All true wisdom is from above. Godly wisdom serves us well as we ascend to the gates of the sanctuary where wisdom, truth, love, mercy, and justice are the rule of the day. Those who are taught heaven's wisdom and apply it to their daily lives gain true knowledge in the ways of God's kingdom. They walk in the light of Christ and shine out with the brilliance of His glory. Those who are taught of the Lord[5] will discern an enemy's deceit, turn their thoughts to God's precepts, and learn to walk on paths of wisdom.

Instruction by Spirit-inspired teachers imparts knowledge of God's Word, feeding our soul and spirit to strengthen us so we may overrule the ungod-

---
3. The author's book, *Treasures of the Kingdom* outlines the ministry of a presbyter, page 221.
4. Psalm 84:6.
5. Isaiah 54:13.

ly yearnings of the flesh. When learners meditate and test what is taught, it opens the Scriptures and serves to light their pathway and appoint their footsteps. They gain godly insights that keep their feet from slipping from the path of truth, righteousness, justice, and mercy.

When I said, "My foot is slipping," your unfailing love, Lord, supported me. When anxiety was great within me, your consolation brought me joy.
(Psalm 94:18–19)

We are not born wise, and we can't download heaven's wisdom with a click. How then do we gain godly knowledge and insight? This pursuit begins with the fear of the Lord.[6] Reverence, awe, and delighted obedience are the groundwork needed to gain wisdom from above. A reverent attitude compels us to know more of our heavenly Father and gives us a hunger for God's Word. When we have saturated ourselves with knowledge and understanding of the Scriptures, our hearts instruct us in the night and awaken us in the morning with a teachable mind.[7] By the power of the Word and the Holy Spirit, wisdom comes to light life's pathway and keep us from stumbling.

As we learn more of heaven's wisdom, we gain a great treasure worth more than silver and gold. It is sweeter than honey from the honeycomb.[8] Hold wisdom close and never let go of it. Stand fast in the fear of the LORD because this wisdom drives us to Christ. As we abide in wisdom our Good Shepherd is present to love, protect and watch over us. Wisdom is taught by means of every inspired Word written by the prophets and apostles. Come, let us gather so we may be taught. Then listen, receive, and cherish every word of wisdom, and it will change our lives forever.

Do not forsake wisdom, and she will protect you; love her, and she will watch over you.
(Proverbs 4:6)

Isaiah reveals an amazing truth about those who teach. When we listen to an inspired teacher, it's easy to see them as a person who has it all together. They speak out with life-saving truths and appear to be free from life's difficulties that weigh everybody else down. We tend to put a charismatic instructor on a pedestal so we can admire and emulate them.

What we don't see is the road a teacher traveled to get to the front of the class. Empathetic teachers weren't born compassionate. They didn't learn to identify with their learners' trials and troubles in an air-conditioned class at a university. No, they came to these necessary qualities through the bread

---

6. Proverbs 9:10.
7. Psalm 16:7.
8. Psalm 19:10.

of adversity and the water of affliction.[9] They, like Christ, learned to know the needs of those whom they teach by overcoming difficult temptations and trials.[10] Teachers who have overcome much are useful vessels the Holy Spirit uses to teach others.

> *Although the LORD gives you the bread of adversity and the water of affliction, your teachers will be hidden no more; with your own eyes you will see them.*
> (Isaiah 30:20)

When an instructor references Socrates or Plato to make their point, they do so to give their own words authority. A professor quotes Martin Luther King Jr. to give her lessons greater impact. A math professor may reference Leonhard Euler, the king of mathematicians, to prove his own equation. Historic experts add credibility to a university lecture, but God's Word is the only authority when we teach spiritual truths.

In the realm of God's kingdom, our words are spoken with authority only when we speak what our heavenly Father is speaking.[11] Our teaching has power to change lives only when we instruct with the words of our LORD and Savior. When we speak our own thoughts, ideas, and musings, our words fall to the ground. Our own reflections are like useless fire and have no eternal impact.[12]

To teach with the authority of Christ, we must store God's Word as treasure in our hearts so we may correctly explain what is written. Teachers are careful to hear, know, and understand every word the Spirit of Christ inspired the apostles and prophets to speak and write. Jesus taught with great authority because He only spoke what He heard the Father speaking.[13] He didn't need to reference Gamaliel[14] or anyone else as an expert because His authoritative words came from above.

> *When Jesus had finished saying these things, the crowds were amazed at his teaching, because he taught as one who had authority, and not as their teachers of the law.*
> (Matthew 7:28–29)

Teachers of the Word are held to a high standard. When it comes to instructing people regarding the truths of Scripture, we must not add to or take away from what the apostles and prophets penned by the inspiration of the Holy Spirit. We do not interpret the Scriptures by our own thoughts or ideas.

---

9. Bread and water of affliction is a reference to a prisoner's diet.
10. Hebrews 4:15.
11. John 8:38.
12. Malachi 1:10.
13. John 12:49.
14. Gamaliel was a leader in the Sanhedrin who taught men like the Apostle Paul (Acts 22:3).

We don't use personal experiences as the arbiter of truth. Teaching truths from the Scriptures is only possible by means of the Holy Spirit opening our understanding and then our mouths to teach the Scriptures with integrity.

Teachers in the church must be diligent students of the Word and stay tuned to what the Spirit is revealing in prayerful research and study. There is no other source of divine truth. The Spirit of Christ inspired the Holy Scriptures, and the same Spirit opens our hearts and minds to its true and faithful message. The Holy Spirit teaches us so that we may teach God's people and open their eyes to see their need of Christ.

A gifted Bible teacher works to become saturated in every book of the Bible because Scripture interprets Scripture. Genesis helps us understand Revelation. The Psalms prepare us to understand the gospels. Deuteronomy opens our minds so we can comprehend the epistles. The words Jesus spoke during His years of ministry have their roots in the prophetic words of the Old Testament. Our Messiah was present with the Holy Spirit when He inspired the prophets to write and speak.

As we teach, the prophets of old stand with the apostles to surround us as a cloud of witnesses. In their honor we conform to Christ and toss aside anything that gets in the way of the true message of the holy Scriptures.[15]

He must hold firmly to the trustworthy message as it has been taught, so that he can encourage others by sound doctrine and refute those who oppose it.
(Titus 1:9)

Anointed teaching in the church changes lives forever. This eternal kind of work cannot be accomplished by our own means and methods. The Spirit of Christ who works in us is the one accomplishing this good work through us. Inspired teaching from the Scriptures keeps the learner focused so we don't turn aside to the right or to the left.[16] The Spirit and the Word empowers a teacher. Then, with their instruction encompassed with earnest prayer, they speak with authority to prepare the learner for service.

The church has a great treasure of wisdom, knowledge, and understanding. We come together to embrace this wisdom and listen to godly teachers who open God's Word to us. When words of wisdom rain down, the congregation blossoms and spreads the fragrance of Christ well beyond the doors of their gathering place.

---
15. Hebrews 12:1.
16. Deuteronomy 5:32.

We teach Christ, and Him crucified, as an essential part of God's design for His temple.

> Do your best to present yourself to God as one approved, a worker who does not need to be ashamed and who correctly handles the word of truth.
> (2 Timothy 2:15)

Chapter 21 Q&A

Teaching the True Word

1. What is necessary for a teacher to effect an eternal change in people's lives?

2. Describe what happens when a teacher speaks out with words of truth to those who gather.

3. Why are teachers of God's Word held to a higher standard?

4. How does teaching the Word fit into God's design and plan for every sanctuary for worship?

My Journey's Journal:

Chapter 22: Proclaiming the True Gospel

Key Scriptures:

- "The one who stands firm to the end will be saved. And this gospel of the kingdom will be preached in the whole world as a testimony to all nations, and then the end will come" (Matthew 24:13–14).

- "And the gospel must first be preached to all nations" (Mark 13:10).

If you have no building materials other than 2x4s, you can't build a house. That pile of river rocks is not enough to build a workshop. It takes a variety of materials, fasteners, and hardware to make a proper structure. A builder must not leave out any necessary part.

Worship is much more than singing songs and listening to an inspirational sermon. In this leg of our ascent, we'll see the essential elements of this sanctuary where we gather in Jesus' name. Preaching the true gospel of Jesus Christ to reveal our Savior is one essential thread that must be woven into every message.

This segment presents a gospel with one faith, one Savior—a gospel path that leads to saving faith.

> A prayer according to Romans 1:16:
>
> May we never be ashamed of the gospel, knowing it is the power of God for salvation for everyone who believes, no matter who they are.

Some churches have a "One Way" sign posted on a wall to remind people that Christ Jesus is the only way to heaven. The gospel of Jesus Christ does reveal that there is only one gate to enter God's presence—through Christ and His saving grace. In truth, there's only one way, and it's a narrow path up the mountain. The good news can't be attained by blazing our own trail. It's more like hiking on a Forest Service trail with signs that say, "Stay on the Path." When trekking through the meadows, you can see the mountain top, but you can't safely reach the summit without hiking through the woods on the designated trail.

The way of salvation is through Jesus Christ and no other. We can only come to the Father as the Holy Spirit leads us to Jesus Christ, who redeems us by the power of his Word. We are called to proclaim only one true and simple gospel of Jesus Christ, "Believe and be baptized."[1]

> *Jesus answered, "I am the way and the truth and the life. No one comes to the Father except through me."*
> (John 14:6)

Are we so ashamed of the true gospel that we must carve out a more pleasant ways to be saved? Is the gospel so simple that we are compelled to make it a challenge to be saved? Is it a fear of people that compels us to preach only comforting promises and bountiful blessings?[2] We must not be ashamed of the good news or the blood of Christ that paid the price for our salvation. We show our contempt when we say, "Your mom and dad are Christians, so you are too." We scorn the good news when we say, "Get your act together then you can be saved."

We are called to stand up and preach God's Word by the inspiration and anointing of the Spirit of Christ. If we choose other words because of fear, discord will overthrow the platform where we stand.[3] We must turn away from these terrors and armor up for battle. Stand up and proclaim to the people what the Spirit is speaking. A preacher of Christ dare not be frightened by people's opinions or demands and stop speaking the truth. Jeremiah warns against being afraid of people's faces in the congregation.[4] An upright minister serves by the power of the Spirit and under the authority of Christ, who is head of the church. There is no other authority and no other means of saving faith.

> *For I am not ashamed of the gospel, because it is the power of God that brings salvation to everyone who believes: first to the Jew, then to the Gentile. For in the gospel the righteousness of God is revealed–a righteousness that is by faith from first to last, just as it is written: "The righteous will live by faith."*
> (Romans 1:16–17)

A gathering that doesn't proclaim Christ and the cross in melodies of praise misses one essential element of worship. An assembly without proclamations of the gospel in song and preaching might just as well lock the doors and go home.

The Apostle Paul proclaims the true gospel as the Spirit of Christ revealed it to him. This message is heard, received, and believed by those who

---

1. Mark 16:16.
2. Proverbs 29:25.
3. Jeremiah 1:17.
4. Jeremiah 1:8.

are called to be sons and daughters of the Most High God. Those who embrace the good news by faith are compelled to repent of their sins, turn from their wandering ways, and be baptized into the Father, Son, and Holy Spirit. This powerful message is then confirmed by an outpouring of the Spirit's power in signs, wonders, and spiritual gifts for the work of the church.[5]

> *Therefore I glory in Christ Jesus in my service to God. I will not venture to speak of anything except what Christ has accomplished through me in leading the Gentiles to obey God by what I have said and done–by the power of signs and wonders, through the power of the Spirit of God. So from Jerusalem all the way around to Illyricum, I have fully proclaimed the gospel of Christ.*
> (Romans 15:17–19)

The story of Philip and the Ethiopian high official overflows with mysterious truths. A eunuch traveled in his chariot while reading from the book of Isaiah on a scroll. He read the words, "he was led like a sheep to the slaughter," but he couldn't puzzle out its meaning. He needed a teacher. The Holy Spirit sent an anointed messenger who opened the mystery of the gospel to him. The Word was hidden like buried treasure until Philip came along and revealed the whole message of Christ, the cross, and a resurrected Savior.

The Ethiopian heard the Word, believed, received the truth, and the seed of faith took root in his heart. When they came to some water, the man couldn't wait a moment longer to be baptized. The joy of salvation overwhelmed him. Then, when he came up out of the water, the Spirit suddenly took Philip away.

This short historic record shows the dynamic power of God's Word and the preaching of the true gospel of Jesus Christ. How can we deny so great a salvation by offering any less than the redemptive miracle the Lamb of God made possible? Jesus offered His body to be broken so that we might be made whole. Why would we proclaim a message that takes anything away from our Savior who gave His blood to be shed to redeem the whole world from sin's clutches?

> *Then Philip began with that very passage of Scripture and told him the good news about Jesus. As they traveled along the road, they came to some water and the eunuch said, "Look, here is water. What can stand in the way of my being baptized?"*
> (Acts 8:35–36)

There are two kinds of wisdom. On one hand there is the earthbound wisdom of human reasoning. This kind of wisdom hears the gospel and asks, "Does it make sense?" Reason typically answers, "No." Human based

---
5. 1 Corinthians 1:6–7, Hebrews 2:3–4.

wisdom empties the cross of its power and therefore, sees the good news as irrational.[6] On the other hand, our heavenly Father's wisdom reigns supreme. The mystery of this redemptive wisdom can't be proven by mathematical formulas. It's impossible to verify it with radiometric dating. Being well informed by our newsfeed won't confirm its veracity. Even so, an honest intellect that seeks to know God is guided by the Spirit and finds this mystery within reach.

Jesus' claim to be the Way, the Truth, and the Life is a stumbling block for those who demand signs from heaven and mystical experiences to reconcile their prideful doubt. The gospel is like a rock in the middle of everyone's pathway. We'll either trip on it or stand upon it. The message of Christ, who is the Cornerstone, will either crush us or serve as the foundation for our lives and make us fruitful in God's kingdom.[7]

> *For since in the wisdom of God the world through its wisdom did not know him, God was pleased through the foolishness of what was preached to save those who believe. Jews demand signs and Greeks look for wisdom, but we preach Christ crucified: a stumbling block to Jews and foolishness to Gentiles, but to those whom God has called, both Jews and Greeks, Christ the power of God and the wisdom of God.*
> (1 Corinthians 1:21–24)

Life on planet earth offers a choice of two backpacks. One comes with a load of depravity, guilt, and shame. Its contents are corrosive, but its outside is bejeweled with glitter, glam, and bright multicolored animations. The other backpack is rather plain looking, only a little better than sack cloth, but inside we find all that is right and good. Comfort, peace, joy, saving grace, mercy, forgiveness, faithfulness, and a humble spirit are among its contents.[8] What is inside is redemptive. The first backpack has an expiration date, while the second holds the promise of life everlasting. When these alternatives confront us, the Light of the World opens our eyes to see what is right. Natural eyes only see the outside of the packs.

Our Savior came to us in weakness. His mother wrapped Him in plain cloth and placed Him in a cow's trough for a cradle. Over thirty years later, soldiers drove nails through his hands and feet, pinning Him to a cruel Roman cross between two thieving bandits. Then Jesus cried out with a loud voice, "It is finished," bowed His head, and died. This is the treasure inside the plain, cloth backpack.

---

6. 1 Corinthians 1:17.
7. Matthew 21:42–44.
8. Matthew 11:30.

Open it and it overflows with delightful treasures. The burden is light, and the benefits are awesome. Sin, death, and the grave are defeated in Christ. We are transformed into overcomers who live victorious lives, free from the clutches of sin and depravity. We are set free to run on our Savior's narrow pathway. We're released from the chains of darkness so we may rejoice in the joy of His salvation.

Now our redeemed hearts hunger to hear instruction about what is right and good so that we can walk in obedience. Christ's abundant love drives us to learn and do what our heavenly Father requires of us. We are given ears to hear, and our hearts soak in words of eternal life.[9] Our ears yearn to hear true preaching on the law of love—the true gospel. We humbly respond to correction according to God's Word because of our love for our Father, His beloved Son, and the Holy Spirit. We are God's children and our hearts delight in obedience.

Everyone who believes that Jesus is the Christ is born of God, and everyone who loves the father loves his child as well. This is how we know that we love the children of God: by loving God and carrying out his commands. In fact, this is love for God: to keep his commands. And his commands are not burdensome, for everyone born of God overcomes the world. This is the victory that has overcome the world, even our faith. Who is it that overcomes the world? Only the one who believes that Jesus is the Son of God.
(1 John 5:1–5)

How can we know beyond doubt that we are redeemed and adopted sons and daughters of the LORD Most High? Why are so many people uncertain? After we come to saving faith in Jesus Christ, the enemy of our soul whispers questions to plant doubt about our salvation. When these temptations assault us, it's good to have proof of our adoption in writing.

We are given three sure witnesses that we are true children of the light. These witnesses serve as anchors for our soul:

a. The Spirit who indwells us and seals us against the day of God's just and righteous wrath. He is the breath from the four winds who breathes life into our spirit.[10]

b. In the water of baptism, we die and are buried with Christ and then resurrected in Him. We are made new creations in Christ in the water and through the water. Then, as newborns, we hunger for God's Word because we want to know our heavenly Father and live according what He desires for us.

---

9. John 6:68.
10. Ezekiel 37:9.

c. The blood of Christ justifies us, reconciles us, and washes us clean so that He may present us for adoption as righteous sons and daughters before our heavenly Father.

And this is the testimony: God has given us eternal life, and this life is in his Son. Whoever has the Son has life; whoever does not have the Son of God does not have life.
(1 John 5:11–12)

A soldier pierced Jesus' side with a spear as He hung on the cross. Blood and water flowed out. This awesome flow is for the cleansing of sins for the whole world—to all who will believe and receive.

The Spirit continually breathes His refreshing wind into us so we may sing out with the joy of our salvation. With the breath of the Spirit, we breathe out exaltations to the great I AM from the rising of the sun until it sets. The Spirit of Christ gives us songs in the night to comfort us. We live our lives in agreement with our baptism, constantly assured of our adoption. Every day we rejoice to be called by our heavenly Father's holy name. In the morning, evening, and when we wake up in the night we come before the Father with prayers and petitions. We believed the gospel, and now we come boldly and with great assurance before him because we have been washed clean in the blood of our Savior, Jesus Christ, and have been given right standing before our heavenly Father.

This is the one who came by water and blood–Jesus Christ. He did not come by water only, but by water and blood. And it is the Spirit who testifies, because the Spirit is the truth. For there are three that testify: the Spirit, the water and the blood; and the three are in agreement. We accept human testimony, but God's testimony is greater because it is the testimony of God, which he has given about his Son. Whoever believes in the Son of God accepts this testimony. Whoever does not believe God has made him out to be a liar, because they have not believed the testimony God has given about his Son.
(1 John 5:6–10)

That's narrow minded! Why is there only one way? To answer this question, we must stop for a moment and consider the serious nature of our sinful condition. Our sin sickness is terminal and there is only one cure that works—Jesus Christ and His atoning sacrifice.

Consider what people of faith do when they move to a new town. They search online for local churches, but usually find more choices than an ice cream shop's many flavors. We can narrow down the choices by noting the churches that proclaim the true gospel's one way. Churches that offer customized ways of salvation get deleted from our list. Knowing that justification is only possible by grace and through faith in Jesus Christ as LORD and Savior is vital to our search. The church that preaches the true gospel of Jesus Christ and remains true to the design of the sanctuary is the best place to gather for worship and fellowship.

> In a loud voice they were saying: "Worthy is the Lamb, who was slain, to receive power and wealth and wisdom and strength and honor and glory and praise!"
> (Revelation 5:12)

Chapter 22 Q&A

Proclaiming the True Gospel

1. What is the cure for the malady called sin?

2. What are the two kinds of wisdom? Which will you choose?

3. Check out your backpack? What is inside it?

4. What proofs do you have that you are an adopted son or daughter of the Most High God?

My Journey's Journal:

Chapter 23: Ministries of Spiritual Gifts

Key Scriptures:

- "There are different kinds of gifts, but the same Spirit distributes them. There are different kinds of service, but the same Lord. There are different kinds of working, but in all of them and in everyone it is the same God at work" (1 Corinthians 12:4–6).

- "There is one body and one Spirit, just as you were called to one hope when you were called; one Lord, one faith, one baptism; one God and Father of all, who is over all and through all and in all" (Ephesians 4:4–6).

It wouldn't be reasonable to expect one climber to do all the heavy lifting so the others can enjoy an easy ascent. A single climber can't carry all the backpacks for the group. It's the same for the construction boss. He can't build a house without the help of skilled craftsmen. A principal without teachers and students is only a desk jockey. The church is not a one man show; everyone, with every kind of spiritual gift, is needed to pitch in to get the job done.

The Scriptures show us that we must not forbid, despise, or redefine the Spirit's good gifts. Those who do so plunder the church of the Spirit's power. Spiritual gifts are an integral part of worship gatherings. They are a sure sign that the true gospel is accomplishing its good work in our assembly. Let's put aside our fears regarding spiritual gifts and learn how they are imparted to each one according to the Holy Spirit's purpose and plan.

This topic helps us to see ourselves as captives in His train who are given good gifts for the ministry of the church so that we may complete the work God prepared in advance for us to do. Every office that is established to equip the saints for this work of ministry is important.[1] With the Spirit's good gifts at work in us, we avoid the wordly spirituality that crowds around us. Instead, our focus is to fulfill our calling in Christ, serving in His royal priesthood of believers for the good of the church. By means of the anointing, gifting, and empowering work of the Spirit of Christ we are raised up as the church victorious.

---
1. Ephesians 4:12–16.

> A prayer according to 2 Timothy 4:17:
>
> God of majesty, stand at our side and give us your strength so that through us your message might be fully proclaimed for everyone to hear.

All Christians are called to serve as priests, doing their part in the work of the Great Commission. We must not be like Israel, who rejected God as King and demanded a man to rule over them and fight their battles. It's human nature to think that the ministries of the Spirit are too hard and demand too much of us. Because of this, we expect a pastor to manifest all the spiritual gifts and perform all the ministries of the church for us. But that defeats the whole purpose of spiritual gifts and exhausts the one who is required to do it all. God's design for the sanctuary brings all the parts of the body of Christ into one functioning body with Christ as the head.[2] It pleases the Holy Spirit to gift and empower the many parts of Christ's body as He determines. We must not demand that the pastor operate in all the spiritual gifts, do all the hard work of ministry, and keep us entertained while doing so. That's what we pay him for, right? But this is not the way of Jesus' church.

The wind of the Holy Spirit breathed into Adam's nostrils to made him a living being. Later, the Spirit of Christ came as a mighty wind with tongues of fire to give life to the church. The Spirit of Truth continues to empower God's people with gifts for the orderly functioning of our worship gatherings. The Spirit of Christ has a unique gift for every Christian, but there is no quiz or formula to determine whom He will gift with each spiritual ability. A paper test can only help you discover your common strengths and talents.

Every local assembly needs all the spiritual gifts at work to be a fully functioning church. The church cannot reject any of the workings of the Spirit without crippling itself. When one part is broken or missing, the whole congregation eventually becomes ineffective. To reject any of the gifts provided to the church is to refuse the fullness of Christ's living and active presence among us. We must not be like the tribes of Israel who would not take full possession of the promised land.[3] Without spiritual gifts ministered in love, those who come into our fellowship will go on their way, asking, "Where is their God?"[4] Those who forbid or despise these good gifts plunder the church of its power.

---

2. Ephesians 1:22.
3. Judges 1:27–33.
4. 1 Corinthian 13:13, Psalm 115:2.

"The wind blows wherever it pleases. You hear its sound, but you cannot tell where it comes from or where it is going. So it is with everyone born of the Spirit."
(John 3:8)

A car that is all pistons and no wheels in no car at all, only parts for the junk yard. A pocket watch that is all face and hands with no gears and springs will not keep time. It is tossed out as useless. Every part in a car or watch is necessary for it to function and be useful. Likewise, a fully functioning church requires many different working parts that minister according to their various gifts.

Paul teaches us that the spiritual gift of prophecy is a useful and necessary part of a church body. He encourages all of us to desire this good gift and use it according to the faith we are given.[5] Too often this gift is denied the church and we suffer for it. Some churches redefine it as only a pastoral sermon, which is easy to do because a pastor may exercise a prophetic gift during a sermon. But prophetic ministry is not limited to the work of one person in the church who stands in a pulpit and claims, this is my territory and don't step into my space.

The true spiritual gift of prophecy is one of the most useful gifts for building up the church, and it's a gift we should all desire.[6] In the New Testament church, the spiritual gift of prophecy often serves to reveal the secrets of a person's heart to convince and convict of sin, leading them to know that "God is really among you." This gift is forthtelling, and rarely foretelling. It's a special gift that must never be denied.

We have different gifts, according to the grace given to each of us. If your gift is prophesying, then prophesy in accordance with your faith.
(Romans 12:6)

Manifestations of spiritual gifts in a local church are sure signs that the true gospel is preached, believed, and obeyed.[7] The various gifts and those who are gifted come together as a vital part of a fully functioning church. In reality, each one of us serves as one part of a talented fellowship. By the power of the Word and in water of baptism, our old self died, we are raised into the power of the resurrected Christ and wrapped in His robe of righteousness. Now, in Christ, we all have equal standing before our God and Father.[8] All who are called by our Savior's name have a job prepared for them to do in the church.[9] Whether we mop the kitchen floor or lead out in prayer, we stand equal before the Almighty. Every job is necessary. No one is excluded.

---

5. Romans 12:6.
6. 1 Corinthians 14:5.
7. For a description of spiritual gifts see author's book *Treasures of the Kingdom,* pages 110 through 132.
8. James 2:1.
9. Ephesians 2:10.

Remember that we don't just find or discover our gift. We can't take a personality test to help us know our spiritual talents. Gifts of the Spirit are only imparted to us by the Spirit of Christ according to the working parts that are needed in the local church. A gifted presbyter may help us discern our spiritual calling. Then, spiritual gifts are imparted to us by laying on of hands and may be confirmed by a word of prophecy.[10]

As we serve according to our spiritual gifts, we must watch out for the hazards. Because of our fallibility, we are often tempted to exalt ourselves." But a person gifted with the spiritual gift of healing[11] can only minister in the strength of the Spirit. Those who serve in the spiritual gift of teacher or prophet must not exalt themselves but test their words to be sure they speak what can be proven true in the Scriptures.

Our natural tendency is to set special people on pedestals, idolizing them so we can identify with them. All too often, we give our pastors, elders, and gifted people an exalted platform and then knock them down when we see they're not perfect. What we ought to do instead is to recognize, love, and respect all our brothers and sisters in Christ, seeing them as equal servants in the sight of our heavenly Father. All servants and every service are of equal value.

> *So in Christ Jesus you are all children of God through faith, for all of you who were baptized into Christ have clothed yourselves with Christ. There is neither Jew nor Gentile, neither slave nor free, nor is there male and female, for you are all one in Christ Jesus.*
> (Galatians 3:26–28)

On the cross, our LORD Jesus triumphed over every enemy. What appeared to be a horrible defeat in the eyes of man was the greatest victory for the salvation of all who will believe. Jesus died in our place for the sins of the whole world. Then He rose victorious, defeating sin, Satan, and death. By the work of the cross, Jesus recovered those held captive to sin. He restored spiritual gifts for the good work prepared for us from the beginning.[12]

The Holy Spirit manifested this truth on the day of Pentecost when He came like a mighty wind and gave good gifts to His church. The great I AM does not change. The gifts that the Spirit poured out as He established the New Testament church are still available to all who will receive. Those who teach that some spiritual gifts were only for establishing the church and are no longer necessary, deny good gifts to God's people. These gifts still serve to confirm that the true gospel is preached, received, and believed.

---

10. 1 Timothy 4:14 ASV.
11. 1 Corinthians 12:9, 28, 30.
12. Ephesians 2:10.

Spiritual gifts ministered by the authority of Jesus' name are the only means available to empower the church so we can complete the good work of the Great Commission. The need for all life-changing spiritual gifts is as great in our day as on the day of Pentecost when the New Covenant church came into being.

This is the beauty and majesty of Christ who gives good gifts to His redeemed captives. He unites us as a holy nation and calls us to worship, serve, and minister in His church.

You have enlarged the nation and increased their joy; they rejoice before you as people rejoice at the harvest, as warriors rejoice when dividing the plunder. (Isaiah 9:3)

When establishing an accredited university, it's necessary to have qualified professors in various disciplines. Math, science, philosophy, psychology, economics, and many other fields of study require highly schooled professors with proper credentials.

As head of the church, Jesus prepared His disciples for their work by teaching them at Jesus' university for three-and-a-half years. He prepared them for the Holy Spirit's empowering work so they could fill vital jobs for the functioning of the church and the work of the gospel. Every person in our gatherings is equally necessary so that we may grow in grace and knowledge until the day of the LORD when we graduate to the eternal presence of our Lord.

Apostles are still necessary in our day, even though we seldom call them apostles. They are missionaries and church planters, who serve to establish and organize local churches by the Spirit's leading. They preach the Word, and they're always prepared to correct, rebuke, and encourage with great patience and careful instruction.[13] An apostle serves by authority of the Spirit of Christ as a presbyter to anoint pastors, elders, deacons, and teachers. He anoints people with spiritual gifts, as the Spirit directs, by laying on of hands. The church planter's job is to impart various spiritual gifts as the Spirit wills. Then, after the church is established, he moves on but returns frequently to check up on their growth and progress in the faith.

Prophets in the church speak only what God is speaking. By the Spirit's prompting, they tactfully admonish where sin creeps in. Speaking by the inspiration of the Holy Spirit, they warn of dangers ahead. Their work is necessary to keep the church serving in submission to Christ and to stir up the fires for the work of the great commission. Gifted prophets in the church may confirm a person's spiritual gift by a prophetic word. But because those

---

13. 2 Timothy 4:2.

who minister in the spiritual gift of prophecy today are fallible, we must prove what they prophesy using the Scriptures to weigh every word they speak.

Evangelists are gifted with an anointing to reach out and touch hearts with the message of the gospel. He or she calls people to the cross where Jesus died for their sins. Their voices ring out, beckoning lost souls to repent of their sin, receive forgiveness, and come to saving faith in Jesus Christ.

Gifted pastors are a blessing to the church because their hearts overflow with love, compassion, mercy, grace, and forgiveness. "Pastor" means "shepherd," and describes one who cares for the flock, anointing wounded souls and infirm bodies with healing oils. He preaches the truths of the Scriptures from Genesis to Revelation with patient, loving care. He proclaims the royal law of love[14] and extends God's mercy and forgiveness for our offenses. He also searches for wandering souls and gently leads them back home. Pastors minister under the authority of Christ to lead the church in true worship.

Teachers serve to improve the spiritual health of the church by opening the Scriptures so the people may grow in grace and knowledge. His or her instructions are more in depth than a pastor as they dig into and explain the Scriptures in context, with historic accuracy, and based on a true understanding of the whole Bible. The aim of their teaching is to give our hearts and minds an eternal perspective that affects how we view the world around us.

Each of the offices is a vital element of every modern-day church, just as it was in the church in Acts. When these offices are actively at work in our churches, we take great strides into the fullness of Christ who is worthy of all praise, honor, and glory.

So Christ himself gave the apostles, the prophets, the evangelists, the pastors and teachers, to equip his people for works of service, so that the body of Christ may be built up until we all reach unity in the faith and in the knowledge of the Son of God and become mature, attaining to the whole measure of the fullness of Christ. (Ephesians 4:11–13)

When there's a railroad crossing sign by the road, it's a good idea to pay attention. If we ignore its warning, we may soon learn that locomotives always come out on top in a crash. All road signs serve a good purpose and it's wise to look and listen.

The Holy Scriptures abound with road signs to guide us on life's pathway. The Bible's signposts warn us and offer direction at every intersection of life. We are called to hear the faithful eyewitnesses who wrote the gospels proclaiming the victorious, resurrected Christ. We can rest assured that where

---

14. Leviticus 19:18, James 2:8.

genuine good news is preached, the message will be confirmed and proven true with signs, wonders, and various miracles.

We must keep our gospel message true. We cannot be distracted from this great salvation by allowing all kinds of worldly spiritualities to creep in. We must also be sure that no irrational fear of squelching the Holy Spirit invades our church. Wise pastors and elders do not allow false displays of spirituality. Instead of acting out of fear, they must discern the spirits and keep the ministries of spiritual gifts within the bounds of truth, love, faithfulness, and saving grace.

> *How shall we escape if we ignore so great a salvation? This salvation, which was first announced by the Lord, was confirmed to us by those who heard him. God also testified to it by signs, wonders and various miracles, and by gifts of the Holy Spirit distributed according to his will.*
> (Hebrews 2:3–4)

It's too easy for our natural desires to overrule a hunger and thirst for righteousness. If we want our redeemed soul and spirit to triumph, we must constantly feed on God's Word. We must be careful, because our default mode is to be consumers who demand that our feelings be assuaged, and our minds humored. It's easy for Christians fall into this trap.

An equally serious detriment to true worship is an attitude of anything goes. This brings disorder into the church and leads to shallow worship. If you feel inspired to show your dancing skills during a time of worship—wait on the Lord. When you're enthused to reveal your awesome voice—wait on the Lord. Prayers designed to show your great spiritual insights need to be prayed in silence until the Spirit opens your mouth to pray from your spirit.

Our heavenly Father provides a design for His sanctuary that has no personal platforms. This plan guides us in the work prepared for the church.[15] We are God's sons and daughters who are called to humble ourselves and serve our part in a royal priesthood. We are all called to do the work of God's kingdom together as a holy nation. We are the Father's special possession, whom He has commanded to proclaim His glorious works and minister to those in need, singing with Psalms, hymns, and spiritual songs.

Every working part of the body of Christ has a purpose. When we stop functioning according to our calling, we soon begin to fester and become cancerous within the church. Demanding that one person manifest all the gifts of the Spirit and do all the work leaves us to stagnate in the shadows on our padded pew. We are called to come out of this darkness and live up to God's

---

15. Ephesians 2:10.

plan as a chosen people. Our calling is to submit to Christ and serve as royal priests in His kingdom.

> *But you are a chosen people, a royal priesthood, a holy nation, God's special possession, that you may declare the praises of him who called you out of darkness into his wonderful light.*
> (1 Peter 2:9)

It's important to clear up a misunderstanding regarding spiritual gifts. The Scriptures speak of one baptism that is salvific.[16] In water and by the power of the Word we are baptized into the name of Father, Son, and Holy Spirit. As we are raised up from the water, we are sealed by the Holy Spirit so we are kept safe from God's just and holy wrath. We are raised up in resurrection power. Now, we're prepared for Jesus' fiery baptism that is most often imparted by fasting, prayer, and laying on of hands. In the fire of the Spirit, we are anointed and gifted with spiritual gifts that empower us to do what is otherwise impossible in the ministries of the church—to preach the true gospel, change lives for eternity, and prove the message is true with signs and wonders. But how does this happen? Jesus instructed us to wait for the anointing fire of the Spirit.[17] This still applies because the fire of our spiritual gifts must constantly be rekindled.[18] The church is called to "repent and do the things you did at first."[19] We must not leave home to minister without first receiving the empowering work of the Spirit as Jesus promised.

First, we must understand that prior to the day of Pentecost, the Apostles had already received the Holy Spirit.[20] Then on the day of Pentecost the Spirit came with a mighty wind, like tongues of fire to empower the people for ministries of the church. Consider Peter, who always put his foot in his mouth and denied Jesus three times. After the Holy Spirit came, appearing as tongues of fire, he preached a powerful message and three-thousand people believed and were baptized.

This powerful baptism is evident in the Apostle's ministries throughout the book of Acts. As the gospel message spread, Gentiles who heard and believed the good news of God's saving grace were baptized in water. Then the Apostles laid hands on the new believers to receive empowering gifts as the Spirit determined. Receiving spiritual gifts came with visible evidence of the grace of God in tongues and prophecies.[21] All those who waited for the Spirit to gift them with His empowering work were then prepared to be sent out

---
16. 1 Peter 3:21.
17. Matthew 3:11, Acts 1:8.
18. 2 Timothy 1:6.
19. Revelation 2:5.
20. John 20:22.
21. E.g., Acts 2:4, Acts 8:15–17, Acts 10:44–48, Acts 11:23, and Acts 19:1–7.

to do the work of the Great Commission, baptizing and making disciples by proclaiming the cross of Jesus Christ.

We are also called to speak the good news with words of wisdom and with proofs of the Spirit and with power.[22] Then, as we do the work of the church, we come into another baptism: a baptism in fiery trials.[23]

> *On one occasion, while he was eating with them, he gave them this command: "Do not leave Jerusalem, but wait for the gift my Father promised, which you have heard me speak about. For John baptized with water, but in a few days you will be baptized with the Holy Spirit."*
> (Acts 1:4–5)

The Holy Spirit has not left the church without anointing oil to feed the flame that empowers us for the work of the Great Commission. Those who work in the harvest field must constantly trim their lamps to keep the fire burning bright. We stir up the flame of Pentecost by constantly being refilled with the oil of the Spirit. Our first love compels us to stir our spiritual gifts into a blaze. Every Christian is called to wait for the Spirit of Christ to gift and empower them before serving in the church and then being sent out to proclaim the good news gospel of Jesus Christ.

> But you have an anointing from the Holy One, and all of you know the truth.
> (1 John 2:20)

---

22. 1 Corinthians 2:2–5.
23. Luke 21:12, 1 Peter 1:6–7.

Chapter 23 Q&A

Ministries of Spiritual Gifts

1. How has the modern-day church limited itself in the work we are called to complete?

2. Is Pentecost only a one-time event in church history?

3. What purpose do spiritual gifts serve in the local church?

4. Are all spiritual gifts necessary as we gather to worship in a congregation today?

5. Can we effectively minister and serve without first being gifted and empowered by the Holy Spirit?

My Journey's Journal:

Chapter 24: Awesome Offerings

Key Scriptures:

- "Each of you should give what you have decided in your heart to give, not reluctantly or under compulsion, for God loves a cheerful giver" (2 Corinthians 9:7).

- "On the first day of every week, each one of you should set aside a sum of money in keeping with your income, saving it up, so that when I come no collections will have to be made" (1 Corinthians 16:2).

When you're on the third leg of your ascent and realize you didn't pack enough of your favorite dried fruit and granola, you flash back to the planning stage. The cost of preparing for an extensive mountain climb stretched your budget. But now you realize you should have spent a little more.

No matter what pastime you enjoy, it seems you never have enough nickels, dimes, quarters, and dollars. The credit limit on the plastic in your wallet is never high enough, especially when inflation surges. Around the world, people work hard to earn rubles, euros, pesos, pounds, and shekels. They're an important means of exchange to keep the wheels of commerce turning. Investors speculate, buying and selling currencies, trying to make a quick profit. But the world-wide economy still thrives on the American dollar. Everywhere you look, there are dollar signs and it's too easy to get caught up in the money, money, money mill.

This study explores the various offerings specified for the people of Israel beginning with firstfruits. Our lesson answers the question, "What does our heavenly Father desire for us to offer today?" The Old Covenant required worshippers to bring burnt, drink, freewill, heave, meal, peace, sin, and firstfruit offerings. What is required of Christians today?

> A prayer according to Isaiah 60:9:
>
> O Holy One, bring your children from afar, bearing treasures to honor you. Oh Lord, give us favor among men by the light of your countenance. Bestow your blessings upon us so the good news may be proclaimed on every island and continent.

The law required people in ancient Israel to bring firstfruits from their harvests during the Festival of Weeks and present them before the Lord.[1] The firstborn male, whether human or animal also belonged to the Lord.[2] The people presented the first and the best fruit from the bounty of their fields as gifts to provide for the priests who served in the temple. With these offerings, the priests had enough to offer help to the poor.

Do Christians have to bring the first and best tomatoes from our garden and offer them to our pastor and elders? That's a good idea, but if that's all we do, we miss the point. Our LORD and Savior fulfilled the law of firstfruits and we who are in Christ are now offered as the firstfruits of the Spirit. With God's blessings in our hands, compassion and generosity are our first thoughts. We, the firstfruits of Christ, receive blessings from the work we do and then open our bounty to provide for our church leaders, for the work of our church, and to help the poor as we eagerly wait for the full revelation of Christ who redeems us.[3]

> *Tell the Israelites to bring me an offering. You are to receive the offering for me from everyone whose heart prompts them to give.*
> (Exodus 25:2)

Picture a Pharisee while he prepares his offering. He stands tall in his flowing robes and instructs his servant to squat down to carefully count mint leaves in his garden so he can give exactly one tenth of them.[4] Now consider what we do today. Do we tithe a tenth, rounding it up to the nearest penny of our earnings, but then cheat our workers out of their wages? Does our calculator figure our offerings down to the nearest decimal point? Do we give an offering on Sunday and then evict a poor widow on Monday when she is short on her rent? This is hypocrisy. When our doing and our giving don't match, our gifts are unacceptable.

---

1. Numbers 28:26.
2. Exodus 13:2.
3. Romans 8:23.
4. Luke 11:42.

Do we hoard for ourselves what really belongs to our heavenly Father? Do we live in our beautiful houses while God's house is in ruins?[5] In reality, all that all we have, home, business, bank accounts, job, and cars, belong to God. He could demand it all from us, but He only asks for a part of it. He makes us good stewards who manage what belongs to Him. He asks for a small sum from our increase to acknowledge that He is King and LORD over all He has provided.[6]

Many precious blessings overflow to those who are cheerful givers.[7] Our boundary lines are set in pleasant places and we give abundantly.[8] The Almighty satisfies our desires with good things and we present our offerings with thanksgiving. Heaven's blessings overtake us and we submit a portion our treasures.[9] We are blessed in our labor and bestow gifts from our bounty. Our Father teaches us how to work the land so that our gardens flourish with good fruit, and we contribute from our plenty.[10]

> *"Bring the whole tithe into the storehouse, that there may be food in my house. Test me in this," says the LORD Almighty, "and see if I will not throw open the floodgates of heaven and pour out so much blessing that there will not be room enough to store it. I will prevent pests from devouring your crops, and the vines in your fields will not drop their fruit before it is ripe," says the LORD Almighty. "Then all the nations will call you blessed, for yours will be a delightful land," says the LORD Almighty.*
> (Malachi 3:10–12)

Every time you leave the grocery store with your trunk full of groceries, there's a guy on the street corner with a sign on a piece of cardboard that says, "Help! Feeding 5 hungry kids." He's asking, but should we give to everyone who claims to have a need? Wisdom tells us that a quick buck tossed to the man or woman on the corner rarely goes toward feeding five hungry children. We need godly discernment to recognize a lie. The panhandler is asking for a quick buck, but there are many better ways to feed hungry children. Real help requires that we invest ourselves in the lives of the poor.

Consider how we respond when a brother in Christ asks for a loan to pay his first, last, and rent deposit? We can see that there's little chance he could ever pay it back, but his family needs a home. How can we loan him the money without ruining our friendship when he can't repay? Jesus taught us to make our loans without expecting repayment.[11] If he starts to avoid us because he can't repay; forgive the debt and invite his family to dinner.

---
5. Haggai 1:9.
6. 1 Corinthians 16:2.
7. 2 Corinthians 9:7.
8. Psalm 16:6.
9. Deuteronomy 28:2.
10. Isaiah 28:26.
11. Luke 6:34.

Give to the one who asks you, and do not turn away from the one who wants to borrow from you.
(Matthew 5:42)

Here we stand with our feet in the dirt of the Pharisee's garden again. He has one big bucket marked "mine" and a showy basket marked "God's." He arranges the produce in the show basket to make it look even better as he carries on his arm to the temple. But even when he is offering his gift, he's planning for the first day of the week when he'll evict his poor tenants. His mind stirs with duplicity. He gathers an offering from his garden while his thoughts plot against his neighbor, "I'm taking that knave to court. His goats got through the fence and chewed up my grape vines."

Today's Christians are just as fallible as the religious Pharisees in Jesus' day. We must overcome our tendency to hold on to our stuff too tightly. Do our offerings have to be wrenched from tight fists? Do we open our wallets under protest? Do we zip our purses up after one minor miscalculation by the church treasurer?

Our faith must not become a religion that's all about assets and gaining more and more wealth. We can't focus our faith on one verse that says, "The blessings of the LORD make a person rich?"[12] Posting this verse on our refrigerator along with a picture of a new Mercedes SUV distracts us from the true roots of our faith. Material riches quickly turn into a trap.[13] It's so easy to slip into greed and forget to extend a just and merciful hand to those in trouble.

Agur the son of Jakeh understood the trap of riches and wrote an inspired proverb to warn us. He asked for neither poverty or riches, knowing that riches would cloud his mind and mislead him.[14] The psalmist, David, wrote about self-assured arrogance that tempts those who prosper.[15] His warning keeps us from joining the meticulous Pharisee in his garden weighing out exactly ten percent of everything for the Lord. Jesus calls us instead to practice compassion, generosity, justice, and mercy with cheerfulness as our motto.

Woe to you, teachers of the law and Pharisees, you hypocrites! You give a tenth of your spices–mint, dill and cumin. But you have neglected the more important matters of the law–justice, mercy and faithfulness. You should have practiced the latter, without neglecting the former.
(Matthew 23:23)

---

12. Proverbs 10:22.
13. Revelation 3:17.
14. Proverbs 30:8–9.
15. Psalm 30:6.

Our jean pockets are nearly empty and toes are sticking out of our sneakers. We pull our pockets inside out and one penny falls to the ground. We don't even have two nickels to rub together. Our wallet has no George Washington's in it, let alone any Ben Franklins. Our bank account is fifty-seven-cents from being overdrawn and its four days until pay day. What do we do when we have nothing to give?

Jesus pointed out a poor widow to the disciples because she had an important lesson to teach them. Her example still applies today. She had next to nothing. What she had would buy only a bit of food at the market, so she gave everything to God.

Do you have a stack of debts and past due bills that add up to more than your paycheck? Then offer two small copper coins to your heavenly Father. Do your groceries run out before you have money to buy more? Then give an offering to the One who provides your daily bread. Is your gas tank empty and your credit card maxed? Open your hands and give cheerfully, even if you can only give some of your time. Give what you have to your heavenly Father who makes a way.

These sayings sound great, but let's get real. What do you do when your cell phone service is cancelled and you're stranded on the side of the road with no spare tire? Lift up your empty hands to the LORD who is an ever-present help in time of trouble.[16] Yes, help is on the way. What can you do when the landlord knocks on your front door and you don't have the rent money? Show the LORD your checkbook balance and open the door. The best you can do when you have nothing is to offer something to God who provides. Even if you can only offer your time, apply your hands to the task with joy. Every cheerful giver soon discovers that their offerings grow and grow because heaven's floodgates pour out blessings on those who give with cheerful hearts.[17]

> *But a poor widow came and put in two very small copper coins, worth only a few cents. Calling his disciples to him, Jesus said, "Truly I tell you, this poor widow has put more into the treasury than all the others. They all gave out of their wealth; but she, out of her poverty, put in everything–all she had to live on."* (Mark 12:42–44)

If you need a new pair of shoes and don't have the money yet, do you have to toss ten bucks into the offering basket? No! That's a giving-to-get offering. Instead, we offer up to our heavenly Father what He asks of us. Abra-

---

16. Psalm 46:1.
17. Malachi 3:10.

ham offers an example by giving Melchizedek a tenth of the spoils.[18] The fact that he offered a tenth is not the point. He gave an offering to acknowledge Yahweh as King. Abraham offered a king's portion to the LORD to proclaim Him as his LORD and King.

Who is your King? Who is LORD of all you have been given to manage as a good steward? Be faithful and prove yourself trustworthy in the little you've been given and then you'll be entrusted with much more.[19] God is faithful to His word.

> *Give, and it will be given to you. A good measure, pressed down, shaken together and running over, will be poured into your lap. For with the measure you use, it will be measured to you."*
> (Luke 6:38)

When your bills are all paid, your savings account is plump, and your retirement account shows some nice gains, it's easy to toss an extra twenty-bucks into the offering. But what about those who don't even have enough money to open a savings account? What do people do who are caught in the clutches of extreme poverty? The Macedonian church teaches us what to do. Their money pouches were nearly empty but their hearts overflowed with joyful bounty. They may have had only two denarii to rub together, but they gave one with a cheerful heart. They were rich in their liberality. Giving an offering to the LORD is not about what we have in your pocket, it's about what is in our heart.

> *And now, brothers and sisters, we want you to know about the grace that God has given the Macedonian churches. In the midst of a very severe trial, their overflowing joy and their extreme poverty welled up in rich generosity. For I testify that they gave as much as they were able, and even beyond their ability. Entirely on their own.*
> (2 Corinthians 8:1–3)

Are we bound by the commandments to give an exact tenth of our paycheck? No, we are compelled by the law of love to acknowledge God as our King. This is a higher standard. The righteousness of God is made known to the church apart from the commandments.[20] But, the Mosaic Law still has great value for us today. All those who have died to sin and live in Christ according to the law of love, abide in Christ, who is the fulfillment of even the smallest punctuation mark in the written law.[21] But instead of being bound by the letter of the law, our hearts are free to overflow with generosity, in keeping

---
18. Genesis 14:20.
19. Luke 16:10.
20. Romans 3:21.
21. Matthew 5:18.

with love and wisdom, and according to all that God has provided. Our offerings are not determined by the law, but by our love. And the love of Christ at work in our hearts fulfills God's Law.[22]

> *Each of you should give what you have decided in your heart to give, not reluctantly or under compulsion, for God loves a cheerful giver. For if the willingness is there, the gift is acceptable according to what one has, not according to what one does not have.*
> (2 Corinthians 8:12)

Whether we have little or much, the essential impulse in generosity is the love of Christ that is written on our hearts. We give a portion of our resources to honor God as our LORD and King. Holding what we have in an open hand lifts up the poor and keeps rich fools from building bigger barns.[23]

Cheerful givers offer what they have, whether time or treasure. We "cast our bread upon the water" to help those who have nothing to harvest.[24] A godly person leaves some of the bounty of their fields for the poor to gather.[25]

> Ascribe to the Lord, all you families of nations, ascribe to the LORD glory and strength. Ascribe to the LORD the glory due his name; bring an offering and come into his courts. (Psalm 96:7–8)

---

22. The law of the tithe is found in Deuteronomy 14:22–24.
23. Luke 12:16—21.
24. Ecclesiastes 11:1.
25. Leviticus 19:10.

Chapter 24 Q&A

Awesome Offerings

1. How does the principle of firstfruits apply to Christians today?

2. What can we give that is more valuable than money?

3. If you only have enough money to buy one bag of groceries for your hungry kids, what do you give?

4. How can we mend the proverbial holes in our pockets?

5. How does the law of love affect our hearts and our stewardship?

My Journey's Journal:

Part VI
Children of Promise[1]

Through the praise of children and infants you have established a stronghold against your enemies, to silence the foe and the avenger.
(Psalm 8:2)

Section six of our journey opens the Scriptures to give us feet like a deer to ascend to the heights of true worship and praise. As we are gathered to worship before Jesus Christ, our high priest, forgiveness overflows from our hearts, our spirit wells up with songs, hymns, and spiritual songs, and we lift up our hands to exalt the LORD of Glory.

---

1. Galatians 4:28.

Chapter 25: Songs of Victory

Key Scriptures:

- "The LORD your God is with you, the Mighty Warrior who saves. He will take great delight in you; in his love he will no longer rebuke you, but will rejoice over you with singing" (Zephaniah 3:17).

- "Shouts of joy and victory resound in the tents of the righteous: 'The Lord's right hand has done mighty things!'" (Psalm 118:15).

Family life often centers around the table where the family gathers at mealtimes. There's good cooking and a chair for everyone. The kids enjoy a sense of security as they dig into mom's good food, accompanied by conversations that bond a family together. At the dinner table, each family member has a chance to share about their daily victories. Jimmy Junior reports: "I got an A on my story about Ruff hiding his dog bone." Emmy Lou proudly declares that she in now first chair in the trumpet section. Mom chortles and says, "I'm so proud of you kids."

In this part of our trek up the mountain we'll answer the question; is it possible for a song to lead the way to victory? The grand songs of the church in our playlist are awesome, but the simple choruses of God's kingdom can also be sung out with great power and effect. We'll consider Gideon, Israel's judge. He was the least among the people of Israel but was the right person to lead them to a great victory from which they surely went home with singing. We'll visit Jesus who is gathered with His disciples around a table, offering them a covenantal meal with bread and wine. They concluded the meal with triumphant hymns.

May God's Word inspire victorious songs in our hearts.

A prayer according to Psalm 118:14–15:

Hear our voices, Oh Lord, for you are our strength and our song. You are the hope of our salvation, and we will praise you.

With the mind of Christ, we picture the ascent that looms before us. Our hearts beat with anticipation as we wait at the base camp. Heroes of faith have made the ascent in the years before we came along, and now cheer us along the way. The summit towers above us as we anticipate setting a banner at the peak. We burst from base camp and surge forward with our eyes fixed on the prize.[1] Throbbing pain can't stop us, and we press on through every trial. To reach our goal and win the victory, we give up our own strength so we can ascend to the heights on the wings of the Spirit's wind.

Our eyes blink as we see frames of God's story flash before our eyes. Finally, initiating a new era of history, Immanuel, who is God with us, was conceived in the virgin Mary. She gave birth to a son and named Him Yeshua. He grew up obedient to His parents.[2] Around the time of His thirtieth birthday He was baptized in the Jordan River by John the Baptist. As He came up from the water a mighty witness from heaven proclaimed, "This is my Son, whom I love; with him I am well pleased."[3] Then, after forty day of being tempted in the wilderness, Jesus ministered and served among the people, healing the sick, blessing the children, and teaching the multitudes.

Several years later, during the Passover meal, just a few hours before He was condemned at an illegal trial, Jesus gave us the Lord's supper—a victorious meal where He offered His disciples a meal with bread and wine. The disciple John, who leaned on Jesus' shoulder during the last supper, later wrote as a witness of Christ's victory. He proclaimed the Anointed One and His victory that overcame the world, even our faith.[4] When did John first see the victory of the Lord's table? The hymn they sang, "I will lift up the cup of salvation and call on the name of the Lord"[5] was certainly enlightening. The beautiful hymn, "Shouts of joy and victory resound in the tents of the righteous"[6] surely edified them.

> *"Blessed be Abram by God Most High, Creator of heaven and earth. And praise be to God Most High, who delivered your enemies into your hand."*
> (Genesis 14:19–20)

Let's rewind for a moment to the time God sent an angel to call Gideon as judge and defender of Israel. The first words from heaven's messenger were, "The LORD is with you, mighty warrior." But Gideon was quick to say, "How can I save Israel? My clan is the weakest in Manasseh, and I am

---

1. Philippians 3:14.
2. Luke 2:51.
3. Matthew 3:17.
4. 1 John 5:4.
5. Psalm 116:13.
6. Psalm 118:15.

the least in my family."[7] As the LORD Almighty heard Gideon's response, He may well have said, "Perfect." Indeed, God's power is best manifested in weak vessels.[8] The angel told Gideon to "go in the strength you have and save Israel out of Midian's hand." The man God saw hiding in the winepress was the weakest among men, but ideal for the job. His human abilities were inadequate, but he served a mighty God. This weakling faced an impossible task, but the LORD turned to him and asked a most pertinent question, "Am I not sending you?"[9]

Gideon gathered a sizeable army, but God pruned them down to just three hundred men, who would face an army that swarmed the valley like locusts. The battle tactics given to Gideon were unconventional, unthinkable according to human logic. But Yahweh, who is mighty in battle, defeated their enemies and restored peace to the lands of Israel for forty years with Gideon as their judge. Under his leadership, the LORD ruled over His people.[10] and they worshipped the Lord, praising the God of Israel with sacrifice and song.

> *When Gideon heard the dream and its interpretation, he bowed down and worshiped. He returned to the camp of Israel and called out, "Get up! The LORD has given the Midianite camp into your hands."*
> (Judges 7:15)

When we are led to worship in a way that is spiritual and real, the wind of the Holy Spirit lifts us up to soar on the wings of the wind.[11] The indwelling Spirit of Christ imprints God's Word in our souls as we sing our Savior's new song. The Spirit's breath utters through us so we may overflow with the blessings of spiritual songs. We gather to worship God where we learn to be hearers and doers of God's Word. We are true worshippers who sing out to our God as He has revealed Himself in Christ.

What is one of the best things you can do when enemies surround you? You are kept safe in the presence of God who is mighty in battle when on your knees with hands uplifted in praise. You are secure under the shadow of His wings, in the shelter of the Most High God where shouts of victorious praise echo on the ramparts.

> *"Rather, worship the LORD your God; it is he who will deliver you from the hand of all your enemies."*
> (2 Kings 17:39)

---

7. Judges 6:12–15.
8. 2 Corinthians 12:9.
9. Judges 6:14.
10. Judges 8:23.
11. Psalm 18:10.

Can an army win a battle without real, live ammo? Can troops without rifles and mortars do anything more than stand at their guard post? What weapons and ammunition are most effective when we're confronted with real threats? Can spiritual warfare tactics win the battle? God taught King Jehoshaphat how to fight these battles. The king prayed earnestly for help and the Spirit of the LORD compelled one of the temple singers to tell him, "Do not be discouraged because of this vast army. For the battle is not yours, but God's."[12] Then the king put the most uncommon defenders—a choir—on the front line of battle. This was God's plan to fight against the Moab and Ammonite troops that vastly outnumbered the armies of Israel.

Jehoshaphat chose singers to march before the armed troops and sing praises, exalting Yahweh for the "splendor of His holiness" with songs of thanksgiving. As their voices echoed from the walls of the gorge in the Desert of Jeruel, the LORD ambushed and defeated the invading army's soldiers. All that was left for Israel to do was plunder their enemies' camp and return home with joy. They gathered in Jerusalem to sing praises at the temple, playing harps, lutes, and trumpets.

> *After consulting the people, Jehoshaphat appointed men to sing to the LORD and to praise him for the splendor of his holiness as they went out at the head of the army, saying: "Give thanks to the Lord, for his love endures forever." As they began to sing and praise, the LORD set ambushes against the men of Ammon and Moab and Mount Seir who were invading Judah, and they were defeated.*
> (2 Chronicles 20:21–22)

To win spiritual battles we must first surrender. Not to the enemy, of course. We surrender ourselves, our very life, and all our heart's desires to the LORD who is mighty in battle. We humble ourselves in the sight of the LORD and He lifts us up victorious.[13] We unburden ourselves by being still, knowing that God is sovereign over all.[14] We can let go of tomorrow's worries and cast all our burdens upon the Lord.[15] With the load off our backs, we are joined together with all overcomers in Christ. Every step we take, every word we speak is committed to and conformed to Christ. Jesus, our Redeemer, must be exalted and we must become less.[16] We subscribe to His words of infinite wisdom. We stand firm at the boundaries of God's kingdom and join in the victory over the kingdom of darkness.

---

12. 2 Chronicles 20:15.
13. James 4:10.
14. Psalm 46:10. Be still, in Hebrew is רָפָה râphah, meaning to drop it, let go of it, be quiet.
15. 1 Peter 5:7.
16. John 3:30.

The Father's children are hearers of the Word so we may do what God's love compels us to do.[17] The sons and daughters of the Lord Most High act justly, love mercy, and walk humbly before our heavenly Father.[18] Then in His light, we shine out like the stars. In the bright light of the Son our justification becomes evident in our victorious songs.

> *Commit your way to the Lord; trust in him and he will do this: He will make your righteous reward shine like the dawn, your vindication like the noonday sun.* (Psalm 37:5–6)

With a click we turn off the light before our head snuggles into the pillow. But tomorrow's dreadful troubles don't have an off switch. They try to edge their way back into our thoughts. Putting our ear to the pillow is often like pressing our ear to the rail to hear the train coming with boxcars full of trouble. Thoughts flood our mind about the boss who is going to call us into her office first thing in the morning and inflict wounds with her sharp words.

But we cast these cares upon the LORD so we can get our proper rest. The Good Shepherd makes us lie down in pleasant pastures and leads us beside still waters so that our soul is restored in Him. The Almighty is our shield. The peace God gives us is beyond anything we can understand. He watches over our hearts and minds through the night hours.[19] Then in the morning, we wake up victorious and greet the new day with praise and thanksgiving. Indeed, fear is driven back with songs of a fruitful vineyard that flow out like a sweet fragrance.

> *You will not fear the terror of night, nor the arrow that flies by day, nor the pestilence that stalks in the darkness, nor the plague that destroys at midday.* (Psalm 91:5–6)

Our voices sing out with harmonies of worship to bless the Almighty who is seated in glory, the Son who sits at His right hand, and the Holy Spirit who inspires us to lift up our voices. True exaltations overflowing from our spirit affect every aspect of our lives. What happens as we gather to worship, minister, and serve in Christ's holy presence? The dynamics are awesome, like the shouts of a triumphant army, spreading through the ranks of believers in a wave we press on to victory in Christ.

By the power of the Word and the work of the Holy Spirit, worshippers who gather together are armored up to fight the good fight. Those who come, hungry to hear the Word and then do it, "will be blessed in all they do."[20]

---

17. James 1:22.
18. Micah 6:8.
19. Philippians 4:7.
20. James 1:25.

They are true overcomers, victors in Christ who is worthy of all praise.

> *Strengthen the feeble hands, steady the knees that give way; say to those with fearful hearts, "Be strong, do not fear; your God will come, he will come with vengeance; with divine retribution he will come to save you."*
> (Isaiah 35:3–4)

From the world's point of view, the kingdom of heaven is upside down. Christians surrender to win. People of faith submit to serve under Christ's authority so they may minister and serve with authority. God's sons and daughters yield themselves to gain a great victory.

We surrender to Christ, who has gained the victory, and join him by faith in overcoming the world.[21] In Christ we are not afraid because He has given our enemies into our hand.[22] Many enemies rise against those who are called by Jesus' name. They attempt to shame us. They insult our faith. They try to disuade us from trusting God's promises. But we are strong in the LORD who protects, honors, and gives us hope. Now we can rest, knowing that we are shielded from all harm. We sing out with joy, having nothing to fear for our God has come to rescue us.

> *Therefore, since we are surrounded by such a great cloud of witnesses, let us throw off everything that hinders and the sin that so easily entangles. And let us run with perseverance the race marked out for us, fixing our eyes on Jesus, the pioneer and perfecter of faith. For the joy set before him he endured the cross, scorning its shame, and sat down at the right hand of the throne of God.*
> (Hebrews 12:1–2)

Picture frames of recorded history flash before our eyes like a movie on fast forward. We see the Lord's table as a constant and undeniable reality throughout all time. This victorious table is first revealed in Melchizedek's time and remains a constant for us in our day like the Rock who provides an anchor our lives.

Our weaknesses and past failings served like chains that bound us in sin, but God is a Mighty warrior who saves. We can be sure that our every struggle and failure can be turned around for good. God's Word teaches us that the weapons we use to fight spiritual battles are not the world's weapons. Instead, the Spirit gives us spiritual weapons to destroy strongholds of fear and doubt.[23] We are made overcomers as we abide in Christ victorious who leads us in songs of victory and shouts of triumph over the enemies of the cross.

---

21. 1 John 5:4.
22. Joshua 10:8.
23. 2 Corinthians 10:4.

> Let them sacrifice thank offerings and tell of his works with songs of joy.
> (Psalm 107:22)

Chapter 25 Q&A
Songs of Victory

1. What do you see in the picture frames of history that strengthens your faith?

_____

_____

_____

2. How do you get from being weighed down with past baggage to getting refined into a useful, precious vessel?

_____

_____

_____

3. What are the weapons of spiritual warfare in a Christian's arsenal?

_____

_____

_____

4. What is effect of the victorious songs we sing in the assembly?

_____

_____

_____

My Journey's Journal:

Chapter 26: Worthy Exaltations

Key Scriptures:

- "Through Jesus, therefore, let us continually offer to God a sacrifice of praise—the fruit of lips that openly profess his name" (Hebrews 13:15).

- "They devoted themselves to the apostles' teaching and to fellowship, to the breaking of bread and to prayer. Everyone was filled with awe at the many wonders and signs performed by the apostles" (Acts 2:42–43).

Have you ever noticed the light in the face of a baby when he sees his mom? When she comes to care for and feed him, he reaches out for mother, who takes him in her arms and lifts him from the crib. His little tummy is empty and he cries out for mother's milk.

This segment of our ascent takes us on a journey with Psalm 48 as our guiding light. We'll follow the tribes of Israel, whose spiritual hunger inspired them to make a pilgrimage, going up the mountains to Jerusalem with songs of ascent. They walked in Abraham's footsteps on the path he followed as he searched for a heavenly city. We join them to walk in his steps because his footprints point the way forward to the greatest goal, Jesus Christ in us, the hope of glory.

> A prayer according to Amos 5:24:
>
> Let our songs be of justice that rolls on like a river. May justice and righteousness flow like a never-failing stream.

Look to the hills and then ascend to the mountain of the LORD because He is the source of all the help you need. In ancient Israel, people made the journey from the lush plains of the Jordan valley. They traveled up the narrow path along the steep cliffs of the mountainside on their way to Jerusalem with singing. Their hearts were filled with anticipation of the moment the great city would come into view on the horizon. They sang out with God's praises to prepare their hearts to enter through the gates of the city where God dwelt among men.[1]

---
1. Revelation 22:14.

We too serve the awesome and unchanging God who is holy, righteous, and abounds with mercy. We press on so we may come to this awesome place of worship where we sing with exaltations before God Most High. He is the great I AM, who is worthy of all praise and glory.

> *Great is the Lord, and most worthy of praise, in the city of our God,*
> *his holy mountain.*
> (Psalm 48:1)

Abraham's footsteps left imprints throughout the land that Yahweh promised to him and his seed.[2] He traveled as far north as the great tree of Moreh at Shechem.[3] He pressed on in his constant search for a city whose builder and maker is God.[4] His heart was overwhelmed with God's promise, and he felt the urge to step onto every field, rolling hill, and mountain, drinking from the springs of promise. His soul's yearning compelled him to search for an eternal city with firm foundations whose designer and builder is the Creator of heaven and earth.

With eyes of faith, he looked forward to see the city's beautiful preeminence in a land of milk and honey. He looked to the mountains to see a city lifted above all others. He climbed on the trails from the valley to the mountain top where his eyes searched as far as he could see. What he found was an eternal hope, a hope that purifies.[5]

Why was Abram so passionate in his search? Did he know the foundations were built with twelve precious stones? Was he persistent because he knew the city would have great, high walls and twelve gates with his son's names engraved on them?[6] Could he have known the streets would be paved with pure gold, so pure they appeared to be transparent as glass?[7] He pressed on because the Father's holy presence encompassed him. By faith, and on a pathway of many troubles and trials, he searched for the promise. Through eyes of faith and hope he saw a city with eternal foundations that God prepared for him and all who come to Christ with a faith like his. As we walk in Abraham's footsteps, our hearts burst out with joyful worship to the LORD God who is above all gods.

> *Beautiful in its loftiness, the joy of the whole earth, like the heights of Zaphon*
> *is Mount Zion, the city of the Great King. God is in her citadels; he has shown*
> *himself to be her fortress.*
> (Psalm 48:2–3)

---

2. Galatians 3:16.
3. Genesis 12:6.
4. Hebrews 11:10.
5. 1 John 3:3.
6. Revelation 21:11–12.
7. Revelation 21:21.

Blessed are all those who hear and believe. We've read the eyewitness accounts recorded by the authors of the four Gospels. The word they proclaimed still plants the seed of faith in our hearts so we may believe that Jesus is the Christ, the only Son of the Living God, who paid the penalty for our sin. Now, with eyes of faith, we enter the city whose builder and designer is God. We receive our Savior's redemptive gift and run to this great city of refuge where we are encompassed in the Father's loving arms, safe and secure from all harm.

The LORD Almighty is robed in majesty and armed with strength. He established the heavens and earth and holds them in the hallow of His hands.[8] He leads us to Mount Zion where our hearts overflow with praise and exaltations.

As we have heard, so we have seen in the city of the LORD Almighty, in the city of our God: God makes her secure forever.
(Psalm 48:8)

We come to the altar of worship to exalt our heavenly Father, who abounds with great and eternal love. Because of His love, He provides a haven of rest where we lie down in pleasant, green pastures. In compassion for His people, the Good Shepherd leads us to His flowing fountain of living water, where we drink deeply and are fully satisfied. Our God's goodness and love follow us every day of our lives,[9] and He is worthy of all praise.

We are separated from the world to follow Christ who leads us into quiet, peace, comfort, rest, security, and faithfulness. Now we are ready to meditate in the safety of our heavenly Father's sanctuary and stand in His loving counsels. The reflections of our hearts cause us to flow out with words of loving worship to honor and glorify our LORD and Savior, who has loved us first.[10]

Within your temple, O God, we meditate on your unfailing love.
(Psalm 48:9)

Victorious shouts rise from the joyful assembly of saints as they ascend to Mount Zion. Worshipful voices are heard praising the Almighty's holy name on every continent and island, giving testimony of His goodness, mercy, and power to save. God's messengers carry the good news and show the mighty works of His strong arm. The gospel message is proven to be true by God's awesome acts—signs of His righteousness, justice, and faithfulness. Faith and hope enlighten us to see the glory of this great city our God builds with precious stones. We stand surrounded by a great cloud of witnesses, a mighty chorus that sings of God's power and might to save.

---

8. Psalm 93:1.
9. Psalm 23:6.
10. 1 John 4:19.

Like your name, O God, your praise reaches to the ends of the earth; your right hand is filled with righteousness. (Psalm 48:10)

Through eyes of faith, we see the city whose builder and maker is God. The bride of Christ longs to see God's promises.[11] When is the Bridegroom coming? Our eyes get sleepy. We yawn and ask, "How long, Oh, LORD?" We keep our lamps trimmed and filled with oil. We check them again to be sure we are ready. We blink away the sleep, and with great hope in our hearts, we know there is a dwelling place being prepared for us where we will be called "Hephzibah" and "Beulah."[12] The bride rejoices with jubilant expectations and sings her songs of delight to the One who has redeemed her. When the truths we sing become part of our daily thoughts, it keeps the flame of faith burning. Songs that we apply to our everyday work, are great treasures that become evident to those around us.

Mount Zion rejoices, the villages of Judah are glad because of your judgments. (Psalm 48:11)

When God's people consider this great city, they stand in awe as they reflect on its beauty, majesty, and perfection.[13] A sense of humility washes over us as we meditate on the perfection of her majestic temple, bulwarks, and fortifications. The perfect design draws us to enter its gates. With our unrighteousness cleansed away, and the righteousness of Christ wrapped around us as our own, we enter His gates with songs of thanksgiving for our children to hear and then sing in harmony.

Walk about Zion, go around her, count her towers, consider well her ramparts, view her citadels, that you may tell of them to the next generation. (Psalm 48:12–13)

There is great comfort in the promise of eternal life, but we need a guide to get us there. With Jesus as our Shepherd, "nothing can ever separate us from God's love. Neither death nor life, neither angels nor demons, neither our fears for today nor our worries for tomorrow—not even the powers of hell can separate us from God's love. No power in the sky above or in the earth below—indeed, nothing in all creation will ever be able to separate us from the love of God that is revealed in Christ Jesus our LORD."[14] Christ's eternal promise keeps on giving by holding us secure and keeping our feet from slipping from His pathway. We serve a Savior who is worthy of all praise, honor, and glory because of His mighty, everlasting acts on behalf of the sheep of His pasture.

---

11. Psalm 119:82.
12. Isaiah 62:4. Hepzibah means "my delight is in you." Beulah means "married."
13. Ezekiel 43:10–11.
14. Romans 8:38:39.

For this God is our God for ever and ever; he will be our guide even to the end. (Psalm 48:14)

We stand on the heights in Abraham's footprints, and with eyes of faith, we see the mighty works that God has done. Our eyes are opened to see the strong right arm of the LORD raised in triumph.[15] In our heavenly Father's awesome presence our knees bow down, we lift our hands to offer sacrifices of praise, and our voices shout victorious exaltations.

God has gathered a people to proclaim His praise.[16] Worthy acclamations of the bride of Christ are true to the design of the sanctuary where we gather to worship the LORD who is worthy of all praise.

> Ascribe to the LORD the glory due his name; worship the LORD in the splendor of his holiness. (Psalm 29:2)

Chapter 26 Q&A

Worthy Exaltations

1. Where is the city of our great and eternal hope?

2. Describe the joy of gathering with the congregation to stand on the heights and offer up worthy exaltations.

3. What is the affectionate name your beloved calls you?

---

15. Psalm 118:16 NLT.
16. Isaiah 43:21.

My Journey's Journal:

Chapter 27 : Our High Priest's Ministry

Key Scriptures:

- "For this reason he had to be made like them, fully human in every way, in order that he might become a merciful and faithful high priest in service to God, and that he might make atonement for the sins of the people" (Hebrews 2:17).

- "Now the main point of what we are saying is this: We do have such a high priest, who sat down at the right hand of the throne of the Majesty in heaven, and who serves in the sanctuary, the true tabernacle set up by the LORD, not by a mere human being. Every high priest is appointed to offer both gifts and sacrifices, and so it was necessary for this one also to have something to offer" (Hebrews 8:1–3).

These steps on our ascent lead us to reflect on Jesus, who powerfully serves before His disciples present and future. His awesome ministry is present with us today, covering us in the shadow of His wings.[1] Our Savior ascended to the right hand of the Father, where He continues to advocate on our behalf and intercede for us constantly.

Jesus Christ, our high priest, knows our every pain, grief, and suffering. Our heartaches touch the chords of His heart, and He sends the Holy Spirit to comfort us. He ministers forgiveness and healing to us. But we must be sure we are not like religious elite of Jesus' day who refused to receive Him.

Our Savior and LORD offered Himself as a once-for-all, sufficient sacrifice for our sin. Our sins are no longer just covered, they are cleansed away because we have a high priest who is made perfect forever.

A prayer according to John 17:3–5:

Teach us, O Lord, so that we may know you as the only true God, and reveal our LORD Jesus Christ, whom you have sent, so that we may be sent out in the authority of Jesus' name to accomplish the good work you gave us to do.

---

[1]. For a teaching on the topic of Jesus' wings, see chapter 11, in the author's book, *The Greatest Love*.

Jesus taught His followers so that they would have peace, and then He said, "In this world you will have trouble. But take heart! I have overcome the world."[2] While the disciples were still trying to grasp this truth, Jesus continued to pray and glorify God. The hour had come for God's only Son to be glorified for the glory of His Father.[3] His prayer honored the Father, who proclaimed by a sure oath that He would establish His Son with authority and place all things under His feet.[4] His words still draws all those to whom He has granted eternal life and teaches them to know His Father as the only true God. By His word, the chosen believe and receive Christ as Savior, recognizing Him as the Son of God, Immanuel, that is, God with us.

He spoke the words of a true Son, who ministers and serves under authority. He prayed saying, "And now, Father, glorify me in your own presence with the glory that I had with you before the world existed."[5] He prayed these powerful words, knowing that on the following day He would offer His body to be broken and His blood to be shed for the sins of the whole world. Jesus' words open our eyes of faith to see Christ as the glorified One, who is the guarantor of a new and better covenant. Today is the day that you are called into covenant with Christ who redeems you.

Because of this oath, Jesus has become the guarantor of a better covenant. (Hebrews 7:22)

Jesus' work among the people of Israel offers a beautiful foretaste of His high priestly ministries on our behalf today. He is our prince who ministers before us at Mount Zion's gates. He is our advocate. He serves as our defense attorney, who presents our case before heaven's courts of justice. He pleads for mercy, knowing that the Father's mercy always prevails over judgment.[6]

We serve with the mind of Christ in the light of His ministries. He is more than able to save every soul whom the Father has given Him for His own. His salvation is complete, making us entirely new creations. The Spirit of Christ draws us with the words we hear from the holy Scriptures, planting the seeds of faith in our hearts. Faith blossoms as we come to God through Jesus, the Christ. We are baptized into Christ to wash away our sins, and He makes us whole as functioning parts of His body, the Church. We can be sure that through every moment of our walk of faith, we have One who intercedes on our behalf. He knows our pain, grief, and sorrow and advocates for us before the throne of grace. He is worthy of all praise, glory, and honor.

---

2. John 16:33.
3. John 17:1–4.
4. Ephesians 1:22.
5. John 17:1–5.
6. James 2:13.

Because Jesus lives forever, he has a permanent priesthood. Therefore he is able to save completely those who come to God through him, because he always lives to intercede for them.
(Hebrews 7:24–25)

We will not toss aside our confidence in Christ, because in Him there is great reward.[7] We live by faith and persevere in doing God's will, knowing that He is living and actively present with us. He is all sufficient for every need, especially in time of trouble. We come to the One who knows our every heart's cry even before we pray. He knows us better than we know ourselves because He formed our very beings and knit us together in our mother's womb.[8] He walked among us on the dusty roads of Galilee with no home where He could lay his head.[9] He became homeless so He could prepare an eternal home for us. He was tempted and tried just as we are, and yet He remained blameless—for He is holy. He sat down at the dinner table with tax collectors and remained faultless.

Jesus walked among us as fully man and fully God. But the pious Pharisees of the day refused to accept God among them. He taught in their synagogues where the religious elite falsely accused Him of violating their rules. The teachers of the law could not see that He was the exalted Son of God, and demanded that He be crucified. But Jesus rose up victorious and now serves and ministers as our High Priest.

Such a high priest truly meets our need–one who is holy, blameless, pure, set apart from sinners, exalted above the heavens.
(Hebrews 7:26)

Jesus Christ is the Lamb of God who is the perfect and unblemished sacrifice. He is the once-and-for-all-time sacrificial Lamb who takes away the sins of the world.[10] Those who lived in the shadow of Christ under the law were required to make many animal sacrifices to cover their sin. But Jesus offered up own His body and blood as a final sacrifice, sufficient for all time. His sacrifice does more than just cover our sins, His blood washes away our sin and every stain of it, "so that we might die to sins and live for righteousness."[11] In this cleansing flow we are made spotless to the very depths of our soul. The weight of our guilty conscience is washed away so we may serve.[12]

---

7. Hebrews 10:35.
8. Psalm 139:13.
9. Matthew 8:20.
10. John 1:29.
11. 1 Peter 2:24.
12. Hebrews 9:14.

Unlike the other high priests, he does not need to offer sacrifices day after day, first for his own sins, and then for the sins of the people. He sacrificed for their sins once for all when he offered himself.
(Hebrews 7:27)

Israel's high priests were anointed, served the people during their lifetime, and then went on to their reward.[13] Those in the lineage of Aaron's priesthood were flawed, mortal men who were required to first offer sacrifices for their own sins. Then, with their own sins covered, they could offer sacrifices for the sins of the people.

Today, we have a Savior who is eternal. He is perfect in holiness. Our Redeemer was tempted just as we are but did not sin. Now He wraps us in His robe of righteousness with loving arms. Our high priest is Jesus Christ who died in our place to pay the debt of our sin. By His vicarious death, burial, and resurrection He defeated sin, Satan, and the grave. Now we have an advocate who is holy and presents us as holy before our heavenly Father. Our Good Shepherd keeps us safe in His fold, separating us from all who would do us harm. In Christ Jesus, we have an all-sufficient high priest who is made higher than the heavens and who sits at the right hand of God to make intercessions on our behalf.

He is worthy of all praise, and honor, and glory.

For the law appoints as high priests men in all their weakness; but the oath, which came after the law, appointed the Son, who has been made perfect forever.
(Hebrews 7:28)

Our high priest, Jesus Christ, serves to unite those who are called to believe in Him through the testimony of the gospel. He serves as our defense attorney. He pleads our case, knowing our human weaknesses and our failings. Day and night He pleads for mercy before the throne of grace on our behalf.

Our Savior serves to make sure that every good work He has begun in us is brought to completion. Jesus' high priestly ministries are an essential element in the design of God's holy sanctuary where we gather to worship in His presence.

> It is he who will build the temple of the Lord, and he will be clothed with majesty and will sit and rule on his throne. And he will be a priest on his throne. (Zechariah 6:13)

---

13. Hebrews 7:23.

Chapter 27 Q&A

Our High Priest's Ministry

1. Describe the power and effect of Jesus' high priestly prayer for the church today?

   _____
   _____
   _____

2. Why is it so comforting to be aware of Jesus' living and active presence in our daily lives?

   _____
   _____
   _____

3. Why does the postmodern church still need the ministry of a high priest?

   _____
   _____
   _____

My Journey's Journal:

Chapter 28: Our High Priest's Prayer

Key Scriptures:

- "I pray for them. I am not praying for the world, but for those you have given me, for they are yours" (John 17:9).

- "My prayer is not that you take them out of the world but that you protect them from the evil one" (John 17:15).

John chapter 17 records the greatest and most powerful prayer recorded for all time. The One who prayed this prayer intercedes for each one of us who are called by His name. Jesus prayed for all His disciples, and His prayer is timeless. We know He prayed in agreement with God's perfect purpose and plan. He is the high priest of the church and He offered His prayer for all who would come to saving faith. He made a powerful appeal on behalf of all who are His. His prayer binds us together in a unity of faith.

This segment of our climb to God's holy mountain opens our minds to understand the power of Jesus' words. He prayed a timeless prayer drawing all of history together like threads of pure silver and gold woven from the beginning of time until the end—an Alpha and Omega prayer. Come, let's enter into agreement and receive the blessings of Jesus' high priestly prayer.

> A prayer according to 2 Corinthians 2:15:
>
> Oh Lord, may the aroma of Christ flow out from your people as we gather to glorify God. May the fragrant fruit of the Spirit be evident in our worship so that those who are being saved will be drawn to Christ with repentant hearts.

Christians tend to seek a pastor's prayers more than anyone else's, thinking that he has a special hotline to heaven. The truth is, that a prayer of faith by any righteous person is powerful and effective.[1] But how can we pray effectively? What makes our intercessions effectual? Priests who serve in the priesthood of all believers have access before our Heavenly Father. Now consider Jesus' intercessions for all His followers. There is no doubt that He

---

1. James 5:16.

prayed in accord with the Father's will and in agreement with all that God purposed for His church. We see His prayers answered in every generation. It is Christ and His prayers that cover us and lead us into the Father's holy presence where we make our petitions in agreement with Jesus' name.

Jesus prayed for the seed of faith to be planted in the hearts of all those who will hear the good news. This gospel seed sprouts and then gets grafted into the true Vine. He petitioned the Father that we may grow to be one in Him and draw on His strength and vitality. His prayer is for us to be fruitful branches nourished by the Vine so we may bear abundant fruit. These splendid branches display plentiful fruit to bear witness to the world that Christ is more than able to save. The fragrance of Christ in us is carried by the wind of the Spirit to beckon the world to come and partake of the fruit of the Vine.

> *"I pray also for those who will believe in me through their message, that all of them may be one, Father, just as you are in me and I am in you. May they also be in us so that the world may believe that you have sent me."*
> (John 17:20–21)

God's glory is miraculous and radiates throughout all creation. The Father glorifies the Son, and the Son glorifies the Father's holy name. Then the LORD of glory responds to the Son with a voice from heaven, saying, "I have glorified it, and will glorify it again.[2]

This is the glory that the Father gives to the Son, and now Jesus extends His glory to all God's sons and daughters so that we may be brought to complete unity, and pray effectively in agreement with Jesus' prayer. The glory of the Father, Son, and Holy Spirit becomes so evident in His people that the world can't help but see that Christ Jesus was sent to redeem us, break the chains of darkness, and give us freedom to run on His pathway. We are set free so we may shine out with His light and lift up the name of Christ Jesus so that all those whose lives we touch will be drawn to Him.[3]

When we come together to glorify the Lord, His name is exalted.[4] When Christ is glorified in us, we are joined together with one mind and voice for the glory of God, the Father of our LORD Jesus Christ.[5]

> *"I have given them the glory that you gave me, that they may be one as we are one–I in them and you in me–so that they may be brought to complete unity. Then the world will know that you sent me and have loved them even as you have loved me."*
> (John 17:22–23)

---

2. John 12:28.
3. John 12:32.
4. Psalm 34:3.
5. Romans 15:6.

We give glory to our LORD and Savior as we complete the good work God has given us to do during our time on earth. When we serve faithfully in our calling, He brings our efforts to fruition and God receives all the glory. Then, at the end of our days, we can stand shoulder to shoulder with Paul and say, "I have fought the good fight, I have finished the race, I have kept the faith."[6]

The glory of our Savior Jesus was manifested by God's love for Him before the first day of creation. Before time began, Jesus was given a work to do—a redemptive, love-inspired work. As the Word spoke and all things were created in the beginning, He looked forward in time to see the cross. Then, at the right time, His finished work on the cross and glorified the Father so that we may see His eternal glory.

> *"Father, I want those you have given me to be with me where I am, and to see my glory, the glory you have given me because you loved me before the creation of the world."*
> (John 17:24)

What is this great love? No greater love has ever been known than the love of Christ who laid down His life for His friends.[7] Our Savior willingly gave His body to be broken. He was scourged, spit upon, had a crown of thorns pressed onto His head, and then endured as nails were driven into His hands and feet on a roughhewn Roman cross. Because of His overwhelming love, He gave up His very life blood to pay the sin debt of all mankind.

All those who believe and confess that Jesus is the Christ are adopted as children of the Most High.[8] Those who by faith believe Jesus walked among us as Immanuel, and are baptized into the Father, Son, and Holy Spirit are made children of resurrection.[9] In Christ we are adopted as sons and daughters of God Most High. Now He gathers us in His loving arms as His friends and covers us in the wings of His high priest's prayer.

> *"Righteous Father, though the world does not know you, I know you, and they know that you have sent me. I have made you known to them, and will continue to make you known in order that the love you have for me may be in them and that I myself may be in them."*
> (John 17:25–26)

The fervent prayers God's people send up are sure to bear fruit because we pray in agreement with all that Jesus first prayed for us. Our Savior inter-

---

6. 2 Timothy 4:7.
7. John 15:13.
8. Psalm 82:6.
9. Luke 20:36.

ceded for all who God gave to Him, and the fruit of His prayer continues to waft out like a sweet fragrance in the Garden of God.

When Jesus prayed, He covered all the sheep of His pasture with the glory of the Father and Son. This glory then shines out through us to give testimony to the world. The people we rub elbows with can see God's mighty work in our everyday lives. They can't help but notice the bond of love that unites us with Christ.

With an abundance of love, God planned to gather us as a family even before time began. This love is the primary thread that Jesus wove into His prayer and is the tie that binds together all those who are called by His holy name.

> He tends his flock like a shepherd: He gathers the lambs in his arms and carries them close to his heart; he gently leads those that have young.
> (Isaiah 40:11)

Chapter 28 Q&A

Our High Priest's Prayer

1. Describe how the prayers of God's people come together in agreement with Jesus' high priestly prayer.

2. What is the key factor that makes our prayers and Jesus' prayer shine out to the world around us?

3. Why is this primary thread, woven into our prayers so vital to true worshippers?

My Journey's Journal:

Chapter 29: Forgiveness

Key Scriptures:

- For he has rescued us from the dominion of darkness and brought us into the kingdom of the Son he loves, in whom we have redemption, the forgiveness of sins" (Colossians 1:13–14).

- In him we have redemption through his blood, the forgiveness of sins, in accordance with the riches of God's grace that he lavished on us. With all wisdom and understanding" (Ephesians 1:7–8).

Without forgiveness, a gathering is not real church. Apart from forgiveness there can be no true fellowship. We all need a safe place where we can pour out our hearts to trusted friends. They know our wrongs and our troubles. Our godly friends show us a lot of mercy and still love us. The perfect place for this ought to be in our gatherings in Jesus' name. Where two or three are gathered in Jesus' name, He is present with us to forgive. This makes our worship assemblies the truest and safest environment for forgiveness.

We may be able to offer proofs of our innocence, but they fall short of complete holiness, showing we're still in need of a Savior. The burden of sin remains and needs to be lifted. How do we want to be forgiven? We show the way we desire to be absolved of our sin by the way we release others from the guilt caused by the harm they have done to us. The Scriptures lead us to throw out the account we've kept of others' offences.

We release our friends from the guilt of the wrong they have done to us. But, what about the consequences? They serve a good purpose—to restrain further sin.

When we begin our worship gatherings with forgiveness, our hearts are opened to worship freely from our spirit. We assemble to exalt our heavenly Father, with Jesus serving as our high priest. By His command, those who minister among us have authority by Christ's command to release a sinner from the burden of guilt.[1] As a forgiven and cleansed church, we come to

---
1. John 20:23.

Jesus, and worship before Him in harmony, raising unclenched hands without anger.[2] In the light of the Word, our sins are exposed and we are compelled to turn from our offences and repent. Then, with contrite hearts, we are prepared to enter the sweet harmony of true worship.

> A prayer according to John 16:8:
>
> Come LORD Jesus, convict us of our sinful, wandering ways. May our repentant hearts turn to you so we may be forgiven and cleansed of all unrighteousness. Wash us clean so we may lift up holy hands to you with reverence and awe.

Pouring your heart out to your buddies at the pub may give you a sense of release from your troubles. But when the bar closes for the night, their approvals and affirmations have done more harm than good. When you need help in time of trouble, there is a Rock where you can anchor your life, and He won't turn your life into a barstool spin.

Church ought to provide a better and safer place for us to be vulnerable. James instructs us to "confess your sins to each other and pray for each other so that you may be healed."[3] Our gatherings should offer a sanctuary where we can be open about our temptations, weaknesses, and failings. This doesn't mean that we have to stand up and shock the congregation with our sins. It's best to pour out our hearts to trusted confidants who offer God's Word as true counsel, keep us accountable, and pray for us earnestly.

A gathering for worship is an assembly of contrite sinners who are saved by grace. There will also be some who are drawn by the Holy Spirit to hear the gospel calling them to repentance. We bow our hearts and join in their repentant plea for forgiveness because we are forgiven and redeemed sinners.

We come into our high priest's sanctuary as repentant sinners. In this holy place it's safe to repent so we may receive Christ's abundant compassion and mercy.

Whoever conceals their sins does not prosper, but the one who confesses and renounces them finds mercy.
(Proverbs 28:13)

We must not trample heaven's courts of justice.[4] It's human nature to try offering a sacrifice of our own making. We justify ourselves by compiling evidence of the great things we have done and add it to our resumé. We give generously to support our claim of a devoted life. But when we present our

---
2. 1 Timothy 2:8.
3. James 5:16.
4. Isaiah 1:12.

boxes full of proofs, our Advocate puts them aside, saying, "You are in need of a Savior. These things cannot redeem you. I have purchased your forgiveness with my shed blood, and that is sufficient."

> *"Come now, let us settle the matter," says the LORD. "Though your sins are like scarlet, they shall be as white as snow; though they are red as crimson, they shall be like wool."*
> (Isaiah 1:18)

Do you want to be completely forgiven? Then forgive in the same way. Do you forgive while still determined to hold it against the person who harmed you? You'll be forgiven in the same way. Do you forgive but make the offender pay dearly for their wrong? You'll be forgiven in the same way. Is your style of forgiveness to never let the offender forget the wrong they did to you? You will be forgiven in the same way.

In forgiveness we put aside our right to retribution. We place our entitlements for victim paybacks on the altar of forgiveness. We do this because it's the only right response to Jesus' generous forgiveness of us. Our Savior knows this is the only way to heal our wounds. When we generously forgive, we can take comfort in knowing we will be forgiven in the same way.

> *For if you forgive other people when they sin against you, your heavenly Father will also forgive you. But if you do not forgive others their sins, your Father will not forgive your sins.*
> (Matthew 6:14–15)

We know it's not right to hold a counter in our hand and click it every time we forgive until we reach seventy-seven times—then the offender is toast. But does this mean we are required to forgive instantly and act like nothing ever happened?

As we hear the truth of Jesus' teaching, it's important to understand that His numbers declare a greater truth than clicks on a tally counter. Some translations record Jesus' words as "seventy times seven." If you do the math, the most you must forgive is 490 times. Is this what Jesus is really teaching us? We can turn to the book of Daniel to see this truth in the proper light. He was inspired to prophesy, "Seventy 'sevens' are decreed for your people and your holy city to finish transgression, to put an end to sin, to atone for wickedness, to bring everlasting righteousness."[5]

With abundant mercy, Yahweh brought about Israel's forgiveness and restoration by imposing consequences that put an end to their sin and idolatry. This truth teaches us that genuine forgiveness often calls for consequences.

---

5. Daniel 9:24.

Here is an extreme example. We can forgive someone who attempted to murder us, but forgiveness does not require us to invite them back into our home. That would not be wise or safe. A pastor who betrays the trust of the people can be forgiven, but he needs a time of separation from ministry to bring an end to his transgressions. But always remember the end purpose of exile is restoration to fellowship in Christ.

We serve an awesome God who abounds with forgiveness and mercy. He is longsuffering with us and forgives us even more than 490 times. Our God of mercy and forgiveness is worthy of all praise and honor and glory.

> *Then Peter came to Jesus and asked, "LORD, how many times shall I forgive my brother or sister who sins against me? Up to seven times?" Jesus answered, "I tell you, not seven times, but seventy-seven times."*
> (Matthew 18:21–22)

What would happen if worship gatherings began with confessing our sins and receiving forgiveness?[6] Consider the atmosphere of grace and mercy created in our gatherings when we begin by making peace with others whom we may have offended. Confession and forgiveness create a powerful setting for prophetic ministry, teaching, preaching the gospel, prayers and petitions, psalms of praise, and spiritual songs.

Confession and forgiveness lift the load of guilt from us so the Spirit of Christ may come like a pent-up flood.[7] When we hold to this teaching, the Spirit breathes new life into us so we may worship in a way that is spiritual and real. Following Jesus' teaching is like a breath of fresh air for our spirit so we may sing out with the joy of our salvation.

> *"And when you stand praying, if you hold anything against anyone, forgive them, so that your Father in heaven may forgive you your sins."*
> (Mark 11:25)

Forgiveness is a key element in the design of the church. If sins are not washed away, how can we call it church? In forgiving others, we fulfill our calling and true purpose. By Jesus' command we are given the authority to do the good work of releasing sinners from the chains of their sin. By the power of Jesus' name, the crushing burden of depravity is removed from our shoulders. It's as if we come into our assemblies lugging a bag of black coal. Then, in forgiveness it is lifted away. Even the stain of it is gone forever and our conscience is clear.

When we need forgiveness, where can we go? We run to a safe sanctuary where forgiveness is generously offered. We come to Jesus, our high priest

---

6. Matthew 5:23–24.
7. Isaiah 59:19.

who gave His blood to be shed for the forgiveness of our sin. This cleansing fountain is ours to wash away all unrighteousness. This abundant mercy is pictured for us in the Pentateuch as the priest takes the basket from the hand of those who were once enslaved and places it before the altar.[8] He takes the produce from the sweat of a man's labor, Adam's curse, and places it before the Lord.[9] This is the forgiveness we have in Christ.

> *Again Jesus said, "Peace be with you! As the Father has sent me, I am sending you." And with that he breathed on them and said, "Receive the Holy Spirit. If you forgive anyone's sins, their sins are forgiven; if you do not forgive them, they are not forgiven."*
> (John 20:21–23)

If we are unable forgive each other, it's impossible to worship together. Our discordant songs are an affront to heaven and we might as well lock the doors and go home. If the congregation is divided into groups with opposing ambitions, our gatherings turn into chaos. It's like having voices singing different songs in various keys. We're all out of tune. Instead, we're called to gather in Jesus' holy name under his spirit of forgiveness so that we may sing out in harmony with the true gospel.

Let's begin our worship with mercy and forgiveness. This is not just a ritual of prescribed confessions and absolution, but genuinely admitting our wrongs, receiving Christ's forgiveness, and forgiving others. If we have been offended, or if we have harmed anyone, we must make it right before we open our mouths to minister and sing out with praise. In forgiveness, our voices are brought into harmonious worship.

> *Bear with each other and forgive one another if any of you has a grievance against someone. Forgive as the LORD forgave you.*
> (Colossians 3:13)

Confessing our negligence, harmful words, and outright sinful acts requires a humble and contrite heart. We enter the presence of Jesus, our high priest, where He leads the congregation to sing His new song. We come into the light of Christ where our sin-bent ways come to light and we're compelled to repent and make things right with our brothers and sisters in our gathering. Then, the Spirit of Christ brings us together in a harmony of grace and mercy. With our hearts washed clean, we are free to lift holy hands to exalt our heavenly Father, our LORD and Savior, and the Holy Spirit who empowers us to shout out with joyful acclamations.

---

8. Deuteronomy 26:1–11, Psalm 81:6.
9. Genesis 3:19.

If we confess our sins, he is faithful and just and will forgive us our sins and purify us from all unrighteousness.
(1 John 1:9)

We enter worship gatherings as sinners saved by grace. This is a safe place where we're forgiven and cleansed so we may ascend to the heights and worship. When a church begins a gathering with confession of sins and receiving forgiveness, the way is opened to spiritual and real worship.

Life stories of the heroes of our faith remind us that forgiveness does not preclude discipline. But we are confident that the consequence of our offences serves to restrain further sin and strengthen us in hope. This vital element of worship frees God's people to overflow with joyful exaltations upon the mountain of the Lord.

> Be exalted, O God, above the heavens; let your glory be over all the earth. My heart, O God, is steadfast, my heart is steadfast; I will sing and make music. Awake, my soul! Awake, harp and lyre! I will awaken the dawn.
> (Psalm 57:5, 7–8)

Chapter 29 Q&A

Forgiveness

1. How can a church create a welcoming atmosphere that draws people to Christ?

2. Why is a chair in church better than a bar stool?

3. Why is it important to consider how we forgive others?

4. When we're forgiven, what good purpose do consequences serve?

5. Why is forgiveness so vital to harmonious worship?

My Journey's Journal:

Part VII
Praise of Children and Infants

Through the praise of children and infants you have established a stronghold against your enemies, to silence the foe and the avenger.
(Psalm 8:2)

The seventh segment of our ascent leads us to a child-like faith so we can let go of anything that weighs us down as we continue our pilgrimage up God's holy mountain.

Chapter 30 : Lift up Holy Hands

Key Scriptures:

- "Therefore I want the men everywhere to pray, lifting up holy hands without anger or disputing" (1 Timothy 2:8).

- "May my prayer be set before you like incense; may the lifting up of my hands be like the evening sacrifice" (Psalm 141:2).

This part of our ascent opens our eyes to see the One who inspires us to lift our hands in worship. Our physical hands have no spiritual power of their own; they were designed to do good things like hold, sooth, lift, twist, and grip. But when our hands are placed in Jesus' hands, they become powerful means of worship and ministry through the Holy Spirit. What are the awesome forces that compel us to lift up holy hands? We have a risen Savior who gave Himself as a perfect, final, and all-sufficient sacrifice for the sins of the world and is worthy of all glory, honor, and praise.

Extending our hands to exalt our heavenly Father is an all-of-us-together kind of praise as each of us supports, strengthens, and lifts the others up. We will look at the great gathering at the dedication of the temple Solomon built for God's holy name. The prayer he offered with uplifted hands set the course for Israel's worship for centuries. When Ezra called the people together to hear the law read, they were compelled to lift up their roughened and calloused hands that rebuilt Jerusalem's walls and temple.

> A prayer according to Psalm 141:2:
>
> Oh Lord, may our lifted hands be like incense before you. May our hands extended to worship you be accepted like an evening sacrifice.

Jesus, our high priest, fulfilled all the demands of sacrificial law when He offered His body to be broken and His blood to be shed to pay the sin debt of all humankind. Jesus is the perfect, once and for all time Lamb of God, given as a sacrificial offering and the ransom to redeem us. His beard was plucked out, and was scourged, spit upon, beaten with a cat-of-nine-tails, and nailed to the cross for our transgressions.[1] Jesus' perfect sacrifice was received as all sufficient. His sacrifice was a fragrant aroma, better than the burnt offerings offered outside the camp. In Christ, who is the Prince of Peace, we are restored to sweet fellowship with our LORD and God. Together we take up our tambourines and go out to dance with the joyful.[2]

Jesus' offering of himself was necessary to fully satisfy the Father, because without the shedding of blood there is no forgiveness of sin.[3] He is the all-sufficient, perfect sacrifice that lifts the basket of slavery from our hands so we may lift holy hands to offer a sacrifice of praise.[4] By the authority of the word, those who lead us in worship bless the LORD and inspire the people to worship in Jesus' name.[5]

> *Then Aaron lifted his hands toward the people and blessed them. And having sacrificed the sin offering, the burnt offering and the fellowship offering, he stepped down.*
> (Leviticus 9:22)

By Yahweh's authority, Moses lifted his hands to defeat the Amalekite warriors, but he got weary and his hands gradually dropped down. To win the battle, Moses rested on a stone while Aaron and Hur held his hands up. How can a person's hands be powerful enough to win a battle? The answer is clear. On our own, our hands have no power or authority. If we stand alone, they grow weak. But we are not alone when we obey what God commands and then join hands with our brothers and sisters to worship before the God of the armies of heaven.

As we raise up holy hands in the assembly, we encourage others. The essence of true worship strengthens us for victory as we exalt the LORD of glory. Together in Jesus' name, we extend our hands to the heavens—to Christ who is worthy of all praise.

> *As long as Moses held up his hands, the Israelites were winning, but whenever he lowered his hands, the Amalekites were winning.*
> (Exodus 17:11)

By Yahweh's command, King Solomon built a temple for His holy name. The solemn moment for dedication arrived when the temple was finished in every detail. Then the king raised his hands upward to the LORD, his King, who is enthroned on high. He stood before God's holy nation, a people called by the Great I AM's holy name. With all of Israel's tribes gathered around the altar, he raised up his hands in prayer. Solomon's petitions were offered

---
1. Isaiah 50:6, 53:5.
2. Jeremiah 31:4.
3. Hebrews 9:22.
4. Psalm 81:6, Hebrews 13:15.
5. Nehemiah 8:6.

in agreement with the heart of God for His holy nation and his prayer guided Jewish supplications ever after.

Today we stand in the company of a great cloud of witnesses who have gone before us.[6] We, like them, are the temple of the Holy Spirit.[7] All those who are called by God's holy name now lift up our hands to exalt and worship our Sovereign LORD. We extend holy hands because He is worthy of all praise. He reigns on high. He is robed in majesty and armed with strength. He is Creator God who established the world and set it on a firm foundation.[8]

Then Solomon stood before the altar of the LORD in front of the whole assembly of Israel, spread out his hands toward heaven.
(1 Kings 8:22)

There are special moments to raise our hands and exalt the Almighty One. There are also times to bow down, bend our knees, and humble ourselves in the sight of the LORD so that He may lift us up.[9]

Ezra stood together with the remnant of people who had returned to Jerusalem after seventy years of exile. Their hands were calloused and hardened from digging through the rubble to rebuild the city. They finished the walls and set the cities gates in place. Now the moment came to read to the people from the Book of the Law. Ezra stood on a stand above the people and opened the book. Then, as "Ezra praised the LORD, the great God," all the people stood up. It was as if a wave of the Spirit washed over them as the Book of the Law was opened and they raised their roughened hands to respond, saying, "Amen! Amen!" Then they bowed down to the Almighty who brought them home from many years of exile in Babylon.

Ezra praised the LORD, the great God; and all the people lifted their hands and responded, "Amen! Amen!" Then they bowed down and worshiped the LORD with their faces to the ground.
(Nehemiah 8:6)

As we lift holy hands to worship, we must open our hands and let go of everything we held onto in our clenched fists. We must release the grip we have on our wallets. Anger, the right to revenge, and disputes all fall away as we open and extend our hands on high.[10]

Pain and sorrow dragged us down. The world's injustice weighed on our heavy hearts. The constraint of societal pressure bound us like a strait jacket.

---

6. Hebrews 12:1.
7. 1 Corinthians 6:19.
8. Psalm 93:1.
9. James 4:10.
10. 1 Timothy 2:8.

But in the power of the Spirit, we are strengthened like Samson who broke his bonds and let them drop from his hands.[11]

Are you bound with the chains of addiction? Is your heart weighed down with grief? Are the pressures of life getting too much for you? Lift up your hands and cry out for mercy. Our heavenly Father offers His mercies with abundance. We lift our praises up and God's mercies shower down.

> *Hear my cry for mercy as I call to you for help, as I lift up my hands toward your Most Holy Place.*
> (Psalm 28:2)

Among the nations, our voices are heard as we celebrate with triumphant delight. Joyful exaltations thunder from our assembly as we worship a holy God. Our uplifted hands accompany our joyful harmonies. We are victors in Christ and we applaud Him with delight. With our hands extended to the heavens, we join in to celebrate before the great I AM who inspires us with reverent awe, for He is Sovereign over all the earth.

> *Clap your hands, all you nations; shout to God with cries of joy. For the LORD Most High is awesome, the great King over all the earth.*
> (Psalm 47:1–2)

May the strength of the Spirit inspire us to lift our hands in true praise and worship. Throw open the church doors so our victorious applause wafts out for all to hear. Oh LORD, shed the light of Christ upon us so we may rejoice in your holy name and praise your mighty works.

May the praise of children and infants be heard in our gatherings. We are gathered in Jesus' holy name, where our little ones sing and applaud in harmony with us. Give us strength, O LORD; be our stronghold against every adversary.[12] Silence our enemies so that we my lift up holy hands with singing as long as we have breath. May your holy name be ever on our lips as we lift up our hands to exalt our LORD and God.

> *I will praise you as long as I live, and in your name I will lift up my hands.*
> (Psalm 63:4)

True worshippers come in reverent awe before the LORD God who set the heavens and earth in place. We put our hands together and come into harmony with all He created. The hands of the congregation sound like the waters of the mighty oceans that roar. The exaltations of the assembly resound like thunder on the mountains that tremble and quake at the presence of the LORD.

---

11. Judges 15:14.
12. Psalm 8:2.

When Israel wandered in the wilderness, the tribes quarreled and threatened when they should have lifted up their hands with petitions and praise to God who provides. Yahweh spoke through Moses to cause the rock to flow out into a pool to refresh His people. By Yahweh's command, springs of water flowed out of the hard rock.[13] God's people drank and were satisfied and watered their flocks. God was faithful, even when Moses, Aaron, and the people were not.[14]

Winds and waves obey God's command.[15] The Almighty makes rivers flow even on barren plateaus.[16] The great I AM causes a refreshing flow to spring up and water the valleys. The God of majesty turns the desert into an oasis. Our heavenly Father changes parched fields into well-watered gardens.[17] Rejoice, oh my soul, and proclaim God's word with authority because we serve a God who is worthy of all praise, glory, and honor.

You split the earth with rivers; the mountains saw you and writhed. Torrents of water swept by; the deep roared and lifted its waves on high.
(Habakkuk 3:9–10)

Jesus led His disciples to a place near Bethany. As He ascended to the right hand of the Father, He lifted up His hands and bestowed a blessing on His disciples. Today He still holds out His hands to strengthen His people and bless them. He ministers in the true sanctuary in heaven and inspires His people to worship in spirit and truth.

Now we are called to serve with our hands open and extended under the covering of and authority of our high priest's lifted hands. We reach out our hands as His hands, lifting them up to worship, reaching out to touch, and opening our hands to serve. May our hands exalt and glorify Christ our Redeemer.

Under the covering of Jesus' parting words, the disciples continued to gather at Jerusalem's temple where they overflowed with praises to the LORD who sent His only Son to walk among men. They prayed and waited just as Jesus commanded them. Then, on the day of Pentecost the promised Holy Spirit came to empower them, descending upon them with tongues like fire. They were empowered and anointed to go and make disciples in Jerusalem, Judea, Samaria, and to the ends of the earth.[18]

---

13. Psalm 114:7–8.
14. Numbers 20:1–13.
15. Psalm 89:9, Luke 8:22–25.
16. Isaiah 43:19.
17. Isaiah 41:18.
18. Acts 1:8.

When he had led them out to the vicinity of Bethany, he lifted up his hands and blessed them. While he was blessing them, he left them and was taken up into heaven. Then they worshiped him and returned to Jerusalem with great joy. And they stayed continually at the temple, praising God.
(Luke 24:50–53)

The passion that led Jesus to suffer the terrible pain and torment of the cross is a love beyond anything we could imagine. The deep darkness of the sixth hour that came over Mount Calvary was driven away with Jesus' final victory over sin, Satan, and death. The triumph of the cross still shines out from Jesus, the Light of the World, who restores us to sweet fellowship with the Father. Jesus' atoning sacrifice put victory in our hands so we may lift holy hands to worship. As we come together, the voices of our children sing in unison with us, and we strengthen each other as we celebrate our resurrected LORD and Savior.

Come and join the refrains of victorious worshippers As our applause is heard among the nations!

> "Stand up and bless the LORD your God from everlasting to everlasting. Blessed be your glorious name, which is exalted above all blessing and praise." (Nehemiah 9:5)

Chapter 30 Q&A

Lift up Holy Hands

1. What is the effect does Jesus' atoning sacrifice have on us when we gather to worship?

___

2. Why are hands such a vital instrument for true worshippers?

___

3. Why do we join hands in a joyful assembly to worship our LORD who is Sovereign over all the earth?

___

4. How is it possible that God's servants can extend their hands as the very hands of Christ?

___

My Journey's Journal:

Chapter 31: Sing a New Song

Key Scriptures:

- "Sing joyfully to the LORD, you righteous; it is fitting for the upright to praise him. Praise the LORD with the harp; make music to him on the ten-stringed lyre. Sing to him a new song; play skillfully, and shout for joy" (Psalm 33:1–3).

- "He put a new song in my mouth, a hymn of praise to our God. Many will see and fear the LORD and put their trust in him" (Psalm 40:3).

Raising our voices to sing from the heart is something that's imbedded in all those created in God's image. When the Holy Spirit breathed into Adam, He gave him a voice to sing. This topic leads us to use our voices to sing in harmony with Christ Jesus new song—a redemptive gospel song. The sheep of His pasture follow the Good Shepherd's voice. He sings out to the flock as He leads them to pleasant green pastures.

Our Savior sets captives free and they come out singing His new song. The LORD watches over the wayfarer. When he comes to a safe harbor, no longer buffeted by storms, he sings out with praise. God's blessings put a song in the farmer's heart and a dance in his step after he harvests the abundance of his fields.

As the bride of Christ, our voices resonate with joy as we look forward to the day we will sing and dance at the great wedding banquet when the Bridegroom returns for His beloved. We will sing in harmony with the voices of the morning stars as we ascend upon the heights of Mount Zion.

> A prayer according to Psalm 111:1:
>
> Give us hearts that overflow with praise to the LORD. May we ascend to extol the LORD with all our heart in the council of the upright and in the assembly.

Creator God put songs in the hearts of all who are created in His image. He gave us voices so we may sing out the joys of His bountiful blessings. It's in our nature to sing during special moments of celebration. A bride in beautiful array walks down the aisle to a bridal chorus. A mother sings sweet lullabies to her newborn child. An athlete wins a gold medal and celebrates to the sounds of his national anthem. Every graduate, from kindergarten to the university, celebrates with songs to inspire them to continue their life's journey.

These are all good moments we enjoy at the intersections of our lives. Now consider the greatest joy—the joy of our salvation. The jubilant songs we sing are not sung with the same voice as a happy birthday song. Our worshipful music overflows by means of the wind of the Spirit who gives voice to our spirit so we may sing out with a jubilant song to the Almighty who is worthy of all praise, honor, and glory. The Good Shepherd holds us so close that we can hear the song of His heart and sing out in harmony to His new song.

> *Sing to the LORD a new song, for he has done marvelous things; his right hand and his holy arm have worked salvation for him.*
> (Psalm 98:1)

When we're at the beach, where ocean waves wash sand around our feet, we look upward and our voices resound with worshipful acclamations. We ascend to the mountain top and lift our hands to sing God's praises. Islands in earth's great oceans echo with the sounds of worship to God Most High. Every continent reverberates with sounds of joyful singing to God Almighty. The seafarer strains his eyes through the storm's murky sky in search of a safe harbor. He shouts with thanksgiving at the first sight of land.

We serve an awesome God who is mighty to save. Those who hear the good news receive it with songs of delight. Our Redeemer sets prisoners free to run on His pathway.[1] Our Savior breaks the bondage of sin that once bound us and He releases us to kick up our heels in His pasture.[2] Every captive who is set free goes out with singing. All those whose chains are broken rise and lift their hands with shouts of joy. Those who are released from crushing oppressions sing out as they are set free. We celebrate a jubilee of the LORD's favor with victorious songs in our assemblies.[3]

> *Sing to the LORD a new song, his praise from the ends of the earth, you who go down to the sea, and all that is in it, you islands, and all who live in them.*
> (Isaiah 42:10)

All those who are drawn into the joyful worship of the saints are encompassed with God's praises. The sound of His holy name is voiced with harmony in the assembly. The notes penetrate to the depths of our soul so we may join our hearts with singing our Savior's new song.

1. Psalm 119:32.
2. Malachi 4:2.
3. Luke 4:18–19.

Every son and daughter who ascends God's holy mountain shouts out with a glad heart. Their souls rejoice with victorious songs as sin's burden is lifted from their shoulders, their debt of sin paid in full. In forgiveness they are protected from God's righteous judgments. The LORD rises up to fight against our enemies and we fear no harm. Our hands once hung limp with dread but now they are lifted with holy praise. We go out with singing and our heavenly Father receives us into His counsels with delight.

> *I will declare your name to my brothers and sisters; in the assembly I will sing your praises.*
> (Hebrews 2:12)

When the Holy Spirit breathed life into Adam, He gave man a voice to sing. Surely, he sang a love song to Eve who also sang out with affectionate songs to her children. As people began to populate the earth, a man named Jubal invented musical instruments. He will always be remembered as the "father of all who play stringed instruments and pipes."[4] Later, the tribes of Israel camped at the foot of Mount Sanai. Sounds of thunder and flashes of lightning shot out from the thick clouds, accompanied by a trumpet-like sound. These awesome sounds heralded the LORD, who descended upon the mountain and called Moses up to receive His commandments. Years later, David, the shepherd psalmist, became a king who sang an abundance of praises to the God of Israel. But over and over, Israel's people forgot God's good gifts. They turned their celebrative feasts into self-gratifying festivals.

Over and over, God raised up true worshippers in the spirit of Moses and David. The Holy Spirit came on the day of Pentecost, accompanied by the sounds of a mighty wind to establish His new covenant church.[5] The Spirit's mighty rushing wind must have sounded like music to the ears of those who gathered to wait and pray. Finally, in the revelation of Jesus Christ, heaven's choirs sing out to the One who is worthy. Voices from every nation join in the chorus to sing our Savior's new song. From beginning to the end, the Alpha and Omega inspires new songs for His people to sing out His praises—for He is worthy of all praise, glory, and honor.

> *And they sang a new song, saying: "You are worthy to take the scroll and to open its seals, because you were slain, and with your blood you purchased for God persons from every tribe and language and people and nation."*
> (Revelation 5:9)

Oh, what glorious songs overflow from the congregation on earth. We sing in harmony with the angels of the churches as we look forward to the

---
4. Genesis 4:21.
5. Acts 2:2.

great wedding banquet when our promised Bridegroom returns for His bride. One day, our eternal home will burst as great choirs of saints gather before God's throne to sing our Savior's new song.

Not one voice will be missing.[6] Revelation's 144,000 Israelites represents the complete number of martyrs and saints who will be redeemed and adorned as the bride of Christ. Every one of them will rejoice to sing our Redeemer's new song, a song that no others can learn.

> *And they sang a new song before the throne and before the four living creatures and the elders. No one could learn the song except the 144,000 who had been redeemed from the earth.*
> (Revelation 14:3.)

All God's created beings are given voices to sing all kinds of music. We sing country, pop, folk, rap, jazz, reggae, and rock songs. All of us can enjoy our favorite music. But those who are born of the Spirit are gifted with voices to sing our Savior's songs of redemption. From the sands of the seashore to the peak of the highest mountain, God's people lift holy hands and voices to sing out God's praises. He has set our voices free so our spirit may sound out with songs of Christ's jubilee.

Come, join in with the joyful assembly to sing God's praises. We sing as we look forward to entering the joy of God's people from all time who are gathered as the bride of Christ.

> Through Jesus, therefore, let us continually offer to God a sacrifice of praise—the fruit of lips that openly profess his name. (Hebrews 13:15)

---

6. John 18:9.

Chapter 31 Q&A
Sing a New Song

1. What is your favorite worship song?

2. Why do we join our voices together to sing in our gatherings?

3. Who invented musical instruments? What purpose did they serve?

4. What song will you sing with heaven's choir?

My Journey's Journal:

Chapter 32: A Sweet-Smelling Fragrance

Key Scriptures:

- "She has done a beautiful thing to me. The poor you will always have with you, and you can help them any time you want. But you will not always have me. She did what she could. She poured perfume on my body beforehand to prepare for my burial. Truly I tell you, wherever the gospel is preached throughout the world, what she has done will also be told, in memory of her" (Mark 14:6-9).

- "Awake, north wind, and come, south wind! Blow on my garden, that its fragrance may spread everywhere. Let my beloved come into his garden and taste its choice fruits" (Song of Songs 4:16).

This leg of our ascent leads us into a sweet fragrance, like a meadow of mountain flowers. Every verse leads us see our heavenly Father's heart that overflows out with love. He looks far ahead, longing to see wandering souls return to be bathed with the aromas of hearth and home. He calls us back to the beginnings of our faith where our roots intertwine with those who gather with us to worship. We have deep roots in a congregation that is as fragrant as the majestic cedar trees of the forest. Together we give off the fragrance of Christ.

This topic opens our eyes to the beauty of being a captive who is brought home in Jesus' victorious parade. We are led home with triumphant songs. Beginning with Abel, we'll consider how our Savior is present throughout all time to inspire true worship.

We'll delight in the joys of our Good Shepherd as He inspires His church to worship. He sends His Holy Spirit to empower our praise, giving wind to our spirit to sing out a fragrant sacrifice of praise.

> A prayer according to Song of Songs 4:16:
>
> Send your Holy Spirit to give wind to our spirit, like blowing on a garden so that its fragrance may spread to all those around us. May the fragrance of Christ draw all who will come into the garden of God's delights.

So many sheep of God's pasture have been scattered and plundered by unfaithful shepherds.[1] Such leaders trample the grass in the Good Shepherd's pasture. Devious shepherds muddied the streams of water with their feet.[2] Gatherings for worship have turned into a stench because of our spiritual duplicity.[3] We need Christ our Deliverer. Who will cleanse us of the stain and filth of our sin and bring us back from our wanderings?

In the moment of our trouble, we cry out with a repentant plea and turn from our wandering ways. The Good Shepherd hears our cry and comes to break the bars of sin that hold us captive. He crushes the yoke of sin's bondage and rescues the sheep from the corruption that enslaved them. Through repentance and forgiveness He gathers us from the nations and leads us into rich green pastures on the mountain heights.[4]

The Father stands at the gate and looks down the long, winding road. He longs to catch a first glimpse of His returning children. His heart yearns for us to return home where we can be surrounded by His love and protection. Then, at the very moment our Father sees us coming, He runs to receive us and celebrate our return.[5]

The comforting fragrances of hearth and home await those who are restored to the joy of His saving grace. Let us come and humble ourselves in true worship, lifting holy hands and jubilant voices in praise to the God of our salvation. All the nations will see that the One we serve is holy. He is mighty to save.

> *I will accept you as fragrant incense when I bring you out from the nations and gather you from the countries where you have been scattered, and I will be proved holy through you in the sight of the nations.*
> (Ezekiel 20:41)

The Bible often likens God's people to sheep. If you've been around sheep, you know they can get mighty smelly. The prophet Hosea shows us how the Father sees the sheep who return to Him with repentant hearts. He sees us as forgiven and cleansed, and He receives us graciously so "that we may offer the fruit of our lips."[6] Then we offer up fragrant fruit as we are led to serve and worship in a way that is spiritual and real. The awesome aromas of the breath of the Holy Spirit waft out from the congregation as we teach truths from God's Word. The true gospel of Jesus Christ flows out from our worship gatherings as we flourish and grow like a grove of fragrant cedar trees.

---

1. Ezekiel 34:1–6.
2. Ezekiel 34:18.
3. Amos 5:21.
4. Ezekiel 34:14.
5. Luke 15:11–32.
6. Hosea 14:2. NIV footnote: alternate translation: "Offer the fruit of our lips like the sacrifices of bulls."

Consider the way a giant cedar tree sends down its deep roots to grow strong and stand against the storms. They grow tall and give off their soothing, woodsy scent. It's much the same in our times of worship. It's good and pleasing to God when we offer up praise and thanksgiving in our prayer closet. But we are encompassed in the greatest fragrances of worship as we are rooted together in agreement with other true worshippers.

> *I will be like the dew to Israel; he will blossom like a lily. Like a cedar of Lebanon he will send down his roots; his young shoots will grow. His splendor will be like an olive tree, his fragrance like a cedar of Lebanon.*
> (Hosea 14:5–6)

Consider Ezra and Nehemiah. They returned to Jerusalem with forty-thousand people after the seventy years of their exile were fulfilled. Ezra led a victorious cavalcade of God's people who were once held captive in Babylon. Today we are blessed to be made captives in Christ's triumphal procession. We were once prisoners of sin, but Christ offered us a great hope.[7] Our Savior rescues us from the cords of sin that entangled us. We were plundered by the enemy of our souls and led away in the chains of wickedness. But we are now forgiven, restored, and set free by the power of Christ's sacrificial love. His blood cleanses us so that we may serve the living God.[8]

The Good Shepherd leads us home as victors. In Christ we overcome the power of sin, Satan, and death. And now, the fragrant aromas of praise and exaltations flow out from this triumphant procession so that people in every nation may know God is mighty to save.

> *But thanks be to God, who always leads us as captives in Christ's triumphal procession and uses us to spread the aroma of the knowledge of him everywhere.*
> (2 Corinthians 2:14)

Noah's ark settled on dry ground after the world-wide flood. There he built an altar and offered burnt sacrifices as a pleasing aroma to God who had saved them from the great "wickedness of the human race."[9] Many years later, Moses instituted a system of worship for the people to offer up all kinds of sacrifices to the LORD. Their offerings were pleasing aromas that foreshadowed Christ, who would offer Himself as the perfect, once-and-for-all-time sacrifice.[10]

---

7. Zechariah 9:12. The prophet proclaimed God's redemptive message with a double blessing for Jewish prisoners who would be delivered from captivity.
8. Hebrews 9:14.
9. Genesis 6:5.
10. Hebrews 7:27.

For we are to God the pleasing aroma of Christ among those who are being saved and those who are perishing.
(2 Corinthians 2:15)

The smell of the sheep in God's pasture is a pleasing aroma to the Good Shepherd. But to the unfaithful hired hand, they are just smelly, dirty sheep.[11] All those who are God's sons and daughters are called by our Savior's holy name and filled with his sweet fragrance. But those who are rebellious and unrepentant smell of death as they come into our worship gatherings where there is hope.

This truth applies to those who serve as shepherds in the church. They are anointed to accomplish an impossible task as servants in the sanctuary. If they try to work on their own, clothed with filthy rags of their own righteousness, they soon become terrified before the people.[12] True ministry and worship are only possible when clothed with power from on high.[13] By means of the Spirit's anointing, gifting, and empowering wind, the sheep radiate with the sweet aroma of Christ. Who can effectively serve and show the way for people to come into His righteous dwelling? Who will do the work of guiding wanderers to the sacred mountain where they are to gather?[14] This good work is only possible through the strength provided by the Spirit of Christ.

Let us offer us a life-giving fragrance of praise to the awesome God we serve.

To the one we are an aroma that brings death; to the other, an aroma that brings life. And who is equal to such a task?
(2 Corinthians 2:16)

In the holy assembly, the fragrance of God's love fills the air. This sweet aroma is sent up with uplifted hands and carried by the harmonious praise of voices. We speak out and sing out from our hearts in Jesus' name. God is in His holy temple where His love reigns supreme. Our songs proclaim His mercy and justice.

Christ's footsteps guide us in the pathway of the greatest and truest love—a sacrificial love. He loved us first so that now we can love Him and all the brothers and sisters He has given us.[15] His abundant love flows out from us with our fragrant offerings of praise. In His love we are compelled to love one another and walk in keeping with God's precepts as we delight in His ways and obey the gospel imperatives. His love inspires us to seasons of singing that blossom like the flowers on the earth.[16]

---
11. John 10:12.
12. Galatians 1:10, Jeremiah 1:17.
13. Luke 24:49.
14. Jeremiah 31:21–23.
15. 1 John 4:19.
16. Song of Songs 2:12.

Follow God's example, therefore, as dearly loved children and walk in the way of love, just as Christ loved us and gave himself up for us as a fragrant offering and sacrifice to God.
(Ephesians 5:1–2)

A fasting and praying congregation makes a dynamic impact. The sweetest aromas of worship waft from a gathering of Jesus' followers as they fervently fast and pray together in one accord. Corporate prayers in agreement with the Word and the Holy Spirit are a vital element in the work of the Great Commission. Our heartfelt petitions are a major part of a frontline defense against the assaults of the world. The prayerful songs of interceding saints tear down the enemy's strongholds.

When the prayers of the saints are inspired in the written Word of the Apostles and Prophets, and lifted up in accord with Jesus' holy name, they are mighty to pull down spiritual strongholds. But when prayers are self-focused, or become pharisaical show prayers, the empty words find the heavens like brass.[17]

Children of hope pray constantly throughout the day. Our quiet-time prayers sustain our family, friends, and our church. We gather in homes during the week to pray together in harmony. When the whole church gathers to fast and pray, it makes a marked difference in people's lives, our community, nation, and the world. Praying in agreement has a mighty influence on our country's leaders, nations in conflict, injustice in our judicial systems, and helps to drive away the fear of calamities. When answers to our prayers wash over us like a flood, we offer praise, shouting out with victorious song before an awesome God.

And when he had taken it, the four living creatures and the twenty-four elders fell down before the Lamb. Each one had a harp and they were holding golden bowls full of incense, which are the prayers of God's people. And they sang a new song, saying: "You are worthy to take the scroll and to open its seals, because you were slain, and with your blood you purchased for God persons from every tribe and language and people and nation. You have made them to be a kingdom and priests to serve our God, and they will reign on the earth."
(Revelation 5:8–10)

The LORD our God shows His mighty arm to save so that all nations will see that He is holy. He transforms us "into His image with ever-increasing glory which comes from the LORD, who is Spirit."[18] In His glory we enjoy

---

17. Deuteronomy 28:23.
18. 2 Corinthians 3:18.

the sweet fragrance of His anointing oil. Think about the great work God accomplishes in each of our lives. We come as stinky sheep and He cleans us up, to be the aroma of Christ. We gather as a church, and the Spirit of Christ leads us into the beautiful fragrances of true and real worship.

Christ's love has a unique fragrance of its own. This great love compels God's dearly loved children to "walk in the way of love, just as Christ loved us and gave Himself up for us as a fragrant offering and sacrifice to God."[19] The aromas of this overwhelming love intensifies as we gather as a church in Jesus' name. How could we ever forsake gathering to delight in this incredible aroma?

> "I will be like the dew to Israel; he will blossom like a lily. Like a cedar of Lebanon he will send down his roots; his young shoots will grow." (Hosea 14:5)

Chapter 32 Q&A

A Sweet-Smelling Fragrance

1. Describe the fragrance of a worshipping congregation.

2. How are we changed from stinky sheep to having a sweet-smelling aroma?

3. What is the difference between a hireling and a godly shepherd?

4. How can a congregation effect change in the world around them?

---

19. Ephesians 5:1–2.

My Journey's Journal:

Chapter 33: A Redeemed People

Key Scriptures:

- "If you use stones to build my altar, use only natural, uncut stones. Do not shape the stones with a tool, for that would make the altar unfit for holy use" (Exodus 20:5).

- "The LORD is not slow in keeping his promise, as some understand slowness. Instead he is patient with you, not wanting anyone to perish, but everyone to come to repentance" (2 Peter 3:9).

- "Praise be to the LORD, the God of Israel, because he has come to his people and redeemed them" (Luke 1:68).

Remember the days filled with swimming and canoeing at teen summer camp? After hours of fun, hiking, meeting new friends, good food, and making mischief, it was time to settle down to sing, listen, and learn at chapel time. These services always ended with a clear gospel message and singing "Just as I am" to encourage kids to come up front to pray, repent of their sins, and confess Jesus Christ as their LORD and Savior.

Campers who heard and believed the good news and received the free gift of saving faith could be baptized before family and friends into the Father, Son, and Holy Spirit. They joined God's redeemed people as new creations in Christ. They were sealed by the Holy Spirit.

In this part of our hike up the mountain, new creations in Christ see how our Savior has been actively present along each step of life's pathway. We'll see the places we've tripped, the deep pits we dug for ourselves, and how Jesus got us out of the mess we made. When we went the wrong way and came to a big dead-end, we felt hopeless. But the Good Shepherd was there to hold out His hand and lift us out of our lost condition.

> A prayer according to Jeremiah 31:7:
>
> May your people sing out, for you have made us a holy nation. May our praises be heard as we call out; "O LORD, save your people, this remnant you have called and chosen as your own."

Take a moment to enjoy a vantage point where you can look back on the road where you started your walk of faith. Whether He used a church youth camp or a friend's witness of Jesus' saving grace, your path began with God's redemptive work that made you a new creation in Christ.

Once, you were caught in the clutches of sin. As hard as you tried, you couldn't get out of the mess you made. You grasped for a lifeline but came up empty handed. You were ready to give up and sink down into the depths of despair. You were held captive in your sin. Darkness pressed in from every direction. But then you heard a voice calling, "Come unto me." Light shined into the thick darkness and you heard a voice saying, "Be Free."[1]

You listened to the call of hope and freedom: "I paid a ransom to redeem you from the chains of sin." You grasped hold of God's Word and it exposed your sin. Your eyes were opened to see your need for a Redeemer. You listened to the Savior's call to you. The seed of faith was planted in your heart as you heard the gospel message, which led you to repent of your sin. You were baptized into the Father, Son, and Holy Spirit and adopted as a son or daughter of the heavenly Father. The Holy Spirit sealed you from God's wrath against sin. You entered His precious rest. Your soul was restored.

Then, as you laid down in the Good Shepherd's peaceful pasture you wondered, "Why have I wasted all these years of my life? Why didn't I listen when I first heard the good news?" But now the gift of saving faith has put you on the right path and the Good LORD restores the years your sin has eaten.[2] You took a long, winding road, but the Savior led you to the joy of God's salvation.[3]

> *The LORD is not slow in keeping his promise, as some understand slowness. Instead he is patient with you, not wanting anyone to perish, but everyone to come to repentance.*
> (Exodus 17:15)

---

1. Isaiah 49:9.
2. Joel 2:25.
3. Psalm 51:12.

Noah steps up to the podium teach us again. Consider this preacher of righteousness.[4] This family of eight, along with the male and female land animals, were sealed in the ark and kept safe from God's holy and just wrath against a world gone bad—completely corrupted and violent. As Noah and family stepped into the ark, they looked forward to a land redeemed from sin that had defiled the earth.[5] They waited aboard the ark through storms and raging flood waters, kept safe for days that stretched out into many months. They looked to the LORD God who would establish the Noahic covenant with man.[6]

When God cuts a covenant, the word literally means, "to allow blood to flow."[7] Creator God revived the earth by means of a world-wide flood. He cleansed it of the stains from man's violent injustice and bloodshed. He sealed Noah's family in the ark, safe from the world's destruction. Then, after the floodwaters receded and the ground dried, God made a covenant promise and gave them a colorful sign in the sky in the form of a rainbow.[8] This was the right moment for an altar of worship. Noah offered animals as burnt offerings to seal the covenant with blood. These offerings foreshadowed Christ, who would offer Himself to make new and better covenant.

> *Then Noah built an altar to the LORD and, taking some of all the clean animals and clean birds, he sacrificed burnt offerings on it.*
> (Genesis 8:20)

Abraham waited a quarter of a century for God to fulfill His promise of a son. Consider Abraham's dismay when he realized that his efforts to help God fulfill His promise were futile and, instead had wounded His wife Sarah. What was it like to have only one son and then be asked to sacrifice him on a mountaintop altar? Then, sometime after returning home with Isaac, what was it like to hear that his brother, Nahor, had twelve sons?[9] Abraham, the man who left his homeland to find a land of promise shows us an amazing example of a tested, enduring, and redemptive faith that is steadfast in God's promise.

Consider how Abraham's faith continues to reveal Christ. When Abraham loaded the wood for the sacrifice on Isaac's shoulders, he offered us a preview of God's only Son who gave His lifeblood on a cross as a sacrifice for the sins of the world. The father of our faith, in this act of amazing obedience, looked forward to God's plan of redemption. Abraham's walk of faith offers us living illustrations that reveal our heavenly Father's nature as a God of redemptive covenants.

---

4. 2 Peter 2:5.
5. Isaiah 24:5.
6. Genesis 6:18.
7. Mark 14:24.
8. Genesis 9:11–13.
9. Genesis 22:20–24.

> *When they reached the place God had told him about, Abraham built an altar there and arranged the wood on it. He bound his son Isaac and laid him on the altar, on top of the wood.*
> (Genesis 22:9)

As we also ascend to worship, we must examine ourselves and our relationships with those who gather to exalt the LORD with us. If there is no confession of sins and forgiveness in our gatherings, true worship is not possible. Without forgiveness, how can we lift up clean hands in praise? When the burden of our sin remains, church services become meaningless rituals. If there is no godly sorrow that leads to repentance, we become overburdened with our sins. Hiding sins in our backpacks as we climb is contrary to salvation.[10]

We ascend to Mount Zion to worship with contrite hearts. We humble ourselves in the sight of the LORD and confess our moral failings. We admit our offenses against our brothers and sisters in Christ so that we may present offerings with clean hearts. We lift up clean hands to worship and exalt the LORD our God. Every gift offered upon the altar is received as a basket from our hands when offered from redeemed hearts that remember God's deliverance with thanksgiving.[11]

> *Therefore, if you are offering your gift at the altar and there remember that your brother or sister has something against you, leave your gift there in front of the altar. First go and be reconciled to them; then come and offer your gift.*
> (Matthew 5:23–24)

Think back over all the years your heavenly Father was so longsuffering with you. He patiently looked for you to return from your wanderings and come home. God longed for you to come back to His dwelling place where there is forgiveness, peace, comfort, joy, strength, and bountiful provision. The lover of your soul yearned to have you come into His sanctuary where there is protection from the storms of life.

There is no one who seeks God. No one seeks the righteousness of Jesus Christ by his own initiative. Does anyone ever desire to do what is right and good on their own? No one! We're born into the clutches of a sinful world and in need of redemption. There is no natural-born desire in us for salvation. But then, by the power of the Word and the Holy Spirit, our ears are opened to hear the gospel message. The seed of faith is planted in our hearts. It takes root and blossoms as it is watered by teaching from the Scriptures.[12]

---

10. 2 Corinthians 7:10.
11. Deuteronomy 26:4.
12. 1 Corinthians 3:6.

No one can come to me unless the Father who sent me draws them, and I will raise them up at the last day.
(John 6:44)

Shadrach, Meshach, and Abednego served as examples of God's redemptive power. They stood strong in their faith, remained obedient to God's command, and ended up in a fiery furnace. Their faith was stronger than their fears. They spoke some of the greatest words of faith recorded in the Bible: "If we are thrown into the blazing furnace, the God we serve is able to deliver us from it, and he will deliver us from Your Majesty's hand. But even if he does not, we want you to know, Your Majesty, that we will not serve your gods or worship the image of gold you have set up."[13]

Those who live as a sacrifice before God Almighty give up their own desires and embrace what our heavenly Father desires. God's purpose becomes the delight of our hearts. Our own ambitions take second place to God's calling on our lives. The children the LORD gave us are not our own, they are only placed in our loving care. Living sacrifices see life's attractions fade in the light of Christ. This is the true spiritual worship the redeemed offer up to our LORD and God.

Therefore, I urge you, brothers and sisters, in view of God's mercy, to offer your bodies as a living sacrifice, holy and pleasing to God–this is your true and proper worship.
(Romans 12:1)

If one mountaineer slacks, they impede the progress of the whole team. It's hard to be refreshed when there is a lot of grumbling around the evening's campfire. In our journey of faith, there are times when sin and depravity presses in all around us to cause great harm. It's lamentable when the fruit of sin weighs us down. In the world, violence envelops us in our streets at every intersection, and God's people grieve and repent. We mourn over sin and injustice like the saints who have gone before us.

Lot grieved over the sins of Sodom and Gomorrah, and God heard his distressed cry. Finally, when the full measure of the people's sin[14] had completely defiled the plains of Jordan and weighed too heavily on the scales of justice, the Almighty came and destroyed the unrepentant cities.[15]

When corruption and violence are rampant in our communities, the redeemed sing laments. There is a time for sorrowful songs when depravity, violence, and idolatry infiltrate the very fabric of our nation. We must pause

---
13. Daniel 3:17–18.
14. Matthew 23:32, 1 Thessalonians 2:16.
15. Genesis 19:13, 2 Peter 2:9.

to grieve over the sins of Balaam that are like lecherous tentacles spreading out to destroy our families.[16] The deceitful promise of illicit drugs destroys whole generations of our children. These horrors provoke us to give voice to a repentant cry. Lamenting sorrow wells up from the depths of our soul, calling out to the heart of God for retribution.

When saints gather to sing sorrowful, repentant songs, our heavenly Father holds our grieving hearts close to His heart. The LORD Almighty longs to show His might and strength on behalf[17] of those who lament over sin's destruction and seek forgiveness.

> *Out of the depths I cry to you, LORD; LORD, hear my voice. Let your ears be attentive to my cry for mercy. If you, LORD, kept a record of sins, LORD, who could stand? But with you there is forgiveness, so that we can, with reverence, serve you.*
> (Psalm 130:1-4)

The years we wasted following our own path are lamentable. But God was patient and continued calling out to us until the day God's Word planted the seed of faith in our heart. By faith, we answered our Savior's call, and He made us a chosen people, a royal priesthood, a redeemed holy nation.

Come and join the joyful assembly as we ascend to worship on Mount Zion. Let the redeemed gather in Jesus' name, confessing our sins and receiving abundant forgiveness to free us to worship God Almighty. We are faithful to gather as a church, pray together, and be strengthened so that the chaos of the world cannot crush us. When we sing songs of lament, God hears our repentant cries and shows His mighty arm at work on our behalf.

> "My heart rejoices in the LORD; the LORD my horn is lifted high.[18] My mouth boasts over my enemies, for I delight in your deliverance." (1 Samuel 2:1)

---

16. 2 Peter 2:7–10, Revelation 2:14.
17. Psalm 21:13.
18. "Horn" represents strength.

Chapter 33 Q&A

A Redeemed People

1. How many twists and turns in your life's path did it take for you to hear the gospel's call and come to saving faith in Jesus Christ?

   _____
   _____
   _____

2. Why are God's covenants sealed with a blood sacrifice?

   _____
   _____
   _____

3. How did the ancients and the patriarchs of our faith look forward to Christ's all-sufficient and perfect sacrifice?

   _____
   _____
   _____

4. How do you use stories of the heroes of faith to strengthen you to rise above the world's chaos?

   _____
   _____
   _____

Chapter 34: Songs of Rest

Key Scriptures:

- "By the seventh day God had finished the work he had been doing; so on the seventh day he rested from all his work. Then God blessed the seventh day and made it holy, because on it he rested from all the work of creating that he had done" (Genesis 2:2–3).

- "Come to me, all you who are weary and burdened, and I will give you rest. Take my yoke upon you and learn from me, for I am gentle and humble in heart, and you will find rest for your souls" (Matthew 11:28–29).

When a man gets down on bended knee to pop the question to his girlfriend, he offers a sign of his love and pledge to marry her—an engagement ring. Our heavenly Father, who loves us with the greatest love, offers us a sign of his promised eternal rest. He gave us a day of rest to guide us into a life of rest in Christ who leads us into an eternal rest. If you're ever unsure about our heavenly Father's loving care for His people, consider the beauty of the rest He offers. As we take a break on our ascent, we'll see the great treasure we have in this sign of His everlasting covenant.

Scripture by Scripture our ears are opened to hear our LORD Jesus as He knocks on our heart's door. Welcome Him in to commune with Him. Answer the gospel's call and come into God's eternal rest.

> A prayer according to Psalm 5:11:
>
> Our Father in heaven, let all who take refuge in you be glad; let them ever sing for joy. Spread your protection over them, so that those who love your name may rejoice in you.

People from every nation hardscrabble through each day of their lives. They're concerned about their next meal, a shirt for their backs, and a place to shelter their family. But the God who provides gave an awesome gift for His people—REST. It's both practical and sacred. A day of rest strengthens us physically and spiritually. Rest is given to us as the sign of an everlasting covenant.[1] One day is set apart so we may know He is the LORD who makes us a holy people.[2] When we come into God's rest, we honor God as Creator of heaven and earth, who rested from His work on the seventh day. The inspired words of the apostles and prophets give us an overwhelming sense of Creator God entering into His rest and saying to all who are called by His holy name "Come, rest here with me."

This is one day out of the week given to refresh workers and worshippers. The Hebrew word for refresh is שָׁפַשׁ, naphash, which gives us a picture of finishing our work and panting from the exertion. Every worker needs God's provided day of respite. Do we think we're beyond the need to rest and be refreshed? Can we just keep pushing ourselves to gain more wealth? Even our Creator rested from His work on the seventh day.

> *It will be a sign between me and the Israelites forever, for in six days*
> *the LORD made the heavens and the earth, and on the seventh day he rested and*
> *was refreshed.*
> (Exodus 31:17)

Do you have a desire for the Holy Spirit to teach you God's ways so that you may continue in His favor six days a week? Is it the desire of your heart to have the Father's presence with you as you perform the work of your hands? It's God's plan for you to be strengthened and refreshed so you can get back to your job with new vitality. Does your soul need to be restored after the week's battles?[3] Then enter the rest God provides for you.

Where do we find this rest? Is it discovered in grand cathedrals? Do we encounter it in a simple roadside chapel? Will we find it in the shade of a giant sycamore tree in nature's wonderland? Entering God's rest is more humbling and awesome than any of these good things.

King Saul raged against David and drove him from his palace with his murderous pursuits. David fled to the wilderness far from the tabernacle where the priests made daily offerings. But he determined to remain in the LORD's presence. He offered up prayers as incense and lifted up his hands as the evening sacrifice.[4] His hideouts in wilderness caves were places of shelter in the hallow of the Almighty's hands, who promised him rest from his enemies in the same way He promised his ancestors.

> *The LORD replied, "My Presence will go with you, and I will give you rest."*
> (Exodus 33:14)

---

1. Ezekiel 20:12.
2. Exodus 31:13.
3. Psalm 23:3.
4. Psalm 141:2.

As Israel's tribes wandered in the wilderness, they were instructed not to gather manna on the seventh day. Yahweh miraculously provided extra food for them to gather and store for the Sabbath.[5] Those who stored up extra earlier in the week found that it was spoiled and full of worms the next morning.[6] But every Friday they gathered extra manna, prepared it for the Sabbath, and it stayed fresh.

It's important for us to realize that God's provision doesn't depend on us and our back-breaking labor. Of course, we have to put our hand to the plow on workdays, but it is the LORD who renews our strength and gives us the health to do the work of providing for our family's daily bread and shelter.

To enter into this rest we must give up our self-dependance and our "I can do it" attitudes. We work hard during the week, but it is God who provides. We enter God's rest with confidence that all our needs will be met.

Does the work you do on your job end up like a bag of worms in your wallet? Do you put money into pockets with holes?[7] Is your money clip empty when you reach for the cash you stuffed in there? The first step out of dead-end pursuits is to honor the God of creation, who rested on the seventh day. We must hear and obey the gospel that calls us into God's rest; a forever kind of rest that is ours through Jesus Christ. Do you truly hear the good news message? Do you see your need of Christ? Then believe and be baptized into the Father, Son, and Holy Spirit. Come to Christ and partake of the tree of life and enter God's eternal rest.

> *Six days you shall labor, but on the seventh day you shall rest; even during the plowing season and harvest you must rest.*
> (Exodus 34:21)

God's provided rest is not for just one day of the week; it is the finished work of creation. This rest is forever. To enter into the fullness of God's rest we must answer salvation's call today.[8] Our Savior, Jesus, ascended to the right hand of the Father, and He is preparing a place for us—a place of rest where we may dwell with Him forever.[9]

We enter God's rest where we find a place to worship, serve, and minister before Jesus, our high priest. In Jesus' name, we come into an oasis of mercy, forgiveness, and refreshing for all who are set apart as God's holy nation. This is a refuge where springs of living water overflow. God's rest is a refuge for a sojourner rescued from the scorching sands of the desert. Let us enter in with

---

5. Exodus 16:23.
6. Exodus 16:20–21.
7. Haggai 1:6.
8. 2 Corinthians 6:2.
9. John 14:2.

thanksgiving and praise for God who provides. Will you pass by this refreshing oasis our heavenly Father provides?

> *This is what the Sovereign Lord, the Holy One of Israel, says: "In repentance and rest is your salvation, in quietness and trust is your strength, but you would have none of it."*
> (Isaiah 30:15)

How can our petitions and praises be more effective? We face difficult times that compel us to present our case before God.[10] But the most effective intercessions are offered from hearts that belong to the truth and rest in God's holy presence.[11] As we come into His presence to petition for our family and friends, we are surrounded by His comfort. We come into the presence of the great I AM to cast our cares upon Him, knowing that He cares for and loves us. He even cares for and loves those who cause us trouble. In rest and trust we enter that special comfort zone in God's kingdom with reverence and awe, totally confident that every word and promise in ours in Jesus' name.

We are not commanded to observe a legalistic day with no work and no play. It's so much better than that. Our day of rest and refreshing offers us a living illustration of a greater and eternal rest.

> *Then he said to them, "The Sabbath was made for man, not man for the Sabbath."*
> (Mark 2:27)

Wisdom's song rings out at every intersection of life and in every season of life.[12] Will you obey your Savior's call? Will you hear and receive the Word and let the seed of faith take root in your life? Right now, today, will you obey the gospel's call? Do you believe that Jesus is the Christ, the Son of the living God, who came in the flesh as Immanuel, God with us? Will you call on the name of our Savior, Jesus Christ, who gave His life to give us eternal life? Will you receive Him who gave His body to be broken so we may be healed? Will you answer the beckoning call of the One who offered up His shed blood for the sins of the world? Will you be baptized into the name of the Father, Son, and Holy Spirit? God's Word opens your heart to enter His rest.

Come and enter God's holy sanctuary where there is rest for your wounded and weary soul. Enter God's presence where He provides a refuge from life's turmoil. In Christ, you are washed clean from the inside out and refreshed in the fountain of life. Drink from the water that gives eternal life and fully satisfies, so you will thirst no more.[13] Come, partake of the bread of

---

10. Isaiah 43:26.
11. 1 John 3:19.
12. Proverbs 8:1–11.
13. John 4:14.

life so you never hunger again.[14] Now lift holy hands to worship the LORD Most High. Lift up your voice to exalt the God of your salvation, for He is high and lifted up.[15]

> *Therefore since it still remains for some to enter that rest, and since those who formerly had the good news proclaimed to them did not go in because of their disobedience, God again set a certain day, calling it "Today." This he did when a long time later he spoke through David, as in the passage already quoted: "Today, if you hear his voice, do not harden your hearts."*
> (Hebrews 4:6–7)

All those who are in covenant with the Creator of heaven and earth may enter His rest. His rest is a sign of the covenant, and its purpose shines out like countless facets of a diamond. God provides this day to refresh those who labor and draw them together as true worshippers. Why then, do people look for rest in all the wrong places. It isn't found by sitting beside a bubbling brook that flows down the mountainside. It isn't found on a sunny southern California beach. We can enjoy God's presence in these special places, but heaven's rest is like a refreshing rain that showers upon God's people when they gather in joyful worship.

Today is the day to enter God's rest. Will you answer the call? Hear our Savior beckoning you. Come into God's holy presence through Jesus Christ who wraps you in His robe of righteousness. Our Redeemer is the bread of life. He offers us living water that fully satisfies us with eternal life. Come into God's rest to be covered in His blessings every day of your life and forever.

> Yes, my soul, find rest in God; my hope comes from him. Truly he is my rock and my salvation; he is my fortress, I will not be shaken. My salvation and my honor depend on God; he is my mighty rock, my refuge. (Psalm 62:5–7)

---

14. John 6:35.
15. Isaiah 57:15.

Chapter 34 Q&A

Songs of Rest

1. What is your favorite place to get away from the daily grind?

2. How does God's rest on the seventh day of creation affect our lives today?

3. How does a day of rest show us our heavenly Father's merciful and gracious nature?

4. How does wisdom's songs open our hearts to God's eternal rest?

My Journey's Journal:

Chapter 35: The Watchman Calls Out

Key Scriptures:

- "Watch and pray so that you will not fall into temptation. The spirit is willing, but the flesh is weak" (Mathew 26:41).

- "The watchmen found me as they made their rounds in the city. 'Have you seen the one my heart loves?'" (Song of Songs 3:3).

Every playground needs supervisors to keep the kids from lurking dangers. Every sport needs umpires who toss their yellow flags and set the ball back ten yards. The church also needs someone to warn us of the hazards on our ascent to worship. Yes, we watch out for each other, but a watchman knows the pitfalls along each step of the way. He warns us when we wander into a danger zone. Our heavenly Father watches over and shelters us, and He sends a watchman to serve His people. This part of our ascent shows us the need for a wise watchman who continually calls us back to the right pathway.

> A prayer according to Romans 13:11–12:
>
> Father of light, wake us up from our slumber in the watches of the night, ever aware that "our salvation is nearer now than when we first believed." Keep us watchful so we may sing as the darkness is driven back and the light of day dawns. Give us ears to hear your warnings and call to put on the armor of light.

Motorhomes are everywhere nowadays: parked beside the neighbor's house, in the right lane on the freeway, and camped at parks in field and forest. The psalmist didn't have these in mind, but rather the tent dwellings of nomads when he wrote, "Your decrees are the theme of my song wherever I lodge."[1] Our God goes with us wherever we camp for the night. The theme of our night songs is God's abundant goodness and mercies that accompany us wherever we go. If we drive our tent stakes into the frozen ground at the gates of the Arctic National Park, God's mercies are present with us. Even as the stars wheel around us as midnight passes, God's Word is with us to

---

1. Psalm 119:54.

keep us mindful of the gospel's precepts. As we pray, or read our Bibles with a flashlight, shivering because of the howling wolves, God's promises serve as a watchman in the night. Then in the morning hours, the birds sing in the treetops to wake us up and inspire songs of praise.

> *On my bed I remember you; I think of you through the watches of the night.*
> *Because you are my help, I sing in the shadow of your wings.*
> (Psalm 63:6–7)

Jesus taught us to keep watch by offering a parable of five wise and five foolish virgins. He made it clear that we must keep watch in the night with enough oil for our lamps as we wait to hear the call announcing, "Here's the bridegroom! Come out to meet him!"[2] Jesus concluded this teaching with a warning, "Therefore keep watch, because you do not know the day or the hour."[3]

Jesus' disciples fell asleep in the Garden of Gethsemane after He posted three of them to be alert through the watches of the night. Then He went a short distance to pray, knowing He was about to be betrayed.[4] When Jesus found them sleeping instead of watching, He told them, "Watch and pray so that you will not fall into temptation. The spirit is willing, but the flesh is weak."[5]

The reality of life is that we don't have enough strength of our own to wait. We need God's Word to strengthen us. The oil of the Spirit needs constant refreshing to keep our lamps burning through the night.

> *Be dressed ready for service and keep your lamps burning, like servants waiting*
> *for their master to return from a wedding banquet, so that when he comes and*
> *knocks they can immediately open the door for him.*
> (Luke 12:35–36)

A watchman keeps us from constructing a spiritual house in our own strength. He warns us when we're building on sand. Building a house of worship by our own means gives us a house that crumbles with the first storm. When we build a church by mortal strength, God's name is not "feared among the nations."[6] How then shall we build? Paul wrote to the Philippian church to encourage them in the right way. The words he penned open our eyes to see that true worship is only possible by the Spirit of God. Real worship glorifies Christ Jesus and puts no confidence in the flesh.[7]

We're a fallible people who fall asleep just like Jesus' disciples. Because of this fallibility, every gathering in Jesus' name must call out a warning to keep

---

2. Matthew 25:6.
3. Matthew 25:13.
4. Matthew 26:40.
5. Mark 14:38.
6. Malachi 1:14.
7. Philippians 3:3.

our eyes from fluttering with complacency and lethargy. We all serve to warn each other lovingly and tactfully with God's word as our standard, and never by our own intuition. We also need a watchman who stands in God's council and hears what the Spirit is speaking.[8] A watchman redirects our attention when no one cares to go up to repair the gaps in the wall.[9] He stands in the gap until we wake up and hear wisdom's call. We must not deny this voice in our assemblies lest it be said of us, "I looked for someone stand before me in the gap, but I found no one."[10]

Unless the LORD builds the house, the builders labor in vain. Unless the LORD watches over the city, the guards stand watch in vain.
(Psalm 127:1)

Who will stand alert through the watches of the night and announce the dawn, calling out, "The night is driven back, the light of day is coming."[11] Those who stand guard don't fold their hands and relax; they come to join hands with the LORD. They attend to the bright flame of the temple's lamp and the altar to make sure the fire never goes out.[12] They stand at the gate of the LORD's house to proclaim God's message to those who come to worship.[13]

We are the temple where the light of Christ burns bright.[14] The oil of the Spirit[15] that burns in us needs constant refreshing to keep the flame lit.[16] A wise watchman keeps watch over the flocks by night to warn of the dangers of creeping spiritual darkness. The church must never silence or despise the watchmen who serve among us.

Praise the LORD, all you servants of the LORD who minister by night in the house of the LORD.
(Psalm 134:1)

There are only two paths in life. It's not possible to sit on the fence for long. One way is a broad, easy downhill slope. The other is a narrow pathway on an ascent to the heights. Moses pointed out these alternate routes when he directed six of the tribes of Israel to stand on Mount Ebal and six to stand on Mount Gerizim. He proclaimed blessings and mercies from Mount Gerizim and curses from Mount Ebal.[17] He made the two paths as obvious as two mountains.

---

8. Jeremiah 23:22.
9. Ezekiel 13:5.
10. Ezekiel 22:30.
11. Romans 13:12.
12. Romans 12:11–12.
13. Jeremiah 7:2.
14. 1 Corinthians 3:16.
15. Isaiah 61:1–3.
16. 2 Timothy 1:6–7.
17. Note: The elevation of the mount of blessing and mercy is higher than the mount of curses. This is an illustration of God's abundant grace.

The prophet Ezekiel takes up this mantle to enlighten us. He reveals the result of both good and evil ways of living. He shows us that no matter which path we take, "they will know that I am the LORD." He makes the outcome clear; whether in judgment or deliverance, we will know Yahweh is LORD over all. We are warned against the wrong path. When the Almighty executes His just and righteous judgments, removes false prophets, and sends plagues, He leaves the wicked in ruins. He cuts off branches that don't abide in the vine and throws them in the fire.[18]

The great I AM delivers us so we may walk on the right path. He separates us as a holy nation, brings us into His rest, and breathes the breath of life into our spirit. He settles us as the sheep of His pasture in His resting place where "you will know that I AM the LORD."[19]

Christians whose feet slip from Jesus' narrow path cry out in their distress. Wanderers tempted by dark pleasures call out to the watchman for the light of day. Those imprisoned by addictions plead for a Redeemer who breaks their chains, sets them free, and restores them to the joy of His salvation.[20] They rejoice—released from the chains of sin. With repentant hearts they give up their careless and self-assured ways to live a life that honors God's holy name. We're fallible people who must call out to the watchman again and again, "What of the night?"

Someone calls to me from Seir, "Watchman, what is left of the night? Watchman, what is left of the night?"
(Isaiah 21:11)

A watchman calls out with a voice as clear as a trumpet. His eyes are alert during his watch so he can warn people to be sober and wait for the light of day. His voice calls to all those who belong to the day. He admonishes them to put on faith and love as a breastplate and the hope of salvation as a helmet.[21] He encourages the people to pray and lift up holy hands, putting aside their anger and disputes.[22] He is faithful in his calling, urging people to repent and turn around when he sees they have set up idols in their hearts and put stumbling blocks in their way.[23] He works with great purpose, calling out to strengthen and encourage people who have heard the Father say, "I will be their God."[24]

The watchman warns the righteous person not to turn from their righteousness to commit sin and do detestable things.[25] He also warns a wicked

---
18. John 15:6.
19. Exodus 6:7, Ezekiel 11:10, 20:38, 36:11, 36:23, 37:6.
20. Psalm 51:12.
21. 1 Thessalonians 5:8.
22. 1 Timothy 2:8.
23. Ezekiel 14:3–8.
24. Ezekiel 14:11
25. Ezekiel 18:24–26.

person to turn away from their sin and do what is just and right so that he may surely live.[26] His work is to warn of sin and call people to repent.

Listen! Your watchmen lift up their voices; together they shout for joy. When the LORD returns to Zion, they will see it with their own eyes.
(Isaiah 52:8)

The land once steeped in darkness now sees a great light. Isaiah prophesied these awesome words about Jesus who came as the light of dawn. The worship of Israel's northern tribes became polluted by paganism and idolatry. They became rejected and despised as they mingled with foreigners and came to be known Samaritans. The descendants of Ephraim and Manasseh slipped into spiritual darkness. They were unfaithful; but God is always faithful. He sent a watchman.

John the Baptizer served as a voice calling out in the wilderness, "Prepare the way of the LORD, make straight paths for him."[27] He prepared the way for Immanuel, God with us, to bring light to the dark land. Jesus grew up in Nazareth and then went to live in "Capernaum, which was by the lake in the area of Zebulum and Naphtali… "the Way of the Sea, beyond the Jordan, Galilee of the Gentiles."[28] The only Son of God descended to live among men. The ascended Christ still calls us out of our spiritual darkness so that we may ascend to Mount Zion to exalt the LORD our God.

There will be a day when watchmen cry out on the hills of Ephraim, "Come, let us go up to Zion, to the LORD our God."
(Jeremiah 31:6)

Those who need to walk home in the late-night hours often see the violence of those who live on the dark side of life. The homeward bound soul cries out in despair. They look up and call out to the watchman, "How much longer will this darkness prevail?" They grieve over the rampant sin that presses in, creating carnage at every intersection. They call out in desperation, knowing the day of the LORD will come soon, like a thief in the night.[29] He will come to gather all the nations and separate the sheep from the goats.[30] The godly people of faith will receive a crown of righteousness,[31] but violent oppressors will hear those dreaded words, "I never knew you. Away from me, you evildoers!"[32]

---

26. Ezekiel 18:21–23.
27. Matthew 3:3.
28. Matthew 4:13,15
29. Matthew 24:44, 1 Thessalonians 5:2.
30. Matthew 25:23.
31. 2 Timothy 4:8.
32. Matthew 7:23.

Those who mourn over evil know the Sovereign LORD is perfect in justice. He does nothing without cause.[33] They grieve, knowing that on the day of the LORD the wicked will hear the righteous Judge read from the scroll written on both sides with words of "lament and mourning and woe."[34] God's people listen to the watchman's warning, knowing that those who walk Christ's narrow pathway will hear their names read from the book of life and hear those precious words, "Well done, good and faithful servant! Enter into the joy of your master."[35]

> *Arise, cry out in the night, as the watches of the night begin; pour out your heart like water in the presence of the LORD. Lift up your hands to him for the lives of your children, who faint from hunger at every street corner.*
> (Lamentations 2:19)

Everyone who is called by Christ's holy name is given a treasure of good gifts that serve to advance God's kingdom. We are given heaven's resources to use so we may accomplish the work of the Great Commission. We come together and serve together, each person doing their part in the body of Christ, the church. We carefully number the days given to us so we may do our work with a heart of wisdom: the heart of a diligent servant.[36] We take an account of our days so we may be faithful in the tasks prepared for us to complete. A faithful watchman stands shoulder to shoulder with us to help us remain faithful in the work of God's kingdom. The church needs constant reminders of Jesus' command to "be dressed ready for service and keep our lamps burning."

> *Be on guard! Be alert! You do not know when that time will come. It's like a man going away: He leaves his house and puts his servants in charge, each with their assigned task, and tells the one at the door to keep watch.*
> (Mark 13:33–34)

In a sanctuary where the saints gather, a watchman serves with us to keep us vigilant and alert to any sign of approaching danger. Jesus emphasizes this principle, warning us to stay awake and keep watch with a plentiful supply of oil for our lamps, to keep our flame burning through the night. We need constant reminders because of our need to be refreshed in the Word to keep the fire of the Spirit burning. We wait with anticipation to hear the shout, "the Bridegroom is coming." We must keep ourselves prepared and ready so we may go out and meet Him with our lamps burning bright.

---

33. Ezekiel 14:23
34. Ezekiel 2:10, Revelation 5:1.
35. Matthew 25:23 NKJV.
36. Psalm 90:12.

> "At midnight the cry rang out: "Here's the bridegroom! Come out to meet him!""
> (Matthew 25:6)

Chapter 35 Q&A

The Watchman Calls Out

1. Have you served as a guard in the military or as a playground supervisor? Describe your responsibilities.

2. Why is it important to encourage the work of a watchman in our congregations?

3. What is included in a watchman's job description?

4. Will you listen to a watchman's warnings to help you prepare for the day when the Bridegroom returns?

My Journey's Journal:

Part VIII
Faithful to the Temple's Design

"Make known to them the design of the temple—its arrangement, its exits and entrances—its whole design and all its regulations and laws. Write these down before them so that they may be faithful to its design and follow all its regulations."
(Ezekiel 43:11)

We press on to the summit to complete the final segment of our ascent. As we approach our destination, we stand in awe as we see the aspects of the sanctuary's design. We consider its plan and then remain faithful to its purpose.

Chapter 36: From the Beginning to Forever

Key Scriptures:

- "For we also have had the good news proclaimed to us, just as they did; but the message they heard was of no value to them, because they did not share the faith of those who obeyed. Now we who have believed enter that rest" (Hebrews 4:3–4).

- "So there is a special rest still waiting for the people of God. For all who have entered into God's rest have rested from their labors, just as God did after creating the world" (Hebrews 4:9–10 NLT).

- "This is what the Sovereign LORD says: The gate of the inner court facing east is to be shut on the six working days, but on the Sabbath day and on the day of the New Moon it is to be opened" (Ezekiel 46:1).

After all the planning, choosing a venue, negotiating with family, wedding dresses, bridesmaid's outfits, scheduling a photographer, managing details from napkins to table settings, following up with caterers, saying your vows, and then dancing in celebration with family and friends, the new husband and wife fall into bed exhausted. They rest together as one and this is a great beginning for a lifetime together.

In the last part of our ascent, we'll learn that rest and worship are joined like love and marriage. They fit together like a hand in glove. The holiness of God becomes evident as we see the joy, beauty, and benefits of God's rest that He established on the seventh day of creation. We serve an awesome God who instituted rest as the final touch of His creation and looks forward to welcoming those made in His image into the blessings of His eternal rest.

> A prayer according to Psalm 23:6:
>
> Oh LORD our God, may your goodness and love follow us every day of our life and bring us to dwell in your house and find rest in you today and forever.

Life's worries and troubles often overwhelm us. Headlines of war, famine, earthquakes, and wildfires assault us from every angle. It's hard to find good news on our news feed. We doom scroll on our phone while trying to choke down a sandwich and chips so we can get right back to the grind. We get frantic text messages from our adult child because Jimmy got expelled from school. This constant barrage of troubles leaves us with a trainwreck of emotions.

Where can we find refuge from the storm? Is there anywhere on planet earth to escape this chaos? It's a matter of who or what we choose to focus on. Many people of great faith have gone before us and suffered the same entanglements of life. The way they lived their lives teaches us that we can survive this mess by throwing off the baggage that drags us down into the dregs of darkness and sin. We can follow their example and fix our eyes on Jesus Christ, the author of our faith, who works in us to complete His good work in us. He has set before us a great joy: the joy of our salvation that gives us strength to endure, bear our cross, and walk in His footsteps.[1] This is the pathway to rest for our souls. This is the awesome goodness of the LORD who is worthy of all praise.

Return to your rest, my soul, for the LORD has been good to you. (Psalm 116:7).

Our Creator God established a day of rest because He is holy. That day embraced His handiwork in holiness. His rest was the apex of all that He made. God rested from His work and delighted in His creation. He received the lowing of the cattle, the trumpeting of the elephant, and the roar of the lion as praise—for He is LORD God, Creator of heaven and earth. His day of rest surely inspired Adam and Eve's songs of exaltation breathed out by the life-giving wind the Holy Spirit breathed into them.

Even today, all that God created continues to acknowledge and honor Him by doing what He created them to do. This is a common form of worship for all creation. The trees of the field clap their hands in the wind. The birds of the air crack open seed pods and sing just as they were created to do. Adam and Eve's sons and daughters cry out with their first breath—a glorious sound to God who formed them in the womb. We serve and awesome God who entered His rest and now calls us to enter this rest with Him.

The New Testament church celebrates God the Son and His finished work of redemption on the first day. The Son glorified the Father by completing the work He was given to accomplish—the work of the cross and the Father in turn glorifies the Son in His presence with the glory that was His before the world began.[2] We, as the sheep of His pasture, are Christ's glory

---

1. Matthew 16:25.
2. John 17:4-5.

and we give Him all praise. We lift up holy hands and sing out with reverent songs because He is worthy to receive all glory, honor, and power, for He created us and by His word we have our being.[3]

> *Thus the heavens and the earth were completed in all their vast array. By the seventh day God had finished the work he had been doing; so on the seventh day he rested from all his work. Then God blessed the seventh day and made it holy, because on it he rested from all the work of creating that he had done.*
> (Genesis 2:1–3).

Life's journey begins with our first breath and our life is continually upheld by constant breathing. When we run a race, we have to catch our breath. Finally, our life ends with a last gasp. With every breath along the way, God's presence goes with us. He is ever-present in the troubles of the night and the challenges of the day. He is present with us in the night hours to counsel our hearts.[4] Then He awakens our ears in the morning as one being instructed.[5]

In every moment along life's pathway the LORD God Almighty walks beside us. He is closer to us than the air we inhale. With our every breath we heed His call: "Make every effort to enter my rest."[6] Then, our heavenly Father beckons us to abide in His rest after we take our last breath.

> *The LORD replied, "My Presence will go with you, and I will give you rest."*
> (Exodus 33:14).

Gold Run Pass near Mount Baker in northwest Washington offers a challenging hike. The path has many steep drop offs, wild animals howling all around, and the wind's haunting sound whistling through the trees. The hike involves an 1,800-foot ascent to the pinnacle of the pass. Then it's a treacherous descent into a mountain valley teeming with huckleberry bushes and trees toppled by snow and winter storms. Finally, at the end of the trail, hikers come to placid Lake Tomyhoi, a crystal-clear lagoon where the weary can rest and enjoy a peaceful calm accompanied by bugling elk.

Such a hike offers an illustration of life's travails and joys. We press on to overcome every obstacle and continue life's journey with a treasure of rest in our hearts. With every plodding step we are assured of the rest awaiting us.[7] Through trials and persecution we press on in a restful pursuit of God, who welcomes us into His rest where He is enthroned on high. Yes, this is what our heavenly Father desires for all His sons and daughters.

> *For the LORD has chosen Zion, he has desired it for his dwelling, saying, "This is*

---
3. Revelation 4:11.
4. Psalm 16:7.
5. Isaiah 50:4.
6. Hebrews 4:11, Hebrews 12:1–3.
7. 2 Thessalonians 1:7.

my resting place for ever and ever; here I will sit enthroned, for I have desired it."
(Psalm 132:13–14).

Can we worship a holy God in whatever way we think is right?[8] Can a mortal man with human strength alone lead God's people into true and real worship before the LORD Almighty, Creator of heaven and earth? Are the keys of the kingdom of heaven entrusted to anyone and everyone?[9] How do we know that the flame burning in His sanctuary is holy fire and not common?[10] These questions may burn in the heart of those who seek God with all their heart, mind, soul, and strength. All who desire to ascend to the heights and enter into genuine worship ought to ask these hard questions of themselves. The answers are found in repentance and rest.[11]

The Apostle Paul taught us that salvation is by grace through faith alone. Trusting in Jesus Christ as LORD and Savior is the only way to redemption. But will we reject these good things because we want to fulfill our selfish ambitions and exalt ourselves in the congregation? Will we be like foolish Galatians who deserted the One who called them by the grace of Christ? They turned back because they preferred man-pleasing religion over God-pleasing worship.[12] Now, put aside the foolishness that holds you back and step into the Good Shepherd's still water.

Are you so foolish? After beginning by means of the Spirit, are you now trying to finish by means of the flesh?
(Galatians 3:3).

Imagine going for a horse ride on a hot, sunny day. Picture how the horse feels when you dismount, take off his saddle and blanket, walk him cool, brush him out, and give him some oats and fresh hay. He knickers his thanks.

The New Testament began with our Savior finding refuge in a stable, a place where lowly animals were cared for. Today, our role continues as people are refreshed, restored, fed, and cared for—a safe place where weary souls find rest. In such a humble place, the wise bring their treasures and bow down to worship. We come with offerings in hand and place them at the LORD's feet. Our Savior ministers saving grace to us as we dwell in the shelter of the Most High. We come into God's strong fortress for refuge. We are covered with His wings as He shields us from the enemy's fiery darts. In this humble sanctuary we need not fear the terrors of night. He protects us from

---

8. Judges 21:25.
9. Matthew 16:18–19.
10. Leviticus 10:1.
11. Psalm 62:5—12.
12. Galatians 1:6–10.

pestilence that stalks in the darkness that would destroy us.[13] He holds us close to His heart and guards us jealously.[14] Come now to rest in Him, a rest that refreshes us to the depth of our souls.

> *"Come to me, all you who are weary and burdened, and I will give you rest. Take my yoke upon you and learn from me, for I am gentle and humble in heart, and you will find rest for your souls."*
> (Matthew 11:28–29).

The Old Testament system of worship served to regulate a person's external actions. The law required that they rest on the Sabbath day and give their farmland a rest every seventh year. But right living and good stewardship of our fields comes by godly wisdom from the heart and cannot be imposed by means of law. If a person is told, "The law says you must drive no faster than fifty-five miles per hour," he'll test that limit and push his car to 61 mph. Israel's rulers tried to overcome this human tendency by writing more and more rules. Keeping the Sabbath holy turned into: "You can't walk more than one kilometer on Shabbat." "You can't heal the sick on the Sabbath because that's work." "You can't carry your bedroll on the seventh day even if Jesus told you to."

What is the measure of a person? Are we righteous if we drive the speed limit and not one mph over on our way to church? You might say, "That's impossible." But this is exactly the point. Precise adherence to the law is not possible, nor it is the means of righteousness. Our right standing with the Father is through Christ and His righteousness alone. A day of rest is a gift given to those who desire Christ who is present with us in restful worship. It is not a day that demands perfect performance. Instead, we are called to come and bow down. We are welcomed to lie down in green pastures where the Good Shepherd ministers to us and leads us into true worship.

> *Then he said to them, "The Sabbath was made for man, not man for the Sabbath."*
> (Mark 2:27).

We are gifted with God's rest today. We must hear God's call and not harden our hearts.[15] Step by step, every day of our lives, we ascend toward our eternal rest where our labors and troubles will be forgotten forever. We cast our cares on the LORD today, knowing that one day we will be totally free from all that has caused us tears, pain, and sorrow.[16] Is it the desire of your heart to come into your Father's eternal rest? Today is the day to answer the Savior's call to enter God's eternal rest.[17]

---

13. Psalm 91.
14. Joel 2:18.
15. Hebrews 4:6–7.
16. Revelation 21:4.
17. 2 Corinthians 6:2.

What we do on our day of rest one day a week affects what we do and say the rest of the week. Our everyday words and deeds follow us into our everlasting reward. Heaven's holy angels will usher us over the threshold into God's eternal glory, forgiven, cleansed, and wearing the bride's attire—the robe of righteousness that is ours in Jesus Christ.

> *Then I heard a voice from heaven say, "Write this: Blessed are the dead who die in the LORD from now on." "Yes," says the Spirit, "they will rest from their labor, for their deeds will follow them."*
> (Revelation 14:13).

When God's creation does what it was created to do, it honors our Creator, who rested from the work of creation on the seventh day. All those who are brought into the new covenant in Jesus Christ enter God's eternal rest. We delight to set aside time in our busy schedules to gather as a church, where we bow before the LORD our Maker and lift our voices with praise.

Come, all who are blessed in the LORD. Enter His eternal rest today. Every day of rest we enjoy in the Lord serves to prepare us as the bride of Christ so we may enter the joy of the LORD in His eternal rest where we will worship Him forever and ever.

> Surely it is you who love the people; all the holy ones are in your hand. At your feet they all bow down, and from you receive instruction.
> (Deuteronomy 33:3).

Chapter 36 Q&A

From the Beginning to Forever

1. What is common worship? Describe this form of honoring the Creator.

   _____
   _____
   _____

2. Describe your journey of faith in Christ. Has it been like a marathon or a perilous hike?

   _____
   _____
   _____

3. Why is it so hard for people to stop and rest? Why is it especially challenging to rest in the LORD?

   _____
   _____
   _____

4. What should we ask ourselves as we take a personal account to know if we're restless or restful in Christ?

   _____
   _____
   _____

My Journey's Journal:

Chapter 37: Put Your Feet in the Water

Key Scriptures

- "Come here and listen to the words of the LORD your God. This is how you will know that the living God is among you" (Joshua 3:9–10).

- "Therefore, this is what the Sovereign LORD says: 'Look! I am placing a foundation stone in Jerusalem, a firm and tested stone. It is a precious cornerstone that is safe to build on. Whoever believes need never be shaken'" (Isaiah 28:16 NLT).

As we approach the mountaintop, we take a moment to reflect on our pilgrimage. We can see that God has accomplished many great things through His sojourners that would be totally impossible in mortal strength. We remember those first steps at the edge of the Jordan River. The floodwaters overflowed the banks with deadly, raging currents. It was there that an entire nation prepared for three days and then stood ready with their tents packed and their flocks herded together. The tabernacle itself was packed for transport. The priests stood with the carrying poles of the ark of the covenant on their shoulders. Then all eyes turned to Joshua. But what can one man do on his own? He simply obeyed the command of the LORD and instructed the priests to step into the water with the ark.

This part of our ascent leads us to step into the impossible. But we can make this pilgrimage by walking in the footsteps of the patriarchs, apostles, and prophets. They didn't ascend upon the mountain of the LORD with one giant leap. They embarked on their pilgrimage one step of faith at a time. They began by putting their feet in the water at the banks of the river.

> A prayer according to Psalm 61:1 and John 4:23:
>
> God of grace and mercy, lead us to you, the Rock that is higher than we are, so we may come before you to worship according to all that is spiritual and true.

When we get close to our goal, it's important to remember how we got there. How is it possible for God's sons and daughters to cross the threshold so they may ascend into real worship? The tribes of Israel show us the way. The Jordan River was at flood stage when God's nation came to camp on its eastern banks. They couldn't build a barge or bridge for the ark of covenant, the tabernacle, or their families and flocks to cross over. The floodwaters would sweep them away if they tried to wade across. Moses' mighty rod no longer accompanied them.

Joshua, by the authority of God's command, instructed the priests who carried the ark of covenant to go stand in the water near the riverbank. The instructions were clear and simple. Joshua's humble obedience offers a perfect illustration of the first steps into worship of a holy God. Disciples of Jesus Christ delight to take this step of obedience. When we take up the cross and obey the gospel's call, we are compelled to cross over into this land of promise where we may truly worship.

> *Tell the priests who carry the ark of the covenant: "When you reach the edge of the Jordan's waters, go and stand in the river."*
> (Joshua 3:8).

When those who are called by God's holy name put their feet in the water, they take a big step toward life-changing worship and praise. We gather in reverent awe to pray, sing, preach, teach, and proclaim the good news. Abundant blessings flow out from our sacred assemblies like a sweet fragrance to fill the land. God's people enter to worship so they may depart in the Almighty's favor. His lovingkindness covers and shields His obedient servants until they meet again.[1] When we obey the command to step into the water, the LORD of Hosts acts with a mighty hand and outstretched arm.[2] Lives are changed forever when people join us in our assemblies. They come through the back door of the church as objects of wrath. Then, we walk with our guests to the front door as they overflow with rich mercies and alive in Christ.[3] They come in weak, and they are sent out in strength. People whose feet are stuck on a path to destruction join us and then depart with a dance in their step because they're on the pathway to glory. When they gather with us, their name may be mud,[4] but they step out as redeemed sons and daughter who are called by God's holy name. Visitors may join us wondering, "Where is their God?"[5] But they depart declaring, "God is truly among you."[6]

---

1. Deuteronomy 28:2.
2. Psalm 136:12.
3. Ephesians 2:3.
4. Psalm 40:2.
5. Psalm 42:3.
6. 1 Corinthians 14:25.

Whoever enters by the north gate to worship is to go out the south gate; and whoever enters by the south gate is to go out the north gate. No one is to return through the gate by which they entered, but each is to go out the opposite gate.
(Ezekiel 46:39).

As God's people prepare to cross over, the flame of the Spirit of Christ keeps burning through the watches of the night to guard us.[7] With flame or cloud, God's presence radiates to guard and guide His people. He protects us through the great battles being waged between the kingdom of light and the kingdom of darkness. We press on, knowing that the light of Christ drives back the darkness. We take our stand on a sure and awesome Word that strengthens and encourages us. We take heart because, "The night is nearly over; the day is almost here."[8] But who will tend the light in the sanctuary? Arise, servants of the LORD, and keep watch through the midnight hours to tend the light that burns in our heart and spirit to make sure the flame is not extinguished by any wind of deceitful teaching.[9]

Praise the LORD, all you servants of the LORD who minister by night in the house of the LORD.
(Psalm 134:1).

God's power is made perfect in weakness.[10] The Almighty's power is best manifested in weak vessels. Consider those who, by faith, have crossed over before us. The great I AM turned Abram, a lone traveler from the land of Ur of the Chaldeans, into mighty nation. The least son of Jesse who tended the family sheep was crowned king of Israel. A simple farmer was raised up to serve as a mighty prophet.[11] Jesus worked as a poor carpenter in Nazareth, then He was exalted as LORD and Savior. The Son of God who was crucified to die on a rugged Roman cross rose again in resurrection power. What appeared as the weakness of the cross is now the power of the cross. The stone rejected by the builders, became the cornerstone. The One they crucified is now Head of the church. Indeed, God's kingdom isn't built by great noblemen, it is raised up among those whom the world counts as foolish.[12] The kingdom of heaven is advanced by those who simply obey. They do the impossible by just stepping into the water.

The stone the builders rejected has become the cornerstone; the LORD has done this, and it is marvelous in our eyes.
(Psalm 118:22–23).

---
7. Exodus 13:21–22.
8. Romans 13:12.
9. Ephesians 4:14.
10. 2 Corinthians 12:9.
11. 1 Kings 19:19.
12. 1 Corinthians 1:26–30.

God's people are refined in fiery trials and persecutions to make them useful vessels of pure gold, fit for His kingdom. We are purified to make us precious stones for building His church. There is only one foundation for building God's temple and that is the Rock, Christ Jesus. There is only one way for people of faith to ascend to worship on God's holy mountain and it begins with putting our feet in the water.

If we attempt to cross over the river by our own means, our boat will sink in the raging floodwater. Abraham and Sarah tried to help Yahweh fulfill His promise of a son with their own plan—and it crumbled into ruin. Jacob tried to help God fulfill His word by deceiving Isaac so that the younger twin would receive the elder son's blessing, and he had to flee in fear and take refuge in a far-off land. These patriarchs of our faith teach us that our own efforts to build the church are futile—only God's plan will endure. Only what we do in Christ by the power and anointing of the Spirit remains solid. Anything else is like wood, hay, and chaff.

All the work we do on behalf of God's kingdom will be tested by fire. If we attempt to fulfill our calling in our own strength and our own means, it will go up in smoke. Why would we build bridges when God's command is simply to step into the water? Those who claim to do the work of the church but do their own work, by their own strength, or to be seen by men will "have no reward from your Father in heaven."[13] They will be saved, but like a burning stick snatched from the fire, or like a lamb rescued from a lion's mouth.[14] Those who submit to God's Word and wait upon the LORD for the anointing, gifting, and empowering work of the Spirit can go forward, armored up and in the strength of the LORD, and build what will endure the test by fire. We serve to build upon the Rock, who is Christ Jesus, and our reward awaits us in the land of everlasting promise.

> *By the grace God has given me, I laid a foundation as a wise builder, and someone else is building on it. But each one should build with care. For no one can lay any foundation other than the one already laid, which is Jesus Christ. If anyone builds on this foundation using gold, silver, costly stones, wood, hay or straw, their work will be shown for what it is, because the Day will bring it to light. It will be revealed with fire, and the fire will test the quality of each person's work. If what has been built survives, the builder will receive a reward. If it is burned up, the builder will suffer loss but yet will be saved—even though only as one escaping through the flames.*
> (1 Corinthians 3:10–15).

---

13. Matthew 6:2.
14. Amos 3:12, Zechariah 3:2.

In the work of the Great Commission, the American church has weighed itself down. We have an abundance of resources at our fingertips. Great Christian universities prepare our pastors and missionaries. The web makes the world our library. We can raise adequate capital for all our programs. When church committees agree on a plan, they immediately think of the resources they can tap into to get the job done. These are good things, but we cannot depend on our own means to do eternal work. God's people must not be strangers to the power of God, who held back the water of the Jordan River at flood stage so His people could cross over on dry ground.

Too often, Christians limit themselves to their own resources. The elders who serve in our churches are turned into board members who adhere to Robert's Rules of Order to accomplish their work. Following an orderly plan is good, but Robert is not the source of the churches power and authority. There is a clear plan for building the church with precious stones set upon a sure foundation of Christ. All God's people are joined together into one house that is raised up to serve as the sanctuary for true worship. We can't build this eternal house with wood and bricks. The work of building God's kingdom begins with one step of obedience.

> *Consequently, you are no longer foreigners and strangers, but fellow citizens with God's people and also members of his household, built on the foundation of the apostles and prophets, with Christ Jesus himself as the chief cornerstone. In him the whole building is joined together and rises to become a holy temple in the LORD. And in him you too are being built together to become a dwelling in which God lives by his Spirit.*
> (Ephesians 2:19–22).

Footprints of faith are imprinted on the road Abram and Sarah walked from Ur of the Chaldeans to the land of promise in Canaan. Their confident trust compelled them to press on day after day and keep putting one foot in front of the other. With the city of God secured in their hearts they went forward to a land they knew nothing about. They looked ahead with eyes of faith for an inheritance promised to them by a loving God. They were bent on a pilgrimage to the land where the Redeemer would be born as the seed of Abraham.[15]

Abraham didn't arrive in Canaan and buy a large tract of land to start building a city with quarried stone. No, he lived in a tent as a foreigner. He showed us how to live in this temporal world. His life teaches us to treasure eternity in our hearts while living in our bodily tents. We find ourselves regularly uprooted. But instead of resenting the change, we look forward to the place our Bridegroom is preparing for us.

---
15. Galatians 3:16.

> *By faith he made his home in the promised land like a stranger in a foreign country; he lived in tents, as did Isaac and Jacob, who were heirs with him of the same promise. For he was looking forward to the city with foundations, whose architect and builder is God.*
> (Hebrews 11:9–10).

The patriarchs of our faith lived in tents while serving as living stones in a city whose Builder and Designer is Creator God. Some Old Testament prophets went about wearing sheepskin and goat hides for clothes. They were destitute, persecuted, and mistreated as they looked ahead to see the city of the living God. His faithful servants lived in in deserts, on mountains, in caves, and in holes in the ground, knowing they were ascending to a better place—the heavenly Jerusalem.[16] Jesus came as Immanuel and had no home where he could lay His head.[17] But He was proven as a tried and tested precious cornerstone for Zion's sure foundation.[18] Paul followed Christ and ended up chained in a dim, putrid, and filthy dungeon. But he pressed on in his calling by writing letters to build the people's faith and strengthen the church triumphant.[19]

Abraham, Isaac, Jacob, Israel's prophets, and the Apostle Paul did not ascend to these heights with one giant leap. They started by taking one step of obedience, as if putting their feet in the water on the riverbank. We, like them, bow to worship the great I AM as sojourners in a strange land. Our tent pegs may be staked in a thirsty land, but we step up to ascend the mountain where living stones are built upon Christ Jesus the cornerstone.

> *As you come to him, the living Stone–rejected by humans but chosen by God and precious to him–you also, like living stones, are being built into a spiritual house to be a holy priesthood, offering spiritual sacrifices acceptable to God through Jesus Christ. For in Scripture it says: "See, I lay a stone in Zion, a chosen and precious cornerstone, and the one who trusts in him will never be put to shame."*
> (1 Peter 2:4–6)

Now that you've read the guidebook, this is your moment to step into the water and begin your ascent into genuine spiritual worship. Ask the Holy Spirit to lead you to take this great step of faith. As you cross over and start on your pilgrimage, sing out with psalms of ascent. The Spirit of Christ will lead you to

---

16. Hebrews 11:36–38.
17. Luke 9:58.
18. Isaiah 28:16.
19. Revelation 7:9–10.

His holy mountain, where you'll find joy in His house of prayer.[20] Your worshipful journey will lead you to walk on ancient paths in Joshua's footprints. His steps prepared the way for you to cross over to the other side of the river, where you can look up with eyes of faith to see the city of the living God.[21]

There will be tests, trials, and persecutions along the way, but they cannot stop you. By the power of the Word and the Holy Spirit, press on to Mount Zion, the city of the living God.

> Your procession, God, has come into view, the procession of my God and King into the sanctuary. (Psalm 68:24)

Chapter 37 Q&A

Put Your Feet in the Water

1. Why must we take the Good Shepherd's hand and put our feet in the water?

2. What is the church's part in changing people's lives for eternity?

3. What burdens keep the modern-day church from doing the work of the great commission?

4. How will you begin your ascent upon God's holy mountain where you will bow down to worship at His footstool?

---

20. Isaiah 56:7.
21. Hebrews 12:22.

My Journey's Journal:

Standing on the Summit

Sailors lift anchor and set their sails to the breeze to glide across the water and reach their destination. Eagles spread their wings and let the wind lift them up to soar upon the heights of the mountain. As we reach the pinnacle of our ascent, we spread our wings and soar in the wind of the Spirit.[1] God's Word compels us to set our sails to the breath of the Spirit of Christ. This is our moment because He is near.[2] The LORD Almighty prepared a way for us so that we might praise Him from the heights and with the heavenly hosts.[3]

Nehemiah, Ezra, and Zerubbabel caught the Spirit's wind and soared like eagles to Jerusalem's heights. They went from strength to strength on a journey back to their homeland in Judah. The seventy years of exile were complete, and they left Babylon behind to return to the land promised to Abraham. They traveled back to Jerusalem, began to rebuild the temple, and put their hands to the task of restoring worship of the one true God.

Zerubbabel worked in the strength of the LORD to build foundations of the temple. He served as Yahweh's signet,[4] and all mountain-sized obstacles became level ground before him. He brought out the temple's capstone to shouts of "God bless it! God bless it!"[5] Yahweh endowed His servant with the authority of His holy name.[6]

Nehemiah led the people to rebuild the walls of Jerusalem. Each family focused on the fortifications nearest their homes.[7] Ezra served as priest and teacher to restore God's law and open the floodgates of God's blessings upon His people.[8]

---

1. Isaiah 40:31.
2. Isaiah 55:6.
3. Psalm 148:1–2.
4. Haggai 2:23.
5. Zechariah 4:7–9.
6. Zechariah 4:9, Haggai 2:23.
7. Nehemiah 3:23, 28.
8. Nehemiah 8:3.

Today, the new covenant priesthood of all believers is called to reach beyond our common strengths and abilities so that we may be strengthened in the Spirit and worship our LORD and God in spirit and in all truth. The wind of the Spirit gives breath to our spirit so we may shout out with true exaltations and praise upon God's holy mountain. Our heavenly Father calls us to Mount Zion where we will worship in spirit, truth, and righteousness.

We have come to an intersection where the voice of wisdom calls out.[9] True worshippers listen to God's call to enter the house that wisdom built and the seven pillars she carved out.[10] Those who desire to worship in a way that is real, embrace the design of God's holy sanctuary—a house of prayer. They minister and serve, clothed with the righteousness of Jesus Christ. Genuine worship leads God's people to go from strength to strength until each appears before God in Zion.[11]

Now, as we stand on the heights, the Holy Spirit empowers us to raise a banner on the hilltop for all the nations.

> May the grace of the LORD Jesus Christ, and the love of God, and the fellowship of the Holy Spirit be with you all. (2 Corinthians 13:14)

---

9. Proverbs 1:20.
10. Proverbs 9:1.
11. Psalm 84:7.

Author's note:

The process of researching and writing this manuscript felt a lot like writing with my keyboard on my knees while riding a raft through class-five rapids. I know I'm not alone in this sense of being tossed around. The world around us is in chaos. We live in turbulent times. Families suffer economic challenges. Emotional trauma pummels children when they get on the school bus and adults when they walk into work. But in Christ, we have a life jacket that keeps us out of the raging depths of despair. After every crashing wave, we take a gasp of fresh air and lift our hands with thanksgiving to the One who saves us. We are brought from despair into praise and worship.

This study's inspiration began with Hebrews 12:22–24. These verses compelled me to pray earnestly. Every prayerful enquiry led to more prayerful questions and Bible searches. The answers came by the wisdom of God's Word and the fear of the LORD. The Spirit answered my troubled thoughts that something was missing in the post-modern church's worship. He led me to ask the question, "What does it mean when Jesus calls us to worship in spirit and truth?" What is spiritual and real worship?

This verse-by-verse ascent to worship upon Mount Zion is written to inspire greater worship of the Father, Son, and Holy Spirit. The goal of this study is for God's Word to be planted like a seed in each reader's heart, where the Holy Spirit will water the seed and make it grow. Then He will lift us up and open our ears to the Spirit of grace, who teaches us.

This guidebook for our ascent to God's holy mountain is a good map to get you started.

> A prayer according to Psalm 123:1, Jeremiah 3:15, and John 4:23:
>
> Oh, LORD Almighty, lift our eyes to see the One whose throne is in heaven. May the Spirit of Christ raise up shepherds after your own heart who will lead us with knowledge and understanding. Holy Spirit, call many workers who will show saints the way to worship the Father in Spirit and in truth.

www.ingramcontent.com/pod-product-compliance
Lightning Source LLC
Chambersburg PA
CBHW050311120526
44592CB00014B/1866